Malbim

משלי

on Mishley

משלי

Malbim on Mishley

*the Commentary of
Rabbi Meir Leibush Malbim
on the Book of Proverbs*

abridged and adapted in English by
Rabbi Charles Wengrov
based on an original draft by
Avivah Gottlieb Zornberg

FELDHEIM
Jerusalem • New York

The Hebrew text is taken
from the notable *Koren Tanach*
by special permission of the publisher
and copyright owner

First published 1982
ISBN 0-87306-280-9

Copyright © 1982 by
Feldheim Publishers Ltd

All rights reserved
No part of this publication may be translated,
reproduced, stored in a retrieval system or transmitted,
in any form or by any means,
electronic, mechanical, photocopying, recording or otherwise,
without prior permission in writing from the publishers

Phototypeset at the Feldheim Press

Philipp Feldheim Inc.
96 East Broadway
New York, NY 10002

Feldheim Publishers Ltd
POB 6525 / Jerusalem, Israel

Printed in Israel

This volume is published
with the aid of
The Alan Chersky Memorial Fund
(Beverly Hills, California)
in memory of

Alan Marshal Chersky

אברהם בן יוסף

זכרונו לברכה

whose spirit sought
human improvement and perfection
and found some fulfillment
in *aliyah* to the Holy Land
till he fell in battle

על קידוש השם

defending our homeland
in the Yom Kippur War

כ״ג תשרי תשל״ד

October 19, 1973

יהי זכרו ברוך

Blessed be his memory

Introduction

His name was Meir Leib ben (son of) Y^echiel Michael, but as he gained renown, he was increasingly referred to by the initials, as *Malbim*, till that became the family name.

A prodigious Talmudic scholar and a gifted preacher, in 1860 he became the rabbi of Rumania's second largest community, in Bucharest. Here began the persecution and calumny, harassment and vexation, that were to plague him for the rest of his life. Prospering German Jews wanted a "Reform Judaism" that would let them live like their affluent fashionable neighbors, unhampered by religious law. When Malbim opposed them implacably, they denounced him to the government. He was imprisoned, then expelled. In his later communities, *maskilim* too (champions of *haskala*, "enlightenment") made his life a torment and drove him out. Reform Judaism wanted to share the wealth of the non-Jewish world; *haskala* wanted to share its supposed intellectual and cultural wealth. Both thrust Malbim and authentic Judaism ruthlessly aside.

Already in 1844, however, Malbim realized that on another battlefield he could counter those whose heady rush toward assimilation was not to be stemmed. A "synod" of Reform leaders in Braunschweig, Germany that year—which he called an assembly of "shepherds who butcher their sheep and call themselves the rabbis, preachers, cantors and *shoch^etim* (ritual slaughterers) of their communities"—made him aware of the dire need for a sound contemporary commentary on the Hebrew Bible. For the Reform camp was producing interpretations of Scripture, supposedly based on the literal or "original" meaning of the Hebrew, which did not so much reform as deform everything sacred in the Jewish heritage. Reform particularly attacked the Talmud's interpretation of Scriptural texts, on which the Oral Law is largely based.

Already in his early years Malbim had a consummate mastery of the Hebrew (especially Biblical) language. In his commentary on Scripture he used three clear-cut principles: (1) The Written Torah has no mere synonyms or superfluous repetitions in other terms. Every word has its own specific sense, its own nuances and shades of meaning. (2) Every phrase and sentence contains Divine thought. In the Written Torah there is no pointless narrative or history, no idle image or metaphor for literary beauty. (3) Seemingly the Talmudic Sages interpret verses of Scripture homiletically, with little regard for literal meaning; yet they had "important principles and fixed rules about the grammatical forms and foundations of the language..."

Here is one example of his first principle, in the present work: In *Mishley* the terms אֱוִיל (*e'vil*) and כְּסִיל (*k^esil*) occur frequently. The standard translations render both as "fool"; Malbim differs. Connecting אֱוִיל with אוּלַי (*'ulai*), he understands it to mean a skeptic, who cynically doubts the wisdom of the Torah's moral laws. Thus Malbim often finds unsuspected depths of meaning in the Book of Proverbs.

Where the same thought occurs more than once in *Mishley*, often in almost identical words, by noting context and minute details Malbim finds a different element of meaning or application for each. At times he sees an entire section of *Mishley* in a new perspective, that gives all an inspired clarity. As often as not he reveals a remarkable grasp of the ways of this world with all its corruptions, hypocrisies and rationalizations; and on this too he finds Scripture illuminating.

With his commentary on the Hebrew Bible, to refute *haskala* and Reform on the home ground of our Holy Writ, Malbim won a lasting triumph. His work ranks with the classic commentaries of such immortals as Rashi and Abarbanel. (The Chafetz Chaim cherished the *chumashim* — Pentateuch — with Malbim's commentary, that he once bought from the author himself on a trip abroad.)

In preparing the commentary on *Mishley* for the reader of today, it was felt best to condense, abridge and adapt. Where the English version of the text differs from other translations, it follows Malbim's explanations, although the explanations are not always apparent in the abridged commentary.

I am indebted to Avivah Gottlieb Zornberg for a splendid first draft, done with deftness and grace, and with a fine command of English. It lightened my task considerably. Paula Rubin Stotland and Sarah Rivka Cohen (of our editorial staff) improved the work appreciably; and Yoel Epstein is responsible for the excellent graphic preparation. Gratitude is certainly due them.

The initiative for the volume came from Dr Joseph Chersky, in his wish to perpetuate the memory of his only son, a courageous soldier in the Israel Defense Forces who was killed in the Yom Kippur War. The young man gave his life for Jewry's homeland, and the stricken father thought it best to have a lasting memorial in a work of Torah learning — for ultimately, as Dr Chersky passionately believes, Jewry's homeland, people, and Torah are one. May this volume make some of our Torah's wisdom more widely known. And may Alan Marshal Chersky's merit and memory live as long as our Torah lives.

CW

Jerusalem, Fall 1981

Malbim

משלי

on Mishley

PROVERBS 1:1-3

א ‎^א‎ מִשְׁלֵי שְׁלֹמֹה בֶן־דָּוִד מֶלֶךְ יִשְׂרָאֵל: לָדַעַת חָכְמָה וּמוּסָר
‎^ג‎ לְהָבִין אִמְרֵי בִינָה: לָקַחַת מוּסַר הַשְׂכֵּל צֶדֶק וּמִשְׁפָּט

1. The classical philosophers have defined the nature of phenomena under four headings: content, form, agent, and purpose.* In this work, the content and form are immediately stated to be *proverbs*, a collection of metaphorical apothegms, in which obscure and profound concepts are made accessible by reference to easily intelligible concepts. The agent is Solomon, who has three titles, corresponding to three modes of acquiring truth: (1) *Solomon*, suggesting his wisdom and power of prophecy; (2) *son of David*, suggesting the truths of tradition, transmitted from father to son; (3) *king of Israel*, suggesting his discernment and empirical intelligence, aided by the availability of a community of the intelligent. The purpose of the book is:

2. TO KNOW WISDOM AND MORAL DISCIPLINE, TO COMPREHEND THE WORDS OF UNDERSTANDING. To know *chochma* (wisdom) is to understand the principles of moral law governing the proper exercise of all the faculties, such as cruelty and compassion, pride and humility, arrogance and bashfulness, self-indulgence and abstinence, holiness and impurity.

This is the function of *chochma*; and it is important to realize that this can never be engendered out of a man's own resources, or demonstrated by proof, but can only be transmitted by God Himself, through His two forms of instruction: the Written and the Oral Torah. Obviously, then, one cannot really "know *chochma*," for knowledge means empirical knowledge, the lucid action of intelligence working on the evidence of the senses or of self-evident truths; while in *chochma*, man goes beyond anything that can be "given" (conveyed) in the facts of experience. Solomon, however, did aim to "know *chochma*," for he explained non-rational truths by

* This is a concept of Aristotle, mentioned by Don Yitzchak Abarbanel in his commentary on the Pentateuch.

10

1 ¹ **The proverbs of Solomon the son of David, king of Israel: ² To know wisdom and moral discipline, to comprehend the words of understanding; ³ to receive the discipline of insight, justice and right**

means of rational ones, so as to make even the principles of *chochma* accessible to human comprehension.

His technique for achieving this paradoxical aim of knowing *chochma* is "to know *chochma* and *mussar* (moral discipline)": that is, to educate the heart and imagination away from their natural tendency to fantasize in terms of pride, jealousy, vengeance, cruelty; and to educate them instead to *chochma*, to conceptions of virtue. No empirical resources come to man's aid in this process of self-education since, as we have explained, the principles of *chochma* are not any logical inference from the facts of experience, and are often even opposed to human nature. It is for this reason that man needs *mussar*, moral discipline, to shape his imagination in the forms of virtue.

The exact definition of *mussar* is given later, in the statement, "The fear of HA-SHEM is the moral instruction of wisdom" (15:33). This means that the human capacity to be afraid has as one of its offshoots the capacity to fear God, which inhibits man's emotions as with ropes, and binds them into the forms of divine *chochma*. Here man experiences the faith that is centered on the *source* of moral law, on sacred fear of the mighty King whose Word is Law. It is a passionate faith in the truth of the One who established the principles of *chochma*; and it is characterized by an intense conviction as strong as any certainty based on empirical or logical grounds. This is what is meant by "fear of HA-SHEM"—a fear that has practical consequences in conditioning human behavior to the forms of *chochma*.

In addition, the book aims to inculcate *bina* (understanding), which differs from *chochma* in that it arises out of the innate human capacity to derive truths and perceptions from

ה וּמֻשָׁרִים: לָתֵת לִפְתָאיִם עָרְמָה לְנַעַר דַּעַת וּמְזִמָּה: יִשְׁמַע
ו חָכָם וְיוֹסֶף לֶקַח וְנָבוֹן תַּחְבֻּלוֹת יִקְנֶה: לְהָבִין מָשָׁל וּמְלִיצָה
ז דִּבְרֵי חֲכָמִים וְחִידֹתָם: יִרְאַת יהוה רֵאשִׁית דָּעַת חָכְמָה
וּמוּסָר אֱוִילִים בָּזוּ:

one another, to discriminate truth from falsehood, to investigate, penetrate, and resolve both the riddles of existence and the cryptic aphorisms that previous sages have formulated to explain them.

3. Here the author refers to the intuitive faculty (*haskel*), as a further generator of moral living. This allows a human being the direct apprehension of spiritual and ineffable truths, by-passing any deductive process. Therefore "moral discipline" (verse 2) and "discipline of insight" (verse 3) refer to two different springs of moral action: the former arises out of that "fear of God" which is in fact fear of punishment for sin, while the latter is the higher faculty of fear, awe before God's sublimity, which makes sin existentially outrageous to the man who is cognizant and aware of this awe. The Book of Proverbs aims, then, to sharpen this kind of sensitivity, too, through its parables and symbolic situations, and at the same time to inculcate "justice and right and equity" — correct behavior in the social and political spheres, tempering legal exactness with that wise flexibility which is true justice.

4. At this point, the author turns to the subject of his intended audience, and shows that, in effect, all sections of the public stand to benefit from his work. First he refers to "the simple" men of a naïve type, who are in need of the antidote of a good dose of acumen and shrewdness; these are the overly credulous who have to learn to be more discriminating and judicious.

Then, subtly distinguished from this category, there is the "youth," whose problem lies merely in his youth. This group of

and equity; [4] to give acumen to the simple, to the youth knowledge and discretion — [5] that the wise man may hear and increase in learning, and the man of understanding may attain wise counsels, [6] to understand proverb (*mashal*) and poetic expression (*m*e*litza*), the words of the wise and their moot sayings. [7] The fear of HA-SHEM is the beginning of knowledge; but the foolish despise wisdom and moral discipline.

readers also may benefit from being exposed to the intellectual scope and subtlety of the mature man — and specifically from this collection of insights culled from a long life dedicated to discernment and penetrating thought.

5. The wise and understanding among Solomon's audience, too, will find in these Proverbs material that will expand and enrich their minds: (1) in wisdom, that is, in knowledge of morality gained from teachers or from intensive Torah study; and (2) in understanding, the deductive faculty that operates through chains of analogy and comparison. Even people rich in both these faculties will find in these Proverbs much to nourish and develop them.

6. The author now turns to the question of form. The book is composed of *mashal* and *m*e*litza*, which he takes to refer to image and meaning respectively. Through the *mashal*, the reader is led to understand hidden spiritual meanings. Thus the book serves as an aid to understanding both the allegorical sections of the Written Torah and the cryptic instructions and parables of the Sages in the Oral Torah ("the words of the wise").

7. Every intellectual discipline is founded on some human

ח שְׁמַע בְּנִי מוּסַר אָבִיךָ וְאַל־תִּטֹּשׁ תּוֹרַת אִמֶּךָ: כִּי ׀ לִוְיַת חֵן
ט הֵם לְרֹאשֶׁךָ וַעֲנָקִים לְגַרְגְּרֹתֶיךָ: בְּנִי אִם־יְפַתּוּךָ חַטָּאִים אַל־
יא תֹּבֵא: אִם־יֹאמְרוּ לְכָה אִתָּנוּ נֶאֶרְבָה לְדָם נִצְפְּנָה לְנָקִי חִנָּם:

faculty that is absolutely essential to it. The natural sciences, for instance, require a capacity for experiment and observation. The wisdom that the Torah speaks of, however, is not rationally attainable but is a received wisdom, resting entirely on man's awed, reverent recognition of God, which makes him emotionally open and receptive to His commands. Fear of God, then, is the only key to Torah wisdom. It is a moral and spiritual receptivity, the attitude of faith, that conditions man to this kind of wisdom. Those who reject this attitude, the agnostics and atheists, question the validity of the moral law and the necessity of moral behavior — and thereby render themselves opaque to the radiance of this wisdom. They are called "fools" — an ethical and not merely an intellectual concept.

8. Solomon now addresses these "foolish" ones in an attempt to demonstrate that there are foundations to the moral laws which people can logically accept. "The moral instruction of your father" here refers to the earliest experience of moral teaching; the first instruction given by a father to his son, which becomes integrated into his subconscious and most fundamental attitudes. This basic layer in the structure of the ethical experience is a paradigm for the whole: both operate in a mode not open to rational doubt, as part of man's deepest sense of himself and the world.

At the same time, "do not forsake the teaching of your mother": this suggests the other aspect of moral discipline, that it is founded on the wisdom of the collective, the total social context of tradition and convention, which, like a mother, embraces the individual and is not lightly to be set aside.

⁸ Hear, my son, the moral instruction of your father, and do not forsake the teaching of your mother; ⁹ for they are an adornment of grace for your head, and chain-ornaments for your neck. ¹⁰ My son, if sinners entice you, do not consent. ¹¹ If they say, "Come with us, let us lie in wait for blood, let us lurk for the innocent without cause;

9. Head and neck serve here respectively as metaphors for a person's intellectual and linguistic faculties, both of which will benefit from the guidance given in this book. The word *livya* ("adornment") has, incidentally, the connotation of something external and ornamental, not intrinsic — since moral wisdom, as we have said, does not arise out of human experience and rationality but is received from a source beyond the human.

10. This is the message of that first instruction given by the father (verse 8). He chooses a deliberately simple and self-evident moral guideline. Even a small child will readily understand that keeping company with murderers and theives is wrong, both intrinsically — through instinctive repulsion from the act of murder — and out of caution — through fear of exposing oneself to danger. Thus by beginning with the most obvious example of crime, the father will hope to instill in his son a feeling of repulsion toward all forms of sin. He begins therefore with a general warning, to avoid all kinds of sinners; and immediately proceeds to his first example, murderers.

11. Two possibilities are suggested here. The murderers may expect resistance from their victims and therefore plot strategically to "lie in wait for blood": they prepare for an encounter that will result in bloodshed on both sides. Or alternatively, they may expect no resistance from their victims, and will simply ambush and slaughter them "without cause" —

יב נִבְלָעֵם כִּשְׁאוֹל חַיִּים וּתְמִימִים כְּיוֹרְדֵי בוֹר: כָּל־הוֹן יָקָר נִמְצָא
יד נְמַלֵּא בָתֵּינוּ שָׁלָל: גּוֹרָלְךָ תַּפִּיל בְּתוֹכֵנוּ כִּיס אֶחָד יִהְיֶה לְכֻלָּנוּ:
טו בְּנִי אַל־תֵּלֵךְ בְּדֶרֶךְ אִתָּם מְנַע רַגְלְךָ מִנְּתִיבָתָם: כִּי רַגְלֵיהֶם
טז לָרַע יָרוּצוּ וִימַהֲרוּ לִשְׁפָּךְ־דָּם: כִּי־חִנָּם מְזֹרָה הָרָשֶׁת בְּעֵינֵי כָל־
יח בַּעַל כָּנָף: וְהֵם לְדָמָם יֶאֱרֹבוּ יִצְפְּנוּ לְנַפְשֹׁתָם: כֵּן אָרְחוֹת כָּל־
בֹּצֵעַ בָּצַע אֶת־נֶפֶשׁ בְּעָלָיו יִקָּח:
כא חָכְמוֹת בַּחוּץ תָּרֹנָּה בָּרְחֹבוֹת תִּתֵּן קוֹלָהּ: בְּרֹאשׁ הֹמִיּוֹת

without even the semblance of an equal struggle or the pretext of self-defence.

12-15. The father elaborates on the various arrangements the bandits may devise for disposing of the loot, and warns his son away from any kind of association with such criminals, however tempting it may appear.

16. In addition to the intrinsic evil of their actions, the father warns his son that he too, in his turn, will become a victim of their lust for blood.

17. A bird, for example, sees the net spread out enticingly with food, and vainly imagines that there will be no price to pay for the feast.

18. Similarly, the bandits lure the unsuspecting apprentice into their nets; once the bird is taken, it is at their mercy, to kill or enslave for life.

19. In conclusion, the inexperienced youth is warned by his father that not only because of the obvious evil of robbery and violence, but also for self-preservation, he should resist any temptation to band together with criminals. From this para-

¹² let us swallow them up alive like the grave, and whole, like those that go down into the pit; ¹³ we shall find all precious wealth, we shall fill our houses with booty; ¹⁴ throw in your lot among us, let us all have one purse" — ¹⁵ my son, do not walk on the way with them, restrain your foot from their path; ¹⁶ for their feet run to evil, and they make haste to shed blood. ¹⁷ For to vain purpose the net is spread in the sight of any winged creature; ¹⁸ and these lie in wait for their blood, they lurk for their lives. ¹⁹ So are the ways of everyone greedy of gain; it takes away the life of its owners.

²⁰ Wisdom cries aloud in the street, she raises her voice in the squares; ²¹ at the head of the noisy

digm, the father will proceed to show the analogous horrors and dangers of all sin.

20. Progressively, through the stages of the child's growth to maturity, wisdom reveals itself. The images chosen by our master of Proverbs express this gradual revelation of moral wisdom: "cries aloud" is a spontaneous and private form of self-expression [like "cries out"] while "raises her voice" requires an audience, demands response and reaction from the growing youth. Similarly, the "street" spoken of here is a private alley where children play — suggesting the embryonic forms of moral principle; while the "squares" refer to the open spaces in front of the house, where the grown residents meet and can be addressed by the call of wisdom.

21. The image intensifies and expands yet further: The verb

כב תִּקְרָא בְּפִתְחֵי שְׁעָרִים בָּעִיר אֲמָרֶיהָ תֹאמֵר: עַד־מָתַי ׀ פְּתָיִם
תְּאֵהֲבוּ פֶתִי וְלֵצִים לָצוֹן חָמְדוּ לָהֶם וּכְסִילִים יִשְׂנְאוּ־דָעַת:
כג תָּשׁוּבוּ לְתוֹכַחְתִּי הִנֵּה אַבִּיעָה לָכֶם רוּחִי אוֹדִיעָה דְבָרַי
כד אֶתְכֶם: יַעַן קָרָאתִי וַתְּמָאֵנוּ נָטִיתִי יָדִי וְאֵין מַקְשִׁיב: וַתִּפְרְעוּ
כה כָל־עֲצָתִי וְתוֹכַחְתִּי לֹא אֲבִיתֶם: גַּם־אֲנִי בְּאֵידְכֶם אֶשְׂחָק אֶלְעַג
כו בְּבֹא פַחְדְּכֶם: בְּבֹא כשאוה ׀ פַּחְדְּכֶם וְאֵידְכֶם כְּסוּפָה יֶאֱתֶה
כז כְּשׁוֹאָה

"calls" suggests a specific appeal to the particular people addressed, not simply a general proclamation; and now wisdom is pictured as standing in the central marketplace or square, where all the citizens throng. Finally, in the fourth stage, wisdom "utters her words," speaks her unique essential message, to an audience of the élite and mature of the city — those who sit "at the entrance of the gates" — the judges and elders. At this stage, wisdom most fully reveals itself, in all its truth. This is its message:

22. HOW LONG, YOU SIMPLETONS, WILL YOU LOVE BEING MISLED? AND HOW LONG WILL SCORNERS DELIGHT IN THEIR SCORNING, AND FOOLS HATE KNOWLEDGE? Three groups of sinners are described: The simpleton is swayed because of his sheer lack of knowledge; wisdom offers him the power of discrimination and judgment. The scorner, on the other hand, mocks wisdom because it can be attained only by faith and the recognition of God that commands commitment; for the scorner only the logically demonstrable wisdom has authority. The fool, finally, knows the moral laws, acknowledges them, and detests them — for they are an obstacle to his desires and cravings.

23-25. Wisdom urges man to repent. Once again the double-barreled argument is used: both the appeal to man to listen to his innermost voice that acknowledges the moral law ("I will

18

marketplaces she calls, at the entrance of the gates in the city she utters her words: ²² "How long, you simpletons, will you love being misled? And how long will scorners delight in their scorning, and fools hate knowledge? ²³ Turn back at my reproof; behold, I will pour out my spirit into you, I will make my words known to you. ²⁴ Because I have called, and you refused, I have stretched out my hand, and no man paid heed, ²⁵ but you neglected all my counsel, and would have none of my reproof— ²⁶ I too in your calamity will laugh; I will mock when your dread comes, ²⁷ when your dread arrives like a storm, and your calamity comes on like a whirlwind; when trouble and

pour out my spirit into you" — like a fountain in the heart) and equally the threat of punishment for disregarding that voice ("I will make my words known to you"). Even though moral awareness flows from man's innermost being, some will yet refuse to acknowledge it; and despite the threat of punishment ("I have stretched out my hand"), "no man paid heed." Both conscience and fear have ceased to function as ethical motives or incentives; wisdom's counsel is ignored, and even its prediction of retribution is rejected.

26. Here wisdom speaks of the inevitable disaster that will befall the scoffers, and of the period of anxiety and fear of the unknown that precedes disaster.

27. The word "storm" *(sho'a)* signifies howling darkness, in which terrors and mysteries breed and abound.

כח בְּבֹא עֲלֵיכֶם צָרָה וְצוּקָה: אָז יִקְרָאֻנְנִי וְלֹא אֶעֱנֶה יְשַׁחֲרֻנְנִי וְלֹא
כט יִמְצָאֻנְנִי: תַּחַת כִּי־שָׂנְאוּ דָעַת וְיִרְאַת יְהוָה לֹא בָחָרוּ: לֹא־אָבוּ
לא לַעֲצָתִי נָאֲצוּ כָּל־תּוֹכַחְתִּי: וְיֹאכְלוּ מִפְּרִי דַרְכָּם וּמִמֹּעֲצֹתֵיהֶם
לב יִשְׂבָּעוּ: כִּי מְשׁוּבַת פְּתָיִם תַּהַרְגֵם וְשַׁלְוַת כְּסִילִים תְּאַבְּדֵם:
לג וְשֹׁמֵעַ לִי יִשְׁכָּן־בֶּטַח וְשַׁאֲנַן מִפַּחַד רָעָה:

28. Wisdom describes a process in which the sufferer who once rejected it becomes more and more alienated from it. Most estranged from it will be the simpletons and scorners described in verse 22 — those who either are entirely unaware of the existence of moral law or refuse to accept any authority not logically demonstrable. The third category described in verse 22 — those who acknowledge the authority of moral law but defy it since it denies them full gratification of their cravings — are still at least within range of moral wisdom, though effectively beyond communication ("Then they will call me but I will not answer").

29. "They hated knowledge" refers to the "fools" of verse 22, who indeed "hate knowledge": they agree that there is moral law, but remain dedicated to their cravings. As we explained earlier (verse 2), the knowledge of moral law is attainable through "fear of God": Through the attunement of our ethical and emotional being to habits of virtue, we can come to an organic knowledge of God's law, as profound as rational or empirical knowledge. This kind of knowledge, then, the "fools" do indeed hate, since they reject its moral existential basis of "fear of HA-SHEM" in their own lives.

30. They spurn moral wisdom, ignoring both its intrinsic appeal to the human sense of right (its "counsel" — see verse 25) and the threat of punishment it carries with it (its "reproof").

31. Retribution comes upon them for two reasons: both for the

distress come upon you. ²⁸ Then they will call me, but I will not answer; they will seek me earnestly, but shall not find me. ²⁹ For they hated knowledge, and did not choose the fear of HA-SHEM; ³⁰ they would have none of my counsel, despised all my reproof. ³¹ So they shall eat of the fruit of their way, and be filled up with their own devices. ³² For the waywardness of the simpletons shall slay them, and the complacency of fools shall destroy them. ³³ But whoever listens to me will dwell secure, and will be tranquil without fear of evil."

evil act itself and, more radically ("be filled up" connotes surfeit, engorgement), for the sin of the mind which has rejected faith and truth. This is the ultimate act of treachery — when a person willfully ignores his best intuitions and allows his inner being to be infiltrated by "devices" that run counter to moral truth.

32. Once again, the "simpleton" will suffer for his moral ignorance and irresponsibility: he is criminally ignorant of the laws of wisdom. The "fool," on the other hand, is doomed to a more absolute retribution: he knows those laws, but deliberately defies them. His deluded complacency takes him on a path that will lead to his utter destruction — in both worlds, here and in the Hereafter: for knowledge immeasurably exacerbates his sin.

33. Wisdom ends its proclamation with a brief depiction of its true reward, as opposed to the deluded peace and well-being that is experienced by those who will not acquire it. This brings inner quietness and absence of all fear of evil from the outside world.

ב א בְּנִי אִם־תִּקַּח אֲמָרָי וּמִצְוֹתַי תִּצְפֹּן אִתָּךְ: לְהַקְשִׁיב לַחָכְמָה
ב אָזְנֶךָ תַּטֶּה לִבְּךָ לַתְּבוּנָה: כִּי אִם לַבִּינָה תִקְרָא לַתְּבוּנָה תִּתֵּן
ג קוֹלֶךָ: אִם־תְּבַקְשֶׁנָּה כַכָּסֶף וְכַמַּטְמוֹנִים תַּחְפְּשֶׂנָּה: אָז תָּבִין
ד יִרְאַת יְהוָה וְדַעַת אֱלֹהִים תִּמְצָא: כִּי־יְהוָה יִתֵּן חָכְמָה מִפִּיו

1. There is a difference between *commandments* and *words*: Commandments have an imperative force; they relate to action; and therefore man is urged to "treasure" them in his heart, keep them constantly dynamic and operative in his life. Words, on the other hand, refer here to the general moral and ideological guidelines of the Torah which man should basically recognize and accept as true. They should be the underpinning of his life, as it were — the basic level of awareness which informs it.

2. Wisdom, as we have previously defined it, is the area of the mind to which the terms "good" and "evil" may be applied — the moral sphere; and it can be arrived at only through tradition, by submitting to the authority of sages who have gleaned it from the Prophets or from study of the Torah. Therefore the master of Proverbs speaks of making one's *ear attend* to wisdom. We must listen and hear what our great Torah instructors teach. Discernment, by contrast, is man's own deductive, analytic power, so that the expression "incline your heart to discernment" is appropriate to the intellectual autonomy of this faculty of the mind.

3–4. Two sets of connotations are brought into play here, to depict the intense desire for understanding. "Seek it like silver" calls to mind the craving of the marketplace for profit and gain by trading, and thus conveys the willingness to exchange all the goods of this world for the prize of understanding. "Search as for hidden treasures" is an image of mining for buried riches, connoting the labor involved in digging out the esoteric, secret truths of understanding.

2

¹ My son, if you will accept my words and treasure my commandments with you, ² to make your ear attend to wisdom, incline your heart to discernment; ³ indeed, if you but call out for understanding, and lift up your voice for discernment; ⁴ if you seek it like silver, and search for it as for hidden treasures — ⁵ then you will understand the fear of HA-SHEM, and find the knowledge of God. ⁶ For HA-SHEM gives wisdom; out of His mouth come knowledge and discern-

5. The paradox of the relations between *chochma* and *yir'a*, between wisdom and fear of God, is expressed by the Sages in the double formula, "Without fear there is no wisdom," and "Without wisdom there is no fear." Wisdom, moral law, cannot be rationally demonstrated; as we have explained, it can be grasped and absorbed only by a person sensitized by fear of God to recognize its truth and accept its practical and sometimes unpalatable implications. On the other hand, true fear of God can only be based on a true comprehension of God, an appreciation of His greatness that moves man ultimately to sacred fear and awe. The paradox expresses the dynamic, circular relationship of fear and understanding: fear induces knowledge, the lucid acceptance of the moral law and its dictates; but man can then press onwards from this quiescent base to a resumed pursuit of the more esoteric "knowledge of God," of the mysteries of His being and His relation to the world; this, in turn, naturally brings in its train a new intensity of awe through the newly comprehended sublimity.

6. Although in general man cannot arrive at wisdom directly but must draw on the traditions and interpretations of the whole corpus of Torah, there are exceptional cases where the

יִצְפֹּן ז דַּעַת וּתְבוּנָה: וְצָפַן לַיְשָׁרִים תּוּשִׁיָּה מָגֵן לְהֹלְכֵי תֹם: לִנְצֹר
ח אָרְחוֹת מִשְׁפָּט וְדֶרֶךְ חֲסִידָיו יִשְׁמֹר: אָז תָּבִין צֶדֶק וּמִשְׁפָּט
ט וּמֵישָׁרִים כָּל־מַעְגַּל־טוֹב: כִּי־תָבוֹא חָכְמָה בְלִבֶּךָ וְדַעַת

desire for wisdom is so intense that God "short-circuits" the process, as it were, granting immediate inspiration. Abraham, for example, is traditionally described as having fulfilled the whole Torah before it was even given: his desire was so great that the Almighty granted him the gift that he could arrive at it directly, existentially. Similarly, in the case of "knowledge and discernment," which are accessible to human reason, to the activity of the senses and deductive faculty: the Almighty will sometimes intervene, to short-circuit their laborious and often erroneous workings, and "out of His mouth" communicate perceptions shattering in their clarity and power.

7–8. The Almighty's providential plan for history assigns an important role to the "upright," to figures of the stature of a Joseph or a Moses. To them He relegates some of His prerogatives and planned steps of historic action, of meting out justice, reward and punishment to their own generation. These actions are, as it were, "stored away" from the beginning of time till the man of destiny and the generation of destiny appear. The Almighty's heroes are the "upright," the people of integrity who can maintain themselves by their own power and conviction on the "right road"; and it is they who may "guard the paths of justice," implement His will and deal out reward and punishment. (The Ten Plagues can be cited as an example, with Moses and Aaron as the "upright" agents who carried out His will.) There is, as well, a category of lesser heroes called "those who walk with integrity": these are simpler souls who follow one unvarying path, but who may be misled or caused to stumble, and thus do not possess the self-direction or ingenuity

ment. **⁷** He stores away providential action for the upright [to do], He is a shield to those who walk with integrity, **⁸** to guard the paths of justice and preserve the way of His pious loved ones. **⁹** Then you will understand righteousness and justice and equity — every good winding path: **¹⁰** For wisdom will come into your heart, and knowledge will be pleasant to your soul;

to outwit the forces of evil. These individuals God promises to "shield," and to keep their path clear of obstacles.

9. In addition to wisdom, discernment and knowledge of God, man is promised an understanding of righteousness and justice — that is, of the proper laws of society. "Justice" refers to the strictly legal relationships between men, and "righteousness" to more flexible and generous behavior beyond the mere letter of the law. Similarly, a person will come to understand "equity" — both the straight middle road of balanced neutral behavior, and the art of the "winding path," of behavior that veers from the golden mean to one extreme or another, in order finally to come to a point of stability in the middle. Cruelty and pride are negative qualities in themselves; but are occasionally indicated as necessary — for instance, in dealing with the wicked.

10. When wisdom enters the heart, essentially the moral struggle is then resolved. With the Almighty's aid, man is promised the crowning title, "wise in heart" — his wisdom becomes second nature, absorbed into the core of his being. Similarly, he is promised that knowledge of God, which comes bitterly and uncertainly to most men, will come to him pleasantly, mellifluously, through Divine inspiration and revelation.

יב לְנַפְשֶׁךָ יִנְעָם: מְזִמָּה תִּשְׁמֹר עָלֶיךָ תְּבוּנָה תִנְצְרֶכָּה: לְהַצִּילְךָ
יג מִדֶּרֶךְ רָע מֵאִישׁ מְדַבֵּר תַּהְפֻּכוֹת: הַעֹזְבִים אָרְחוֹת יֹשֶׁר לָלֶכֶת
יד בְּדַרְכֵי־חֹשֶׁךְ: הַשְּׂמֵחִים לַעֲשׂוֹת רָע יָגִילוּ בְּתַהְפֻּכוֹת רָע: אֲשֶׁר
טו אָרְחֹתֵיהֶם עִקְּשִׁים וּנְלוֹזִים בְּמַעְגְּלוֹתָם: לְהַצִּילְךָ מֵאִשָּׁה זָרָה
טז מִנָּכְרִיָּה אֲמָרֶיהָ הֶחֱלִיקָה: הַעֹזֶבֶת אַלּוּף נְעוּרֶיהָ וְאֶת־בְּרִית
יז אֱלֹהֶיהָ שָׁכֵחָה: כִּי שָׁחָה אֶל־מָוֶת בֵּיתָהּ וְאֶל־רְפָאִים
יח מַעְגְּלֹתֶיהָ: כָּל־בָּאֶיהָ לֹא יְשׁוּבוּן וְלֹא־יַשִּׂיגוּ אָרְחוֹת חַיִּים:

11–12. Discretion, the counsels of wisdom, will watch over a man in his moral life, in matters of good and evil — preserving him from the devious, nefarious persuasions of desire, the "way of the evil." On the other hand, discernment, which has to do with matters of truth and falsehood, of straight and twisted ideology — this will save a man from heretical philosophies which tempt him away from a true vision of the world.

13. This follows on from the image of the "way of evil" — the moral danger that a man is exposed to. The "ways" are the main roads, and the "paths" are the side-roads branching off to particular destinations. The master of Proverbs asserts that in the Torah not only the main roads but even the side paths are all straight: all the detailed commandments which derive from the main commandments lead in one blessed direction of Divine light. In evil, however, not only the side paths but the main road itself is covered with darkness.

14. This expands on the theme raised in verse 12, of the "man who speaks in treacherous fickleness," of the ideological hazards that the believer is exposed to. It is only the heretics who "rejoice to do evil." The person who sins out of passion or moral weakness is afterwards filled with remorse; but heretics

¹¹ discretion will watch over you, discernment will guard you, ¹² to deliver you from the way of the evil [person], from a man who speaks in treacherous fickleness, [margin: "FROWARD"] ¹³ who leave the paths of uprightness to walk in the ways of darkness; ¹⁴ who rejoice to do evil, and delight in the treacheries of evil; ¹⁵ [men] who are perverse in their ways, and perfidious in their winding paths; — ¹⁶ to deliver you from the strange woman, from the alien woman who smooths out her words, ¹⁷ who forsakes the suzerain of her youth and forgets the covenant of her God; ¹⁸ for her house sinks down to death, and her winding paths to the shades; ¹⁹ none who go to her will

who pervert truth in thought and speech revel in their evil. More than that, if misfortune befalls the righteous, heretics are delighted, for they are apparently vindicated yet again in their denials of Divine providence. (This "delight" is a joy that is experienced afresh, and so expresses the feelings of the heretics on seeing the recurring tragedies that come upon the righteous, the "treacheries of evil.")

15–17. The dangers pictured here are again two-fold: the moral dangers of dissolute living, exemplified by sin with a married woman; and the hazard of heresy represented by the "alien woman" who has abandoned the religion of Judaism and tries to sway others to follow her.

18–19. The first kind of sin, the sexual sin, shortens life, debilitates physically and leads only to death; while the second, the sin of heresy, involves a man in distortions of truth — it

כא לְמַעַן תֵּלֵךְ בְּדֶרֶךְ טוֹבִים וְאָרְחוֹת צַדִּיקִים תִּשְׁמֹר: כִּי־יְשָׁרִים
כב יִשְׁכְּנוּ־אָרֶץ וּתְמִימִים יִוָּתְרוּ בָהּ: וּרְשָׁעִים מֵאֶרֶץ יִכָּרֵתוּ
וּבוֹגְדִים יִסְּחוּ מִמֶּנָּה:

leads him down winding paths from which he can never return to the high road: Even if he should decide to repent, the heresy works within him like yeast in the dough, so that he can never find his way back to whole-hearted faith.

20–22. The distinction between the "way of good men" and the "path of the righteous" can be seen through an incident recounted in the Talmud (*Bava Metzia* 83): Rabba bar bar Chana hired porters (moving-men) to move his wine-casks. One cask broke, and in accordance with law and custom Rabba bar bar Chana confiscated the porters' coats as security for its value. The case was brought before the court (*beth-din*), and Rav, the judge, told Rabba bar bar Chana to return the coats. "Is that really the law?" asked Rabba bar bar Chana. "Yes indeed," replied Rav, citing our verse, "so that you may walk in the way of good men." The porters spoke up again, "We are poor men

return, nor will they reach the paths of life;—
[20] so that you may walk in the way of good men and keep to the paths of the righteous. [21] For the upright will dwell in the land, and the men of integrity will remain in it; [22] but the wicked will be cut off from the land, and the treacherous will be plucked out of it.

and have been working all day. Must we go home now without any money for food?" The judge ruled, "Give them their wages." Again Rabba bar bar Chana asked, "Is that really he law?" — and the judge replied, "Yes — keep to the paths of the righteous."

From this story, it is clear that the "way of good men" refers to a general attitude of compassion and kindness, while the second principle invoked, the "paths of the righteous," has reference to the particular circumstances of these laborers — the fact that they were poor and in desperate need of their wages. The righteous are flexible and open to the appeals and needs of each specific case.

PROVERBS 3:1-6

גּ א בְּנִי תּוֹרָתִי אַל־תִּשְׁכָּח וּמִצְוֺתַי יִצֹּר לִבֶּךָ: כִּי אֹרֶךְ יָמִים
ג וּשְׁנוֹת חַיִּים וְשָׁלוֹם יוֹסִיפוּ לָךְ: חֶסֶד וֶאֱמֶת אַל־יַעַזְבֻךָ קָשְׁרֵם
ד עַל־גַּרְגְּרוֹתֶיךָ כָּתְבֵם עַל־לוּחַ לִבֶּךָ: וּמְצָא־חֵן וְשֵׂכֶל־טוֹב
בְּעֵינֵי אֱלֹהִים וְאָדָם:
ה בְּטַח אֶל־יְהוָה בְּכָל־לִבֶּךָ וְאֶל־בִּינָתְךָ אַל־תִּשָּׁעֵן: בְּכָל־דְּרָכֶיךָ

1. The young man is urged to commit to memory the whole of the Almighty's Torah (teaching), which includes commandments that are not in practice today, as well as narratives that tell of providence, prophecy, reward and punishment. These are all to be studied and absorbed so that they become part of the person's being. The commandments are specifically those that do affect action; and the heart — the emotional center of the person — is the place where they should exert their dynamism. If the emotions are imbued with the Almighty's will, then all will cohere harmoniously in the psychological self.

2. The master of Proverbs promises three levels of well-being here. "Length of days" is a promise of *quality* of life — days filled with goodness. "Years of life" is literally the blessing of a long life. And, finally, these many good years will be a flowing time of "peace," of physical and material and domestic serenity, unthreatened with any kind of harm.

3. "Kindness and truth" can be seen as categories covering most of the Torah. The practical commandments are directed at the area of interpersonal relationships, the area of loving-kindness between human beings, while the theological aspects of the Torah have to do with "truth" — the cognitive content of Torah. Both of these will become an integral part of the person who is involved in the study and practice of Torah. He is told to "bind them around your neck": to speak of them constantly (the association is with the neck or throat as the

3 ¹ My son, do not forget my teaching, and let your heart keep my commandments; ² for length of days, and years of life, and peace, will they add to you. ³ Let loving-kindness and truth not forsake you; bind them about your neck, write them on the tablet of your heart. ⁴ Then you will find grace and good sense in the sight of God and man.
⁵ Trust in HA-SHEM with all your heart, and do not rely on your own understanding. ⁶ In all your ways know Him, and He will make straight your

source of speech), till they become part of his thought-structure. And he is told to "write them on the tablet of your heart": the heart, as we have indicated (verse 1), is the emotional and imaginative center of man, the core of his personality, the most sensitive place where fantasies and desires breed. Just there, the moral law should be indelibly engraved: then evil will have no power over him.

4. Through his own human resources of intellect, a man can achieve social recognition as possessor of "grace and good sense." But only through contact with the Divine wisdom of the Torah can a man achieve grace "in the sight of God" and also "*good* sense," which denotes the action of Divine inspiration within man, opening up to him an immediate intuitive comprehension of truth.

5–6. If a man will try to "know" God, to imitate Him in the major facets of the godly personality, in the large "ways" of being, such as compassion, generosity, humility (following the basic imperative of "You shall walk in His ways: as He is merciful, so you be merciful...."), then He assures the man that the detailed "paths" of the commandments, the *how*, *when*

ז דָעֵהוּ וְהוּא יְיַשֵּׁר אֹרְחֹתֶיךָ: אַל־תְּהִי חָכָם בְּעֵינֶיךָ יְרָא אֶת־
ח יְהוָה וְסוּר מֵרָע: רִפְאוּת תְּהִי לְשָׁרֶּךָ וְשִׁקּוּי לְעַצְמוֹתֶיךָ: כַּבֵּד
י אֶת־יְהוָה מֵהוֹנֶךָ וּמֵרֵאשִׁית כָּל־תְּבוּאָתֶךָ: וְיִמָּלְאוּ אֲסָמֶיךָ
שָׂבָע וְתִירוֹשׁ יְקָבֶיךָ יִפְרֹצוּ:
יא מוּסַר יְהוָה בְּנִי אַל־תִּמְאָס וְאַל־תָּקֹץ בְּתוֹכַחְתּוֹ: כִּי אֶת

and *where* of doing, rather than being, will follow smoothly and correctly.

7. Since the moral law is not something that can be known empirically, there are men who conclude that whatever way they choose is *ipso facto* moral. This is an individualistic, relativistic morality, that acknowledges no superior absolute authority. True morality, however, says the master of Proverbs, comes only from the Almighty, and is often uncongenial to man's wishes; and it can therefore be accepted only if there is a prior experience of "fear of God" ("The beginning of wisdom is fear of HA-SHEM") which can lead a man to abdicate his own autonomy in defining his moral code.

8. Living within the limitations of Torah morality may seem to imply sacrifice of physical vitality; but in fact, the master of Proverbs asserts, it only serves to invigorate even the physical faculties and the life of the senses.

9–10. The master of Proverbs turns from the physical restrictions of the moral law which will, nevertheless, prove themselves even physically salutary, to the area of material possessions. Here, again, man is told to give of his first-fruits to the Almighty, as a demonstration that all prosperity comes from Him. Then the Almighty will bless the man, who has this moral wisdom to recognize the origin of things, with an abundance of material prosperity. "Returning the first-fruits" to Him is also

paths. ⁷ Do not be wise in your own eyes; fear HA-SHEM, and turn away from evil. ⁸ It will be a healing to your navel, and medicinal drink to your bones. ⁹ Honor HA-SHEM with Your substance and with the first-fruits of all your produce, ¹⁰ so that your barns will be filled with plenty, and your vats will be bursting with new wine.

¹¹ My son, do not reject the moral discipline of HA-SHEM, and do not revile His reproof; ¹² for

a symbolic action, and can be seen as a surrender of the foundations of a person's inner life, his intellectual autonomy or "wisdom," to God's rule. This verse is then an expansion of the idea of verse 7: "Do not be wise in your own eyes": Surrender your intellectual arrogance to His will — and from a life attuned to Divine wisdom, prosperity and well-being must follow.

11. Moral discipline and reproof are two different modes of intervention by the Almighty in human life. Moral discipline denotes suffering imposed on a man as punishment for wrongdoing: this, a man tends to reject — it is obviously an unpleasant experience. Reproof is the intellectual mode of persuasion, convincing a person of a true vision of life. This is not intrinsically unacceptable — reason is persuasive — but a man will nevertheless sometimes object even to such a rational "correction." He is urged here not to shut his mind and heart to such interventions of the Almighty, since there is a profound sense in which suffering, correction, is sent precisely to those whom God loves. The process of redemptive, loving chastisement can only work, however, if a man *accepts* it in love, and makes use of it to mend his ways. This is the thrust of the next verse, that "whomever God loves He reproves, like a father the son in whom he delights."

יג אֲשֶׁר יֶאֱהַב יְהוָה יוֹכִיחַ וּכְאָב אֶת־בֵּן יִרְצֶה: אַשְׁרֵי אָדָם
יד מָצָא חָכְמָה וְאָדָם יָפִיק תְּבוּנָה: כִּי טוֹב סַחְרָהּ מִסְּחַר־כָּסֶף
טו וּמֵחָרוּץ תְּבוּאָתָהּ: יְקָרָה הִיא מִפְּנִינִים וְכָל־חֲפָצֶיךָ לֹא יִשְׁווּ־
טז בָהּ: אֹרֶךְ יָמִים בִּימִינָהּ בִּשְׂמֹאולָהּ עֹשֶׁר וְכָבוֹד: דְּרָכֶיהָ

12. Correction becomes a dynamic expression of the Almighty's love, His desire that the loved one should reach higher levels of goodness. This is the force of the image of fatherly love, which involves a propulsion toward the future, to the increasing achievements of the son; and it therefore sometimes expresses itself sternly, in terms of discipline and effort.

13. Wisdom, as we have defined it, is always "found": it comes to a man by revelation, or tradition. Its source is outside himself, but once "found," it becomes his and forms part of him. Understanding, on the other hand, arises from a man's own intellectual resources; it is "derived" from empirical data.

14. The distinction is followed through here. Wisdom, which has to be discovered in the world beyond the self, can be likened to a rare gold providentially found deep in the mountains, a chance gain bestowed by our Maker; whereas understanding is achieved by an internal "exchange and barter," a process of give-and-take in the mind, to infer and derive new conceptions from knowledge previously gained; hence it is comparable to the "merchandise of silver" acquired by trading. Unlike gold and silver, however, wisdom and understanding remain forever to enrich the spirit.

15. The analogy of pearls is based on the fact that, like wisdom, pearls are found in an element that is not human — not on the

whomever HA-SHEM loves He reproves, like a father the son in whom he delights. ¹³ Happy is the man who finds wisdom, and the man who derives understanding; ¹⁴ for its merchandise is better than the merchandise of silver, and better its gain than fine gold. ¹⁵ It is more precious than pearls, and nothing of all you desire can compare to it. ¹⁶ Length of days is in its right hand; in its left hand are riches and honor. ¹⁷ Its ways are ways of pleasantness, and all its paths are peace.

earth, but in the sea. Wisdom is found not in the earthly or the material aspect of things but in the far more exalted spiritual sources that are God's. This is why it is worth giving up all one's human, physical desires in order to attain it.

16. Just as pearls and silver and gold are means to an end — the acquisition of wealth and honor — so does wisdom give a man the same blessings. These, however, are grasped in wisdom's "left hand": they are relegated to a clearly inferior position; for in its "right hand" wisdom holds a far more precious gift: "length of days" — signifying both the best of this world, and the life to come, which is eternal life in the heavenly realm of the spirit.

17. The ways of wisdom (the reference again is to the main road, as opposed to the side-paths) lead to the general destination of "pleasantness," of psychological and spiritual serenity; while the "side-paths" in the life of every individual, with his own family and affairs, are also "peace" — paths graced with wholeness and security in every aspect — physically, domestically, materially, and politically.

יח דְּרָכֶיהָ דַרְכֵי־נֹעַם וְכָל־נְתִיבוֹתֶיהָ שָׁלוֹם: עֵץ־חַיִּים הִיא לַמַּחֲזִיקִים בָּהּ וְתֹמְכֶיהָ מְאֻשָּׁר:

יט יְהֹוָה בְּחָכְמָה יָסַד־אָרֶץ כּוֹנֵן שָׁמַיִם בִּתְבוּנָה: בְּדַעְתּוֹ תְּהוֹמוֹת נִבְקָעוּ וּשְׁחָקִים יִרְעֲפוּ־טָל: בְּנִי אַל־יָלֻזוּ מֵעֵינֶיךָ נְצֹר תֻּשִׁיָּה

כב וּמְזִמָּה: וְיִהְיוּ חַיִּים לְנַפְשֶׁךָ וְחֵן לְגַרְגְּרֹתֶיךָ: אָז תֵּלֵךְ לָבֶטַח

כד דַּרְכֶּךָ וְרַגְלְךָ לֹא תִגּוֹף: אִם־תִּשְׁכַּב לֹא־תִפְחָד וְשָׁכַבְתָּ וְעָרְבָה

כה שְׁנָתֶךָ: אַל־תִּירָא מִפַּחַד פִּתְאֹם וּמִשֹּׁאַת רְשָׁעִים כִּי תָבֹא:

18. Those who have to "hold fast" to wisdom are actually in constant conflict with morality, since their egoistic drives are powerful and put them in a position of confrontation and embattlement when they want to achieve wisdom. Of this type of person, the master of Proverbs does not feel it necessary to state that he will attain happiness when he succeeds in grasping hold of wisdom; that is an obvious consequence of the intensity of the struggle. What *is* unexpected, and therefore worth saying, is that the struggle, so far from debilitating and shortening the life of the victor, becomes a "tree of life" to him — an actual source of vitality and vigor.

The other kind of moral personality indicated here is the saintly, serene type, whose inner needs are attuned to the dictates of wisdom. He does not have to "hold fast" frantically to wisdom, but can calmly "uphold" it; and of him we are told that in spite of his lack of struggle, he too receives reward, and is called "happy."

19–21. Both action and thought are to be guided by wisdom: there is a special emphasis here on the need for study and thought in plumbing the depths of the moral law. True morality has to be based on profound analysis and understanding.

22. The soul comes alive only when it functions in the mode of

¹⁸ It is a tree of life to those who hold fast to it, and those who uphold it are happy.

¹⁹ HA-SHEM by wisdom founded the earth; He established the heavens by understanding. ²⁰ By His knowledge the depths were broken up, and the skies drop down the dew. ²¹ My son, let them not escape from your eyes; keep providential action and prudent thought. ²² So they will be life for your soul, and grace for your neck. ²³ Then you will walk on your way securely, and will not injure your foot. ²⁴ When you lie down, you will not be afraid; and as you repose, your sleep will be sweet. ²⁵ Do not be frightened of sudden terror, nor of the stormy destruction of the

wisdom — in its own organic mode; otherwise, the body may be alive and thriving, but the soul is dead — a vacuum in place of a center of vital energy. "Grace for your neck" refers again (see verse 3) to the faculty of speech: discussing and teaching the ways of wisdom will bring a person affection from both God and man.

23–25. The promise here is of Divine protection from any kind of accident. Each verse deals with a different area of danger and protection: verse 23 speaks of the peril faced by a traveller; verse 24 of a person's vulnerability in sleep; and verse 25 of danger in times of destruction. In each case there is implied a double assurance, both of a psychological serenity and confidence in the Almighty's protection, and of an objective protection from any kind of evil. One dimension of security without the other is clearly inadequate: even objective security and well-being is useless, if the mind is tormented by irrational fears and anxieties.

PROVERBS 3:26-35

כו כִּי־יְהוָה יִהְיֶה בְכִסְלֶךָ וְשָׁמַר רַגְלְךָ מִלָּכֶד: אַל־תִּמְנַע־טוֹב
כח מִבְּעָלָיו בִּהְיוֹת לְאֵל יָדְךָ לַעֲשׂוֹת: אַל־תֹּאמַר לְרֵעֲךָ לֵךְ
כט וָשׁוּב וּמָחָר אֶתֵּן וְיֵשׁ אִתָּךְ: אַל־תַּחֲרֹשׁ עַל־רֵעֲךָ רָעָה וְהוּא־
ל יוֹשֵׁב לָבֶטַח אִתָּךְ: אַל־תָּרוֹב עִם־אָדָם חִנָּם אִם־לֹא גְמָלְךָ
לא רָעָה: אַל־תְּקַנֵּא בְּאִישׁ חָמָס וְאַל־תִּבְחַר בְּכָל־דְּרָכָיו: כִּי
לג תוֹעֲבַת יְהוָה נָלוֹז וְאֶת־יְשָׁרִים סוֹדוֹ: מְאֵרַת יְהוָה בְּבֵית רָשָׁע
לד וּנְוֵה צַדִּיקִים יְבָרֵךְ: אִם־לַלֵּצִים הוּא־יָלִיץ וְלַעֲנִיִּים יִתֶּן־חֵן:
לה כָּבוֹד חֲכָמִים יִנְחָלוּ וּכְסִילִים מֵרִים קָלוֹן:

26. The image here is of a complete serenity that sees no danger and no need to guard oneself from danger. In a time of real trouble, however, this can appear to be naïveté. Here, the Almighty promises a protection that will objectively support and justify the confidence and faith of man.

27. On a literal level, this is a simple moral appeal, to do good to whoever deserves it, if one can. There is a metaphorical allusion, however, to the soul, which desires a man to do it "good" — that is, to walk in the ways of God. Since a person has it in his power to deal kindly with the soul, he should not withhold this form of spiritual "charity" from his own self.

28. Postponement of a good action is an evil in itself. This applies on the human, charitable level, and also on the metaphorical level of a person's relationship to his own soul. "Do not put off till tomorrow the essential business of penitence and improvement," says the master of Proverbs, "since you have it fully in your power to act today."

29. Again, there are two levels of meaning here: the social — not to plot against your neighbor and plan him any harm; and

wicked, when it comes. ²⁶ For HA-SHEM will be your confidence, and He will keep your foot from entrapment. ²⁷ Do not withhold good from one to whom it is due, when it is in the power of your hand to do it. ²⁸ Do not say to your neighbor, "Go away, and come back, and tomorrow I will give" — when you have it with you. ²⁹ Do not devise evil against your neighbor, while he dwells trustingly beside you. ³⁰ Do not quarrel with a man for no cause, if he has done you no harm. ³¹ Do not envy a man of violence, and choose none of his ways; ³² for the perfidious man is an abomination to HA-SHEM, but His private counsel will be with the upright. ³³ HA-SHEM's curse is in the house of the wicked, but He blesses the dwelling of the righteous. ³⁴ As for the scorners, He puts them to scorn, but to the humble He gives grace. ³⁵ The wise shall inherit honor; but as for fools, disgrace shall surge over them.

the spiritual — not to "victimize" your own soul, which dwells in all innocence within your body. The Creator has placed the soul in such close conjunction with the body, for the person's ultimate benefit; if the body works against the soul, this is a betrayal of its function and purpose.

30–35. The honor and the disgrace spoken of here are inherent aspects and developments of the very experiences of virtue and vice. A life lived according to "wisdom," according to Torah ethics, is rooted and nurtured in the essential dignity of the soul fulfilling its own nature. Sin, on the other hand, diminishes and

PROVERBS 4:1-6

ד א שִׁמְעוּ בָנִים מוּסַר אָב וְהַקְשִׁיבוּ לָדַעַת בִּינָה: ב כִּי לֶקַח טוֹב
נָתַתִּי לָכֶם תּוֹרָתִי אַל־תַּעֲזֹבוּ: ג כִּי־בֵן הָיִיתִי לְאָבִי רַךְ וְיָחִיד לִפְנֵי
אִמִּי: ד וַיֹּרֵנִי וַיֹּאמֶר לִי יִתְמָךְ־דְּבָרַי לִבֶּךָ שְׁמֹר מִצְוֹתַי וֶחְיֵה: ה קְנֵה
חָכְמָה קְנֵה בִינָה אַל־תִּשְׁכַּח וְאַל־תֵּט מֵאִמְרֵי־פִי: ו אַל־תַּעַזְבֶהָ

enfeebles the soul; the impulse to evil rises from the subconscious depths, and sweeps away the lofty aspirations to goodness, so that the soul is overwhelmed and its nobility lessened. The human being grows mean and small, as his animal nature increases in strength and importance.

---

1. The master of Proverbs begins to pass on the teachings he received from his father. This is, then, a real father speaking, and not merely an assumed "fatherly" figure. In addition, he urges his pupils to pay attention to his own conclusions, the results of his own meditations.

2. Doctrine, *lekach*, denotes the sacred lore that is *received*, the traditions passed on from father to son. The Teacher informs us that they are "good" in themselves, apart from their revered authority. His own thinking on ethical matters he also urges on his pupils: "Do not forsake my teaching."

3. The master of Proverbs, i.e., King Solomon, demonstrates the precious value of the teaching by describing how loved and nurtured he was by his parents who transmitted it to him. More than an ordinary love of father to son is described here: this is the love for the chosen son, the heir, both spiritual and temporal, to all the father's kingdom. To his father (King David) he was not an only son, yet he was treated as *the* son (*ben*) who would be the builder (*boneh*) of the future of the

4 [1] Hear, O children, the instruction of a father, and pay heed to know understanding; [2] for I give you good doctrine; do not forsake my teaching. [3] For I was a son to my father, tender, and an only one in the sight of my mother. [4] And he taught me, and said to me, "Let your heart hold fast my words; keep my commandments, and live. [5] Get wisdom, get understanding; do not forget, nor turn aside from the words of my mouth. [6] Do not forsake it,

dynasty. To his mother he was literally an only son; and her intense affection for him communicated itself to his father too, when they were together. The verse implies that when King David was "in the sight of my mother," because of his love for her, he would regard Solomon as his only son.

4. The basis of this doctrine and teaching was his father's life: the precepts of wisdom that he acted out, observed and fulfilled in a real context, in his decades of kingship. Example is the most effective ethical guidance. In addition, however, his father gave him verbal guidance: he "said to me": The heart, which is volatile, constantly vulnerable to every gust of passion, should take tight hold of the words of ethical stability; moreover, it should keep the Almighty's commandments simply because they *are* His will. This loving obedience will generate true vitality.

5. Both wisdom and understanding, both moral and intellectual teaching, are to be acquired in such a way that they become an integral part of one's being — safe from both accidental "forgetting" and the willful side-trackings of desire.

6. Here we have intensifying levels of attachment to wisdom;

ז וְתִשְׁמְרֶךָּ אֱהָבֶהָ וְתִצְּרֶךָּ׃ רֵאשִׁית חָכְמָה קְנֵה חָכְמָה וּבְכָל־
ח קִנְיָנְךָ קְנֵה בִינָה׃ סַלְסְלֶהָ וּתְרוֹמְמֶךָ תְּכַבֵּדְךָ כִּי תְחַבְּקֶנָּה׃
ט תִּתֵּן לְרֹאשְׁךָ לִוְיַת־חֵן עֲטֶרֶת תִּפְאֶרֶת תְּמַגְּנֶךָ׃ שְׁמַע בְּנִי
יא וְקַח אֲמָרָי וְיִרְבּוּ לְךָ שְׁנוֹת חַיִּים׃ בְּדֶרֶךְ חָכְמָה הֹרֵיתִיךָ
יב הִדְרַכְתִּיךָ בְּמַעְגְּלֵי־יֹשֶׁר׃ בְּלֶכְתְּךָ לֹא־יֵצַר צַעֲדֶךָ וְאִם־תָּרוּץ

to love wisdom is much more than simply not to forsake it. This is the ultimate demand that the master of Proverbs makes: not simply to live according to the principles of Torah ethics for prudential, practical reasons, but to love and desire the good purely for itself.

7. The difference between wisdom and understanding is again indicated here. Because wisdom is an organic ethical system, with no necessary rational indices or guidelines in the natural world, the only way to acquire it is simply to accept it as a whole. Understanding, however, is a rational inductive process: from data outside itself, the mind constructs a model of truth. Its "beginning" or trigger is therefore in experience, in various forms of knowledge and observation on which it can work: "with all your accomplishments," with all the resources of the world and with all its sciences of which you learn, acquire understanding. Wisdom, however, has no "beginning," no triggers outside itself; it cannot be attained on the basis of some prior perception. It is its own basis, as it were. "The beginning of wisdom is — simply — Get wisdom": accept the principles of ethics from God, and accept a whole perspective on ethical truth.

8. This is a mutual process of growing esteem: by appreciating the importance of wisdom, a man will himself increase in moral stature. And in embracing it in loving union, he will absorb its beauty and dignity.

and it will guard you; love it, and it will keep you. ⁷ The beginning of wisdom is: Get wisdom; with all your attainments, get understanding. ⁸ Esteem it, and it will exalt you; it will bring you honor when you embrace it. ⁹ It will give a wreath of grace to your head; a crown of glory will it bestow on you." ¹⁰ Hear, my son, and receive my sayings; and the years of your life will be many. ¹¹ I have taught you in the way of wisdom; I have led you in winding paths of uprightness. ¹² When you go, your step will not be hampered; and if

9. Finally, wisdom will give a man "grace" — attractiveness, both to humans and to the Almighty; and particularly, a power of intellectual conviction (connoted by "to your head") and a "crown of glory," symbolizing eternal honor.

10-11. The way of wisdom is the straight road of moral behavior, the way of mercy, modesty and loving-kindness. It is sufficient for the Almighty to "teach" this to man — to merely indicate the highway of normative morality. Often, however, one has to diverge from this highway, onto the winding side-paths of extreme behavior, when moderation is not sufficient to cure a person of some moral defect. (A very miserly person, for instance, has to re-condition himself by a period of spendthrift behavior, before he can return to the golden mean of controlled generosity.) These side-paths veer perilously far from moderation, however, carrying the implicit danger, described earlier (2:15), of the condition of those who are "perfidious in their winding paths"; and the traveller needs the Almighty's special guidance in these corrective periods — not simply, "I have taught you," but "I have *led* you."

יב לֹא תִכָּשֵׁל: הַחֲזֵק בַּמּוּסָר אַל־תֶּרֶף נִצְּרֶהָ כִּי־הִיא חַיֶּיךָ: בְּאֹרַח
יג רְשָׁעִים אַל־תָּבֹא וְאַל־תְּאַשֵּׁר בְּדֶרֶךְ רָעִים: פְּרָעֵהוּ אַל־
יד תַּעֲבָר־בּוֹ שְׂטֵה מֵעָלָיו וַעֲבוֹר: כִּי לֹא יִשְׁנוּ אִם־לֹא יָרֵעוּ וְנִגְזְלָה
טו שְׁנָתָם אִם־לֹא יַכְשִׁילוּ: כִּי לָחֲמוּ לֶחֶם רֶשַׁע וְיֵין חֲמָסִים יִשְׁתּוּ: יכשילו טז יז

12. Here two modes of spiritual life are described. The first is the ordinary "going" or progress of a life according to Torah law; in this the danger is that custom and habit will blunt and stale the eagerness and religious devotion of the pupil. The second mode is the enthusiastic "running" to cling to the Almighty and His will: the tendency to excesses of asceticism and rarefied religious experience. In this the danger is of "stumbling" and committing error through enthusiasm and overreaching spiritual ambition.

13. "Take fast hold," says the master of Proverbs, of that fear of God which alone can restrain the passions and keep them within the bonds of wisdom. "Take fast hold...do not let it go": what is needed is an extreme effort to retain contact with one's awareness of the Creator: an effort against nature, almost against gravity ("Let go for an instant, and it slips away from you"). What wisdom means to the soul (as we explained earlier, in 3:22) is no less than life itself: without it, in the spiritual sense, the soul is dead.

14. Again, the path referred to is the particular area of wickedness that a man may choose to make his own: the side-road leading off from the main road to a specific destination. "Evil men," however, are those whose evil is radical, a fundamental distortion in their vision of the world. These are on the *highway* of sin; the fact that they do or do not indulge in a particular vice is secondary. The pupil is warned not to be misled by the often attractive intellectual sparkle of their arguments, their philosophical disquisitions and scientific

you run, you will not stumble. ¹³ Take fast hold of instruction, do not let it go; keep it, for it is your life. ¹⁴ Do not enter the path of the wicked, and do not walk in the way of evil men. ¹⁵ Avoid it, do not cross on it; turn from it, and pass on. ¹⁶ For they will not sleep unless they have done evil; and they are robbed of sleep, unless they have made someone stumble. ¹⁷ For they eat the bread of wickedness, and drink the wine of violence. ¹⁸ But

researches: these can never be of benefit in a way conducive to happiness ("walk" here, *tᵉ'asher*, has the root, *'osher*, "happiness"); they can never be turned to use in providing a believer's vision of the world.

15. If a person cannot destroy its arguments with full force, then he should keep far from temptation, warns the Teacher. And if someone has already come into contact with the intellectual poison of such writings, he should then veer away and return to the way of Torah and faith.

16. About the heretics, our master of Proverbs sardonically comments that they cannot sleep if they have not perpetrated some evil themselves; moreover, their missionary zeal is such, that if they have not succeeded in infecting others with their views, their sleep is disturbed — almost as if they feel they have not earned a right to rest — they are "robbed" of their restful slumber.

17. Now, the Teacher turns from heretics to those who fall into the category of "the wicked" — those who commit vices in action. Of them, he says that the source of all their livelihood is crime.

יח וְאֹרַח צַדִּיקִים כְּאוֹר נֹגַהּ הוֹלֵךְ וָאוֹר עַד־נְכוֹן הַיּוֹם: דֶּרֶךְ
יט רְשָׁעִים כָּאֲפֵלָה לֹא יָדְעוּ בַּמֶּה יִכָּשֵׁלוּ: בְּנִי
כ לִדְבָרַי הַקְשִׁיבָה לַאֲמָרַי הַט־אָזְנֶךָ: אַל־יַלִּיזוּ מֵעֵינֶיךָ שָׁמְרֵם
כא בְּתוֹךְ לְבָבֶךָ: כִּי־חַיִּים הֵם לְמֹצְאֵיהֶם וּלְכָל־בְּשָׂרוֹ מַרְפֵּא:
כב מִכָּל־מִשְׁמָר נְצֹר לִבֶּךָ כִּי־מִמֶּנּוּ תּוֹצְאוֹת חַיִּים: הָסֵר מִמְּךָ
כג עִקְּשׁוּת פֶּה וּלְזוּת שְׂפָתַיִם הַרְחֵק מִמֶּךָּ: עֵינֶיךָ לְנֹכַח יַבִּיטוּ

18. To the sinner, the lifestyle of the good man seems narrow and constricted (a mere "path"); but this is true only at the outset. The way of the righteous is compared to the first light of dawn: it is a faint shimmering, a mere reflection of the sun's rays in the morning mists, but it gains rapidly in strength and beauty till the full glow of noon. This is the development of the soul — at first tentative and obscured by clouds of physicality, but ultimately radiant in full splendor and clarity.

19. The man at the mercy of his passions seems initially to be treading a broad highway; as far as anyone sees, he enjoys enviable liberty of movement and choice. But what becomes evident finally is that even in his largest, most far-reaching decisions, he is hemmed in by ignorance and impotence — *aféla*, the "thick darkness" that held Egypt in thrall for three days (Exodus 10:22). This is in obvious contrast to the righteous, who may appear constricted but actually move in the light of clarity and assurance, even in their smallest actions.

20–22. The words of wisdom are again described as bringing a vigor that is both spiritual ("life") and physical ("healing") to the man who integrates them fully into his being.

23. The heart is the main source of a person's vitality and development in life — the dynamic focus. If all is well there,

the path of the righteous is as the light of dawn, that shines more and more till full day. [19] The way of the wicked is like thick darkness; they do not know over what they stumble.

[20] My son, pay heed to my words; incline your ear to my sayings. [21] Let them not escape from your eyes; keep them well within your heart. [22] For they are life to those who find them, and healing to all their flesh. [23] Above all that you guard, keep your heart; for from it come the issues of life. [24] Remove from yourself perversity of mouth, and perfidy of lips put far away from you. [25] Let your eyes look directly forward, and your eyelids look

then apparent wrongs in superficial action are accounted trivial, if done in good conscience.

24. Nevertheless, warns the Teacher, externals do have their importance, and the righteous man should make every effort not to give outsiders any opportunity to speak evil of him. This is the import of "perversity of mouth" and "perfidy of lips" — one should behave in such a way that no whisper of slander can attach itself to him.

25. "Eyes" and "eyelids" here refer respectively to open eyes (which allow these organs to be seen) and closed eyes (which leave only the lids to view). In spiritual matters one should be alert and open-eyed, his mind fully focused on God, to know Him and, in imitating Him, to fulfill one's own nature. In physical matters, however, a person should try to keep his eyes shut: his interest in bodily satisfactions should be as simple and direct as possible, so as to keep his main object steadily in focus. There is also a suggestion in the word *negdecha* ("straight ahead

כו וְפַלֵּס מַעְגַּל רַגְלֶךָ וְכָל־דְּרָכֶיךָ יִכֹּנוּ:
כז אַל־תֵּט־יָמִין וּשְׂמֹאול הָסֵר רַגְלְךָ מֵרָע:

of you" or "in front of you") of the idea of confrontation, or conflict — implying that the "closed-eye" policy will be in opposition to the interests and desires of the body. The way of spiritual rectitude does involve a constant battle with the demands of man's physical nature.

26. Once again (see verse 11) the Teacher speaks of the occasions when it becomes necessary to deviate from the highroad of the golden mean; to condition oneself through some form of extreme behavior away from his natural tendency to an opposite extreme (for example, to practice extreme humility, in order to cure oneself of pride — but with the

straight ahead of you. ²⁶ Calculate the path of your foot, and let all your ways be set firm. ²⁷ Do not turn to the right or to the left; remove your foot from evil.

ultimate aim of returning to the golden mean of a healthy moderate humility). Such deviations have to be "calculated," exactly and shrewdly controlled, so that one does indeed return afterward to a normal and firmly set medium of regulated behavior.

27. In spite of the previous verse, which allows for moral extremism as a therapeutic corrective measure, the chapter ends with a general warning against such extremism. In the main, a person should try to avoid any deviation from the golden mean of virtue; for this is the surest way to avoid evil.

PROVERBS 5:1-6

ה א בְּנִי לְחָכְמָתִי הַקְשִׁיבָה לִתְבוּנָתִי הַט־אָזְנֶךָ: לִשְׁמֹר מְזִמּוֹת
ג וְדַעַת שְׂפָתֶיךָ יִנְצֹרוּ: כִּי נֹפֶת תִּטֹּפְנָה שִׂפְתֵי זָרָה וְחָלָק מִשֶּׁמֶן
ה חִכָּהּ: וְאַחֲרִיתָהּ מָרָה כַלַּעֲנָה חַדָּה כְּחֶרֶב פִּיּוֹת: רַגְלֶיהָ
ו יֹרְדוֹת מָוֶת שְׁאוֹל צְעָדֶיהָ יִתְמֹכוּ: אֹרַח חַיִּים פֶּן־תְּפַלֵּס נָעוּ
מַעְגְּלֹתֶיהָ לֹא תֵדָע:

1-2. Once again our master of Proverbs turns his attention to the two sources of ethical principle: (1) "wisdom," the received moral law, to which man is urged simply to "pay heed," for it teaches "prudent considerations," the results of the supra-rational insights of a revealed system; and (2) "understanding," which has its source in man's own rational, inductive powers, taking as its material all the evidences of reason and the senses, and yielding a clear, indubitable knowledge.

3. There are two levels of meaning here. On the one hand, the description is of the hypocrisies and dangers inherent in immorality, whose allurements are so persuasive and apparently harmless. The "strange woman" is also, however, a metaphor for the attractions of alien philosophies: The arguments of heretical writings are deceptively congenial and even seem to have the ring of truth ("smoother than oil," they slip down with the greatest of ease).

4. The ultimate consequences of yielding to her blandishments, however, are in stark opposition at every point to the original impression. "Bitter as wormwood" is counterpointed against "drip honey"; "sharp as a two-edged sword" is contrasted against "smoother than oil."

5. Those who go in her footsteps (following her invitation to sin) will be led to death; even those who merely move in her direction, who have not yet fully yielded to her, will be gripped

5 ¹ My son, pay heed to my wisdom, incline your ear to my understanding, ² to preserve prudent considerations, and that your lips may guard knowledge. ³ For the lips of a strange woman drip honey, and her palate is smoother than oil; ⁴ but the end with her is bitter as wormwood, sharp as a two-edged sword. ⁵ Her feet go down to death; her steps take hold of the netherworld. ⁶ Should you perhaps think to calculate the highway of life, her paths wander, and you will not know how.

in an experience of hell-on-earth from which they will not be able to escape. These two levels of involvement apply also on the metaphorical plane: spiritual death for one who has sold his soul to heresies, and a more insidious yet irrevocable entanglement for a person who tries merely to flirt with pagan ideas.

6. This is a reference to the idea, explained previously (4:11, 26), that sometimes it is legitimate and worthwhile to leave the highway of median, balanced virtue and deliberately venture onto side-paths of moral extremism. Here, the master of Proverbs warns that the pupil should not think such side-paths may include a visit to the harlot's house, that there is any place in his moral strategy for such an experience, even with the intention of ultimately returning to the way of virtue. From this experience, there is no return to the highroad: the paths of sexual sin veer too wildly from the golden mean of virtue. In a similar way, on the metaphorical level, the Teacher warns against thinking one can make use of heretical writings in order to prove rationally the truth of the religious vision. The mind will be infected by doubts; the skeptical approach cannot easily be shaken off, and the clear light of faith will be forever lost.

PROVERBS 5:7–14

ח וְעַתָּה בָנִים שִׁמְעוּ־לִי וְאַל־תָּסוּרוּ מֵאִמְרֵי־פִי: הַרְחֵק מֵעָלֶיהָ
ט דַרְכֶּךָ וְאַל־תִּקְרַב אֶל־פֶּתַח בֵּיתָהּ: פֶּן־תִּתֵּן לַאֲחֵרִים הוֹדֶךָ
י וּשְׁנֹתֶיךָ לְאַכְזָרִי: פֶּן־יִשְׂבְּעוּ זָרִים כֹּחֶךָ וַעֲצָבֶיךָ בְּבֵית נָכְרִי:
יא וְנָהַמְתָּ בְאַחֲרִיתֶךָ בִּכְלוֹת בְּשָׂרְךָ וּשְׁאֵרֶךָ: וְאָמַרְתָּ אֵיךְ שָׂנֵאתִי
יג מוּסָר וְתוֹכַחַת נָאַץ לִבִּי: וְלֹא־שָׁמַעְתִּי בְּקוֹל מוֹרָי וְלִמְלַמְּדַי
יד לֹא־הִטִּיתִי אָזְנִי: כִּמְעַט הָיִיתִי בְכָל־רָע בְּתוֹךְ קָהָל וְעֵדָה:

7. It is the principles of the moral law (*chochma*), received and absolute, that are referred to here.

8. Again there is a double warning: against a full commitment to sin, and against even a tentative approach to it. This applies both on the literal level of sexual wrongdoing, and on the metaphorical level of exposure to heretical thinking.

9. The "splendor" mentioned here is a person's spiritual eminence, that is blotched and spoiled by debauchery; while the "years" given "to the merciless one" refer, on the other hand, to the shattering physical consequences of promiscuity. Again, the metaphorical meaning is equally clear: This is a warning against surrendering one's intellectual faculties to alien philosophies, which will eventually destroy health and well-being.

10. Relations with the "stranger-woman" will mean a waste both of the pupil's physical virility ("your strength") and of his material property ("your labors") — what his work and toil have amassed). His property will end up in the possession of his children born from the "stranger-woman," who have no connection with him.

11. Ultimately, physical decay and exhaustion will be the fate of the licentious person; then, too late, he will be filled with

⁷ Now therefore, O children, listen to me, and do not turn away from the words of my mouth. ⁸ Remove your way far from her, and do not go near the door of her house; ⁹ lest you give your vigor to others, and your years to the merciless one; ¹⁰ lest strangers have their fill of your strength, and your labors be in the house of an alien; ¹¹ and you moan when your end comes, when your flesh and your body are consumed, ¹² and you say, "How I hated moral instruction, and my heart despised reproof! ¹³ I did not listen to the voice of my teachers, nor incline my ear to those who instructed me. ¹⁴ I was almost in all evil in the midst of the congregation and assembly."

remorse. Equally, on the level of intellectual heresy: too late, when all power of physical enjoyment has waned, the pupil will realize for what he has sold his eternal birthright of the Divinely given Jewish heritage. Then he will regret his intellectual infidelities to truth and faith, which he committed, basically, to furnish himself with pretexts for a self-indulgent or unprincipled life.

12–13. Teachers and instructors here represent two different intensities of commitment to the educational process. The first type is the teacher who simply points out facts or arguments; while the second type is the one who is dedicated to an intensive relationship, to communicate his own skills and ideas. Even this kind of sincere instruction the pupil has ignored.

14. The word *kimeʻat* in the text, usually translated "almost," can also connote "for so little": for a mere bagatelle of physical

טו שְׁתֵה־מַיִם מִבּוֹרֶךָ וְנֹזְלִים מִתּוֹךְ בְּאֵרֶךָ: יָפוּצוּ מַעְיְנֹתֶיךָ חוּצָה
טז בָּרְחֹבוֹת פַּלְגֵי־מָיִם: יִהְיוּ־לְךָ לְבַדֶּךָ וְאֵין לְזָרִים אִתָּךְ: יְהִי־
יח
יט מְקוֹרְךָ בָרוּךְ וּשְׂמַח מֵאֵשֶׁת נְעוּרֶךָ: אַיֶּלֶת אֲהָבִים וְיַעֲלַת חֵן
כ דַּדֶּיהָ יְרַוֻּךָ בְכָל־עֵת בְּאַהֲבָתָהּ תִּשְׁגֶּה תָמִיד: וְלָמָּה תִשְׁגֶּה בְנִי

appetite, worth nothing and lasting but a moment, the pupil has sold his birthright, and now he finds himself swamped in "all evil," and publicly exposed, moreover, in his true character. Remorse, self-contempt and shame are all conveyed here.

15. Instead of drinking from alien sources — the broken well of physical lusts that are doomed to frustration — the pupil is urged to drink the blessed waters of wisdom and knowledge. Cistern and well have distinct connotations: the cistern holds standing water — at first the pupil will receive knowledge in a passive way; but later he will become like a surging well of living water, creatively flowing with perceptions and ideas, himself a source of instruction to others. In this vein the image is developed in the next verse.

16. At first, his ideas will find disciples among his own children and pupils, and ultimately they will become a formative influence on the whole nation. This is an image of swelling intellectual and moral vitality, affecting a whole generation.

17. Even though the pupil's teachings will be so widely dispersed and disseminated, he alone will be accredited as their source. And though his disciples will themselves become teachers and share his credit, they are not to be thought of as "strangers," but as sons.

18. The fountain is the pupil's mind, which will be granted

¹⁵ Drink water from your own cistern, and flowing water from your own well. ¹⁶ Your springs will be dispersed abroad, and streams of water in the streets. ¹⁷ Let them be only your own, and not strangers' with you. ¹⁸ Let your fountain be blessed, and have joy of the wife of your youth. ¹⁹ A beloved hind and a graceful doe, let her breasts satisfy you at all times; with her love may you be intoxicated always. ²⁰ Why will you then be intoxicated, my son, with a strange woman, and embrace the bosom of an alien?

felicitous concepts and intuitions. The "wife of your youth" is a metaphor for the Torah, which the people of the Torah received in the early days of its history.

19. The powerful metaphor develops the theme of the sublime delight experienced by one who is totally involved in Torah study and Torah life.

20–23. The chapter closes with a warning about the inevitable retribution that eventually befalls the wicked. Motivated by egoistic drives, they find pretexts for their sins in pagan permissive philosophies. Their end is a miserable, unredeemed death, since they have trained themselves to a skepticism that inures them even to punishment and reproof; nothing can instruct and save them. The ultimate sin, then, is the sin of the mind, seeing the world as empty of God. Such a mind will transform all perceptions and revelations into parts of its own petty egoistical vision of things. Nothing real can get through to it — till, robbed of enlightenment and direction, it reels and totters, and dies.

כא בִזְרֹה וּתְחַבֵּק חֵק נָכְרִיָּה: כִּי נֹכַח ׀ עֵינֵי יְהוָה דַּרְכֵי־אִישׁ וְכָל־
כב מַעְגְּלֹתָיו מְפַלֵּס: עֲווֹנוֹתָיו יִלְכְּדֻנוֹ אֶת־הָרָשָׁע וּבְחַבְלֵי חַטָּאתוֹ
כג יִתָּמֵךְ: הוּא יָמוּת בְּאֵין מוּסָר וּבְרֹב אִוַּלְתּוֹ יִשְׁגֶּה:

²¹ For the ways of man are before the eyes of HA-SHEM, and He calculates all his paths. ²² His own iniquities shall ensnare the wicked, and he will be held in the bonds of his sin. ²³ He will die for lack of moral instruction, and in his abundant folly he will reel.

PROVERBS 6:1-6

א וֹ בְּנִי אִם־
ב עָרַבְתָּ לְרֵעֶךָ תָּקַעְתָּ לַזָּר כַּפֶּיךָ: נוֹקַשְׁתָּ בְאִמְרֵי־פִיךָ נִלְכַּדְתָּ
ג בְּאִמְרֵי־פִיךָ: עֲשֵׂה זֹאת אֵפוֹא ׀ בְּנִי וְהִנָּצֵל כִּי בָאתָ בְכַף־
ד רֵעֶךָ לֵךְ הִתְרַפֵּס וּרְהַב רֵעֶיךָ: אַל־תִּתֵּן שֵׁנָה לְעֵינֶיךָ וּתְנוּמָה
ה לְעַפְעַפֶּיךָ: הִנָּצֵל כִּצְבִי מִיָּד וּכְצִפּוֹר מִיַּד יָקוּשׁ:
ו לֵךְ־אֶל־נְמָלָה עָצֵל רְאֵה דְרָכֶיהָ וַחֲכָם: אֲשֶׁר אֵין־לָהּ קָצִין

1. This refers to a case where a solemn promise of some kind, backed by a guarantee, has been made to a friend, and then it becomes impossible to keep, because the same promise is made to another person. (In fact, the image of a handshake implied a *stronger* commitment, legally, to the second man.)

2–3. The pupil is caught in a double-bind dilemma: he is committed to both men, and cannot fulfill his obligations to both. One solution is to try to get a release from the *second* promise, since the obligation to the first is prior, and hence stronger. The other possibility is to try to placate his first friend, so that *he* will agree to forgo his rights.

4. "Sleep" (*sheina*) refers to the regular hours of rest, and "slumber" (*t*e*numa*) to a snatched brief nap. In such a dilemma one cannot allow himself even to doze off.

5. The gazelle can save itself from the trap by sheer bodily force, while the bird can flutter its wings so desperately in the clutch of the snare that some of its feathers are plucked out and it can then fly off free. So the pupil is advised to gain release either by sheer physical labor and toil, or by "shedding" externals, such as clothing, money or valuables, to placate his creditor.

 The whole episode is really to be read as an allegory, however. On a more meaningful level, this is the dilemma of the soul, which is promised or pledged to its first Friend,

6 ¹ My son, if you become surety for your neighbor, you give your handshake for a stranger, ² you are snared by the words of your mouth, you are caught in the words of your mouth — ³ do this now, my son, and save yourself, since you have come into the hand of your neighbor: Go, humble yourself, and importune your neighbor. ⁴ Give no sleep to your eyes, nor slumber to your eyelids. ⁵ Save yourself like a gazelle from the hand [of the hunter], and like a bird from the hand of the fowler.

⁶ Go to the ant, O sluggard; regard her ways, and

God — committed to study His Torah and keep His commandments — and then entangles itself in the desires of the flesh, which makes contrary demands. The only solution is to "humble yourself," stamp out in the psyche the claims of the later, physical drives and give more and more power to the spiritual voice within the self; indeed to go without a moment's rest in the unabated struggle against the domination of the physical drives; and if he finds himself caught, to escape their clutch either ("like a gazelle") by the full force of his whole being or, if necessary ("like a bird"), by plucking out all his "feathers," all the external trappings of his life, by relinquishing his money and material goods and saving his spiritual integrity in a life of asceticism and rigor.

6. Man was created as a microcosm: a concentration of all the virtues and energies of the universe. Moreover, all these energies and faculties that are found among the various species are intended, over and above their natural function in helping those species survive, for a man's good: to rouse him to a realization of the equivalent energies in his own being. The

ט שֹׁטֵר וּמֹשֵׁל: תָּכִין בַּקַּיִץ לַחְמָהּ אָגְרָה בַקָּצִיר מַאֲכָלָהּ: עַד־
י מָתַי עָצֵל ׀ תִּשְׁכָּב מָתַי תָּקוּם מִשְּׁנָתֶךָ: מְעַט שֵׁנוֹת מְעַט
יא תְּנוּמוֹת מְעַט ׀ חִבֻּק יָדַיִם לִשְׁכָּב: וּבָא־כִמְהַלֵּךְ רֵאשֶׁךָ וּמַחְסֹרְךָ כְּאִישׁ מָגֵן:
יב אָדָם בְּלִיַּעַל אִישׁ אָוֶן הוֹלֵךְ עִקְּשׁוּת פֶּה: קֹרֵץ בְּעֵינָו

natural world is the primary text-book for a man: Were there no Revelation to give us the Torah, he could yet fulfill his moral potential simply by studying the world around him. Even the minuscule ant, for instance, can be a teacher of diligence to a human being: she busily accumulates thousands of seeds, far beyond her own needs, as an object-lesson to man to apply himself to a similar diligent accumulation of wisdom.

7. The ant is described as acting autonomously, without the kinds of motivation, direction and regulation that operate in human society. The three synonyms in this verse express different nuances of social influence: "chief" is the trend-setter in society, the role-model figure, whom all slavishly copy; "overseer" is the executive power which enforces the directives of the "ruler," who dictates social norms, by force of law. The ant does not act under the impulsion of any of these forces.

8. Thus the ant provides a lesson in forethought and diligence. She spend the harvest-time, when the grain is lying around, in gathering her store for winter. After that, in summer, when there is no more grain to be had, she organizes her stock, arranges it safely and in good order for consumption in winter. The moral is clearly that a man should spend his youth accumulating Torah wisdom, a stock to last him into old age. The next stage is the thorough analysis and comprehension of what he has learned, so that he will have nourishment for his soul for as long as he lives.

be wise: ⁷ Without having any chief, overseer, or ruler, ⁸ she provides her bread in summer, and gathers her food in the harvest. ⁹ How long will you lie abed, you sluggard? When will you arise from your sleep? ¹⁰ "Yet a little sleep, a little slumber, a little folding of the hands to lie abed" — ¹¹ and your poverty shall come like a vagabond, and your want like an armed man.

¹² An irreligious person, a man of iniquity, walks with a perverse mouth; ¹³ winking with his eyes,

9. The habit of sloth is to sleep late into the day and then lie around in a pleasant stupor even after waking. These two stages have their reflected metaphorical meaning: In his youth, the sluggard is entirely unaware of eternal things, and of the urgency of action; and even when he does come to his senses and realize the purpose of life, and his own need to immerse himself in Torah, he remains too stupefied by the habits of sloth to do much about it.

10. These are the stages of withdrawal from consciousness and purposeful activity: deep sleep, the transitional light slumber before waking, and, after waking, the sluggish reluctance to rise.

11. These are the consequent stages of disaster — at first swift and unexpected, so that a person is defenseless against it; and then, in its acute form ("your want"), even though man tries to combat it, it is "armed" and conquers all resistance.

12-14. An irreligious man who flaunts the commandments between man and his maker and is evil toward his fellow-man, can be recognized by seven characteristics, listed here: (1) his speech (verse 12): he attacks wisdom, the principles of the

יד מוֹלֵל בְּרַגְלָו מֹרֶה בְּאֶצְבְּעֹתָיו: תַּהְפֻּכוֹת ׀ בְּלִבּוֹ חֹרֵשׁ רָע
טו בְּכָל־עֵת מִדְיָנִים יְשַׁלֵּחַ: עַל־כֵּן פִּתְאֹם יָבוֹא אֵידוֹ פֶּתַע
יִשָּׁבֵר וְאֵין מַרְפֵּא:
טז שֶׁשׁ־הֵנָּה שָׂנֵא יְהוָה וְשֶׁבַע תּוֹעֲבַת נַפְשׁוֹ: עֵינַיִם רָמוֹת
יח לְשׁוֹן שָׁקֶר וְיָדַיִם שֹׁפְכוֹת דָּם־נָקִי: לֵב חֹרֵשׁ מַחְשְׁבוֹת
יט אָוֶן רַגְלַיִם מְמַהֲרוֹת לָרוּץ לָרָעָה: יָפִיחַ כְּזָבִים עֵד שָׁקֶר
כ וּמְשַׁלֵּחַ מְדָנִים בֵּין אַחִים: נְצֹר בְּנִי מִצְוַת

moral law; in verse 13 we have (2) his actions: "winking with his eyes" denotes that he disregards the command, "you shall not turn astray after your eyes" (Numbers 15:39); (3) his movements: "scraping with his feet" implies that he rushes to do evil; (4) his hands: "he points with his fingers"; in verse 14 (5) his thoughts: "treacherous fickleness is in his heart" — in matters of faith he is heretical, and (6) "he devises evil" — in his relations with others; (7) "he sows discord" among others, acting as a source of social tension.

15. Because of the abruptness of his fate, the sinner will have no time to repent.

16. The first six characteristics just listed (in verses 12–14) are hateful to God, but the seventh — sowing discord among people — is the worst of all, since it means the destruction of society.

17–19. The following list is parallel to the previous one (in verses 12–14), but these reprehensible traits are in a higher dimension of evil, as it were: in verse 17 — (1) "Haughty eyes"="winking with his eyes," and refers specifically to the intellectual pride of the heretic in rejecting faith; (2) "a lying tongue"="a perverse mouth," and refers to the abuse of

scraping with his feet, pointing with his fingers. [14] Treacherous fickleness in his heart, he devises evil continually; he sows discord. [15] Therefore his calamity shall come suddenly; all at once he will be broken, and without remedy.

[16] There are six things that God hates, and the seventh is an abomination to Him: [17] haughty eyes, a lying tongue, and hands that shed innocent blood; [18] a heart that devises wicked thoughts, feet that are swift in running to evil; [19] a false witness who breathes out lies, and one who sows discord among brothers.

[20] My son, keep the commandment of your father, and do not forsake the teaching of your mother.

human understanding, twisting logic to arrive at heretical conclusions; (3) "hands that shed innocent blood"="pointing with his fingers"; in verse 18 — (4) "a heart that devises evil thoughts"="he devises evil continually"; (5) "feet that are swift in running to evil"="scraping with his feet"; in verse 19 — (6) "a false witness that breathes out lies"="treacherous fickleness in his heart" — in matters of faith; (7) "he that sows discord among brothers"="he sows discord."

20. The commandment of the father denotes the rule of law that imposes specific actions and restraints on a man, even against his natural instinct. If a man will imprint these commandments on his heart, he will be unlikely to forsake the general moral and philosophical system, the guidelines to thought and feeling, that are indicated in "the teaching of your mother." The insight expressed here is that most heretical thinking is motivated by an urge to discard the yoke of the laws — to live a freer, more self-indulgent life.

כא אָבִיךָ וְאַל־תִּטֹּשׁ תּוֹרַת אִמֶּךָ: קָשְׁרֵם עַל־לִבְּךָ תָמִיד עָנְדֵם
כב עַל־גַּרְגְּרֹתֶךָ: בְּהִתְהַלֶּכְךָ ׀ תַּנְחֶה אֹתָךְ בְּשָׁכְבְּךָ תִּשְׁמֹר
כג עָלֶיךָ וַהֲקִיצוֹתָ הִיא תְשִׂיחֶךָ: כִּי נֵר מִצְוָה וְתוֹרָה אוֹר וְדֶרֶךְ
כד חַיִּים תּוֹכְחוֹת מוּסָר: לִשְׁמָרְךָ מֵאֵשֶׁת רָע מֵחֶלְקַת לָשׁוֹן
כה נָכְרִיָּה: אַל־תַּחְמֹד יָפְיָהּ בִּלְבָבֶךָ וְאַל־תִּקָּחֲךָ בְּעַפְעַפֶּיהָ: כִּי
כו בְעַד־אִשָּׁה זוֹנָה עַד־כִּכַּר לָחֶם וְאֵשֶׁת אִישׁ נֶפֶשׁ יְקָרָה תָצוּד:
כז הֲיַחְתֶּה אִישׁ אֵשׁ בְּחֵיקוֹ וּבְגָדָיו לֹא תִשָּׂרַפְנָה: אִם־יְהַלֵּךְ

21. Of the rule of the commandments, the Teacher says that, uncongenial as they may seem at first to human instinct, it is just to the area of the emotions and the instincts that they should be addressed, "bound upon the heart," till they are fully integrated into the self. Similarly, "tie them around your neck" (i.e., throat) — speak of them often, as a means of attuning your feelings and instincts to their meaning.

22. This verse refers to the "teaching of your mother," applying it to the three situations described or implied earlier (3:23-24): when you are walking on the way, when you are lying down, and when you wake and rise up in your house. The person will be protected from the dangers of travel, from the terrors to which he is vulnerable in the helpless state of sleep, and he will have a mind-nourishing subject for meditation when he returns to consciousness.

23. The individual commandment is compared to a lamp, which requires oil and a wick in order to burn: similarly, the mitzva has force only as long as a man's spirit is contained in a body. The Torah ("teaching"), on the other hand, is light itself, general, diffuse and intangible, radiating in a man's spirit even after his death. And as the lamp is lit from another source of light, so the individual commandments are illumined by the essence of light, the study of Torah: "an ignoramus cannot be

²¹ Bind them upon your heart always; tie them about your neck. ²² When you walk, it will lead you; when you lie down, it will watch over you; and when you wake, it will talk with you. ²³ For a commandment is a lamp, and Torah is light, and reproofs in moral instruction are the way of life: ²⁴ to guard you from the evil woman, from the smoothness of the alien tongue. ²⁵ Do not lust after her beauty in your heart, nor let her take you captive with her eyelids. ²⁶ For on account of a harlot [one is brought low] to a loaf of bread, and the adulteress hunts for the precious life. ²⁷ Can a man take fire in his bosom, and his clothes not be burned? ²⁸ Or can one walk upon hot coals, and

pious." Fundamental to both the Torah and the commandments is a proper way of living, and this is achieved by listening to "reproofs of moral instruction," to warnings that restrain a man from unwise conduct.

24. On the level of warning against immorality, the reference here is to harlots, both of one's own people and of foreign origin.

25–26. These are two categories, bringing two different levels of sin and danger: the prostitute who is single and merely ruins a man financially, and the married courtesan, who sets her sights on the élite members of society.

27–31. The comparison here points out that even a thief is in a better situation, morally, than an adulterer. The thief steals out of necessity, because he is hungry; and when he is discovered, there is a definite limit to his punishment: he pays four times

PROVERBS 6:29-35

כט אִישׁ עַל־הַגֶּחָלִים וְרַגְלָיו לֹא תִכָּוֶינָה: כֵּן הַבָּא אֶל־אֵשֶׁת
ל רֵעֵהוּ לֹא יִנָּקֶה כָּל־הַנֹּגֵעַ בָּהּ: לֹא־יָבוּזוּ לַגַּנָּב כִּי יִגְנוֹב
לא לְמַלֵּא נַפְשׁוֹ כִּי יִרְעָב: וְנִמְצָא יְשַׁלֵּם שִׁבְעָתָיִם אֶת־כָּל־הוֹן
לב בֵּיתוֹ יִתֵּן: נֹאֵף אִשָּׁה חֲסַר־לֵב מַשְׁחִית נַפְשׁוֹ הוּא יַעֲשֶׂנָּה:
לג נֶגַע־וְקָלוֹן יִמְצָא וְחֶרְפָּתוֹ לֹא תִמָּחֶה: כִּי־קִנְאָה חֲמַת־גָּבֶר
לה וְלֹא־יַחְמוֹל בְּיוֹם נָקָם: לֹא־יִשָּׂא פְּנֵי כָל־כֹּפֶר וְלֹא־יֹאבֶה
כִּי תַרְבֶּה־שֹׁחַד:

the value of the ox, and three times the value of the lamb, besides returning the stolen animals, and pays off his debt to society, therefore, with mere money (even if it *is* "all the substance of his house.")

32. The adulterer, on the other hand, does not have the mitigating defense of a need to satisfy his appetite, because there is no real appeasing the sexual urge — on the contrary, the more it is gratified, the more demanding it becomes ("destroy his *nefesh* — his own soul" is understood to mean "exacerbate his own lust," in a contrasting parallel to "satisfy his *nefesh* — his appetite" in verse 30).

33. The adulterer's punishment will not be simply a matter of money, but a fate of social disgrace and even physical retribution that will not be resolved by any payment.

his feet not be scorched? **29** So he who goes in to his neighbor's wife: whoever touches her will not go free of punishment. **30** Men do not despise a thief if he steals to satisfy his appetite when he is hungry. **31** Yet if he is found, he will restore sevenfold, he will give all the substance of his house. **32** He who commits adultery with a woman lacks sense; one who would destroy his own soul is the person who would do it. **33** Wounds and dishonor shall he get, and his disgrace will not be wiped away. **34** For jealousy is the rage of a man, and he will not forgive on the day of vengeance. **35** He will not countenance any ransom, nor will he be placated though you multiply gifts.

34. This means the jealous rage of the betrayed husband, a fire that will be impossible to quench when he has the chance to avenge his dishonor.

35. The wrong that has been done the husband is so great — his wife is, in effect, lost to him, and his children are disgraced — that obviously no money can wipe it out.

PROVERBS 7:1-9

א בְּנִי שְׁמֹר אֲמָרָי וּמִצְוֹתַי
ב תִּצְפֹּן אִתָּךְ: שְׁמֹר מִצְוֹתַי וֶחְיֵה וְתוֹרָתִי כְּאִישׁוֹן עֵינֶיךָ:
ג קָשְׁרֵם עַל־אֶצְבְּעֹתֶיךָ כָּתְבֵם עַל־לוּחַ לִבֶּךָ: ד אֱמֹר לַחָכְמָה
אֲחֹתִי אָתְּ וּמֹדָע לַבִּינָה תִקְרָא: ה לִשְׁמָרְךָ מֵאִשָּׁה זָרָה
מִנָּכְרִיָּה אֲמָרֶיהָ הֶחֱלִיקָה: ו כִּי בְּחַלּוֹן בֵּיתִי בְּעַד אֶשְׁנַבִּי
ז נִשְׁקָפְתִּי: וָאֵרֶא בַפְּתָאיִם אָבִינָה בַבָּנִים נַעַר חֲסַר־לֵב: ח עֹבֵר
בַּשּׁוּק אֵצֶל פִּנָּהּ וְדֶרֶךְ בֵּיתָהּ יִצְעָד: ט בְּנֶשֶׁף־בְּעֶרֶב יוֹם בְּאִישׁוֹן

1. The difference between "commandments" and "words" has been explained previously (2:1): "commandments" denote practical directives, requiring obedience, while "words" mean the general philosophical and ethical insights of Torah.

2. The commandments are the means to life itself, while the Torah ("my teaching") and its modes of thought and feeling function like sight, giving a man orientation and perception. As a man values his eyes, so should he cherish God's teaching.

3. The fingers symbolize action, which should be controlled by Torah; similarly, the heart — the emotions and instincts — should be conditioned to respond to the Torah's way of perception.

4. Wisdom, or the moral law, is given to man — he has little creative role or choice in the formation of its content. So the image of the sister is appropriate: the relationship here too is given, a fact of nature, bringing in its train a host of assimilations and accommodations, and mutual affection. A friendship, on the other hand, is a relationship of choice, usually a cumulative process of growing knowledge and fondness. This is the metaphor for understanding, also an autonomous cumulative process, by which man constructs his conceptual model of the world.

7 ¹ My son, keep my words, and reposit my commandments with you. ² Keep my commandments and live, and my teaching as the apple of your eye. ³ Bind them upon your fingers, write them on the tablet of your heart. ⁴ Say to wisdom, "You are my sister," and call understanding "friend": ⁵ that they may preserve you from the strange woman, from the alien woman who makes her words smooth. ⁶ For at the window of my house I looked out through my lattice, ⁷ and I saw among the simpletons, I discerned among the youths, a boy lacking in [self-disciplining] heart, ⁸ passing through the street near her corner, stepping along the way to her house, ⁹ in the twilight, in the evening of the day, in the

5. The strange woman denotes anyone except his own wife — even if she is of his people; the alien woman is a foreigner, who generally has to go to greater lengths to attract: she has to "make her words smooth." Figuratively, the strange woman, again, represents alien philosophies — of which there are two degrees: one could conceivably be "married" or integrated into the Torah vision, while the other is irredeemably alien, heretical, but employs all the techniques of logic to allure the intellect.

6. The window suggests full, clear vision, while the lattice suggests a partial, secret glimpse. The Teacher speaks, then, of two kinds of insight: of revealed and of hidden things.

7-14. The harlot inveigles her victim at first with the lure of a supposed mitzva, a purportedly commendable pious deed: it is

PROVERBS 7:10–22

י   לָיְלָה וַאֲפֵלָה: וְהִנֵּה אִשָּׁה לִקְרָאתוֹ שִׁית זוֹנָה וּנְצֻרַת לֵב:
יא הֹמִיָּה הִיא וְסֹרָרֶת בְּבֵיתָהּ לֹא־יִשְׁכְּנוּ רַגְלֶיהָ: פַּעַם ׀ בַּחוּץ
יב פַּעַם בָּרְחֹבוֹת וְאֵצֶל כָּל־פִּנָּה תֶאֱרֹב: וְהֶחֱזִיקָה בּוֹ וְנָשְׁקָה לּוֹ
יג הֵעֵזָה פָנֶיהָ וַתֹּאמַר לוֹ: זִבְחֵי שְׁלָמִים עָלָי הַיּוֹם שִׁלַּמְתִּי נְדָרָי:
יד עַל־כֵּן יָצָאתִי לִקְרָאתֶךָ לְשַׁחֵר פָּנֶיךָ וָאֶמְצָאֶךָּ: מַרְבַדִּים
טו רָבַדְתִּי עַרְשִׂי חֲטֻבוֹת אֵטוּן מִצְרָיִם: נַפְתִּי מִשְׁכָּבִי מֹר אֲהָלִים
טז וְקִנָּמוֹן: לְכָה נִרְוֶה דֹדִים עַד־הַבֹּקֶר נִתְעַלְּסָה בָּאֳהָבִים: כִּי
יז אֵין הָאִישׁ בְּבֵיתוֹ הָלַךְ בְּדֶרֶךְ מֵרָחוֹק: צְרוֹר־הַכֶּסֶף לָקַח בְּיָדוֹ
יח לְיוֹם הַכֵּסֶא יָבֹא בֵיתוֹ: הִטַּתּוּ בְּרֹב לִקְחָהּ בְּחֵלֶק שְׂפָתֶיהָ
יט תַּדִּיחֶנּוּ: הוֹלֵךְ אַחֲרֶיהָ פִּתְאֹם כְּשׁוֹר אֶל־טֶבַח יָבוֹא וּכְעֶכֶס

a righteous act to have the meat of these sacrifices at a repast, and the pleasure she offers at first is therefore a supposedly religious one.

15. At first she speaks as though she had simply seen him pass by and decided to invite him: "I came out as you were coming." Then, she shamelessly admits that she came out looking for a "guest."

16. Her brazenness continues, as she invites him to stay with her, tempting him with the luxury of her furnishings.

17–19. This is to reassure the young man that he will not be caught in the act: all is supposedly safe.

20. She continues to reassure him, that her husband will have no need to return home unexpectedly, that indeed he has a definite date when he plans to arrive.

blackness of night and the darkness. ¹⁰ And behold, there was a woman to meet him, decked out like a harlot, and wily of heart. ¹¹ She is volatile and rebellious, her feet do not abide in her house; ¹² now she is outside, now in the wide streets, and at every corner she lies in wait. ¹³ So she gripped him and kissed him, she made her face brazen, and said to him, ¹⁴ "Sacrifices of peace-offerings I owed; today I have paid my vows. ¹⁵ Therefore I came out as you were coming, to seek your face eagerly, and I have found you. ¹⁶ I have decked my couch with coverlets, with colored spreads of fine Egyptian linen. ¹⁷ I have perfumed my bed with myrrh, aloes, and cinnamon. ¹⁸ Come, let us take our fill of lovemaking till the morning; let us delight ourselves with loves. ¹⁹ For my husband is not at home, he has gone on a long journey; ²⁰ he has taken the bag of money with him; at the full moon he will come home." ²¹ With her abundance of fair speech she sways him; with the smoothness of her lips she entices him. ²² All at once he goes after her, as an ox that goes to the slaughter, or as a viper to the

21-22. He follows her impulsively and automatically, for if he delayed and thought it over, he would not go. At first, he is drawn after her, with a measure of reluctance and unwilling compulsion — "like an ox to the slaughter"; then he moves willingly; nevertheless, the image of the viper, which hisses as it approaches its victim ("to the chastisement of the fool"), sug-

כג אֶל־מוּסַר אֱוִיל: עַד יְפַלַּח חֵץ כְּבֵדוֹ כְּמַהֵר צִפּוֹר אֶל־פָּח וְלֹא־יָדַע כִּי־בְנַפְשׁוֹ הוּא:
כד וְעַתָּה בָנִים שִׁמְעוּ־לִי וְהַקְשִׁיבוּ לְאִמְרֵי־פִי: אַל־יֵשְׂטְ אֶל־
כה דְּרָכֶיהָ לִבֶּךָ אַל־תֵּתַע בִּנְתִיבוֹתֶיהָ: כִּי־רַבִּים חֲלָלִים הִפִּילָה
כו וַעֲצֻמִים כָּל־הֲרֻגֶיהָ: דַּרְכֵי שְׁאוֹל בֵּיתָהּ יֹרְדוֹת אֶל־חַדְרֵי־
מָוֶת:

gests the voice of conscience within the young man, which warns him even as he moves toward his poisonous delights.

23. The liver is traditionally the seat of the emotions (filled with blood, symbol of desire and craving), and here the arrow of passion transfixes the young man so that he seethes with eagerness and hastens on to his goal, all scruples left behind.

24–25. The young man is urged not to yield to the harlot — neither in her major "function" of harlotry ("her ways") nor even in any of the minor forms ("her paths") of

chastisement of a fool, ²³ till an arrow strikes through his liver; as a bird hastens to the snare — unaware that it is at the cost of his life.

²⁴ And now, O children, listen to me, and pay heed to the words of my mouth. ²⁵ Let not your heart veer off into her ways, do not go astray in her paths. ²⁶ For many stricken victims has she felled, and a mighty host are all her slain. ²⁷ Her house is the way to the netherworld, going down to the chambers of death.

relationship with her, in which he thinks he may safely engage — such as conversation, or simply looking at her.

26. Any approach to her is perilous, since she has been the doom of many men of great spiritual force, who thought that they could resist her blandishments. Therefore, "Do not [even] go near the door of her house"(5:8).

ח

א,ב הֲלֹא־חָכְמָה תִקְרָא וּתְבוּנָה תִּתֵּן קוֹלָהּ: בְּרֹאשׁ־מְרֹמִים
ג עֲלֵי־דָרֶךְ בֵּית נְתִיבוֹת נִצָּבָה: לְיַד־שְׁעָרִים לְפִי־קָרֶת מְבוֹא
ד פְתָחִים תָּרֹנָּה: אֲלֵיכֶם אִישִׁים אֶקְרָא וְקוֹלִי אֶל־בְּנֵי אָדָם:
ה הָבִינוּ פְתָאיִם עָרְמָה וּכְסִילִים הָבִינוּ לֵב: שִׁמְעוּ כִּי־נְגִידִים

1. The chapter opens with the call of wisdom, which is contrasted in every way with the call of the harlot. Unlike her, wisdom makes its claim in the open, in daylight: it is a widespread unashamed challenge from above and beyond man; and even understanding, whose voice issues from the depths of man's own being, is not a surreptitious voice, but a clear call to contemplate the world and arrive at conclusions.

2. Unlike the harlot, who haunts the streets and squares, wisdom descends from on high. At first, it stands "by the way," on the public highway, and then it moves to the narrow paths, where people walk alone, to encounter the individual in his privacy.

3. It moves on to the main entrance to the city, and then to the private doorways of the houses. The image conveys a progression: [in verse 2] from the popular, basic teachings of ethics, which are accessible to all segments of the people ["by the way"], to the teachings of Torah, which are revealed only to the scholars, following their own "paths"; then [in verse 3] it stands "beside the gates" of the city, where the judges and learned elders sat — symbolizing the rigorous laws and principles of the Torah, learned only by the great scholars who master the Oral Torah and render decisions of law. Finally it "declaims at the entrance of the portals" — conveying the hidden, mystic insights of Torah to the very few, studying alone in their private chambers.

4. The call of wisdom is addressed primarily to those who

8 ¹ Does not wisdom call, and understanding raise its voice? ² Atop the heights by the way, where the paths meet, it takes its stand; ³ beside the gates, at the entry of the city, at the entrance of the portals, it declaims: ⁴ "To you, O men, I call, and my voice is to the sons of men. ⁵ O you simpletons, understand sagacity, and you fools, understand [with a self-disciplining] heart. ⁶ Listen, for I will speak noble matters, and the

deserve the name of "men" (*ishim*) — the great ones. Secondarily it reaches also the smaller "sons of men" as well. For wisdom can fully come only to minds and hearts that are properly prepared to receive it, that are cleared of all impurities and ugly images. Nevertheless, wisdom does convey its message to all human beings, so that it may be accepted by each according to his own degree of readiness.

5. The simpleton has regressed from wisdom, because he is undiscriminating and open to any persuasion. What he needs is sagacity, discrimination, a thoughtful, critical capacity to respond with shrewdness; and this is what wisdom offers him. The fool, on the other hand, is sometimes highly sophisticated and knowledgeable, but is controlled by his drives and desires, and he therefore disputes the authority of the moral law. What he needs is to educate his "heart," his will and passions, so that wisdom can find a place in it.

6. The Teacher now deals with four main categories of revealed wisdom; each is addressed to both the élite and the masses — the ordinary people. The first is indicated by the word "speak" (*dibbér*) as opposed to the second, which is indicated by "say" (*amar*): "say" refers to the original form in which the mitzva was articulated in the Written Torah, while "speak" refers to

ז אֲדַבֵּר וּמִפְתַּח שְׂפָתַי מֵישָׁרִים: כִּי־אֱמֶת יֶהְגֶּה חִכִּי וְתוֹעֲבַת
ח שְׂפָתַי רֶשַׁע: בְּצֶדֶק כָּל־אִמְרֵי־פִי אֵין בָּהֶם נִפְתָּל וְעִקֵּשׁ: כֻּלָּם
י נְכֹחִים לַמֵּבִין וִישָׁרִים לְמֹצְאֵי דָעַת: קְחוּ־מוּסָרִי וְאַל־כָּסֶף

the elaboration of the mitzva, which was conveyed and transmitted orally. The third is the category of rationales for the mitzvoth; and the fourth is the area of the esoteric, of mystic, kabbalistic teachings.

The verse begins with the Oral Torah, the extensive commentary on the laws and mitzvoth, which is indicated by "*speak* noble matters." This phrase, more literally, "princely things," is a reverential way of referring to the authority and greatness of these major mitzvoth, which are transmitted to the wisest of the people to interpret and implement, and which are therefore linked to the appeal of verse 4: "To you, O *men*, I call." Equally, however, the Teacher mentions the simpler levels of "speaking," in regard to the Oral Law: the "opening of my lips" suggests something external, fairly superficial, and accessible to all; while "rightnesses" suggests the sensible, pragmatic, universal appeal of these simpler elements of revelation.

7. This is a reference to the third of the Teacher's categories — the rationale (literally, the *taste* — to "my palate") of the mitzvoth. This is also an oral category of the Torah: the explanations of the mitzvoth are transmitted to all men to meditate on them, but again, they are absorbed by the élite and by the masses to very different effect. The élite will reach out for eternal truths, for modes of attaching themselves to the Source of all existence: through a deeper understanding of the mitzvoth, they will grasp the inner kernel of the Divine that is hidden within each mitzva. The masses too will benefit from the explanations of the mitzvoth, though theirs will be mainly a moral gain: the mitzvoth will bring additional power to deter them from evil. The explanations will serve the masses of the

opening of my lips shall be rightnesses. [7] For my palate shall utter truth, while wickedness is abomination to my lips. [8] All the sayings of my mouth are in righteousness; there is nothing crooked or perverse in them. [9] They are all plain to one who understands, and right to those who find knowledge. [10] Receive my moral instruction

people, then, by making wickedness an "abomination to their lips."

8. "Sayings" indicates the second of the Teacher's categories: the Written Law. This again is addressed to two levels of the people: the ordinary folk, who will learn simple righteousness from the formulations of the Written Law, and the élite, who will appreciate the unique infallibility of the Divine language. "There is nothing crooked or perverse" in the formulations of the Almighty. Unlike human language, which is prone to inaccuracies and redundancies, the language of the Torah, just at those points where it may *seem* inaccurate or redundant, is a vehicle for the most complex insights — for those who are graced with the intellectual and spiritual light to discern them.

9. This is the fourth of the Teacher's categories: the mystical plane of revealed wisdom, which will be made directly and intuitively available to those who have the required understanding and knowledge.

10. By silver the Teacher invokes the idea of coinage and hard currency that can be exchanged and used to acquire goods. This is the purpose of "moral instruction" or self-discipline, which induces the reverent fear of the Holy One. By imbuing himself with this holy fear, a person prepares his soul and mind for wisdom. Such "moral instruction" therefore has the

יא קְחוּ־מוּסָרִי וְאַל־כָּסֶף וְדַעַת מֵחָרוּץ נִבְחָר: כִּי־טוֹבָה חָכְמָה מִפְּנִינִים וְכָל־חֲפָצִים לֹא יִשְׁווּ־בָהּ:
יב אֲנִי־חָכְמָה שָׁכַנְתִּי עָרְמָה וְדַעַת מְזִמּוֹת אֶמְצָא:
יג יִרְאַת יהוה שְׂנֹאת רָע גֵּאָה וְגָאוֹן ׀ וְדֶרֶךְ רָע וּפִי תַהְפֻּכוֹת

implemental function of silver, which will "buy" wisdom, and store it up in the treasury of the heart. It is, indeed, to be preferred to silver, because it purchases the most precious and enduring goods possible. "Choice gold," on the other hand, is not used for barter and purchasing; it is the stored treasure itself. This is the most cherished good of all, knowledge of the Almighty and of His providential dealings with the world.

11. Here the Teacher elaborates on the images of the previous verse. Whatever we can buy for silver, even precious pearls, is surpassed by the wisdom that we acquire through moral instruction and self-restraint. (Note 3:15, "It is more precious than pearls.") Here the beauty of pearls, the attractive glow they lend to the wearer, is the basis of the comparison: This is a merely human attractiveness, while the grace reflected by wisdom on those who "wear" it appeals to both God and man (note also 3:4). Furthermore, even though silver buys all the delights that the body desires and enjoys, for the sake of wisdom these delights often have to be sacrificed and our desires frustrated. Nevertheless the exchange is unquestionably worthwhile: "all things desirable cannot compare to her."

12. "Sagacity" (*'orma*) here denotes the faculty of foresight, the shrewd weighing of consequences, before acting. It can be turned to good or evil use, depending on whether the guiding principle is wisdom, i.e. a sense of ethics, or not. The term "perspicacities" (*m^ezimoth*) in the verse means the penetrating analyses of ethics that lead to a clear and full comprehension of the principles of the moral law. This "knowledge" is the aim of the pursuit of moral wisdom.

and not silver, and knowledge rather than choice gold. ¹¹ For wisdom is better than pearls, and all things desirable cannot compare to her. ¹² I, wisdom, dwell with sagacity, and find knowledge of perspicacities. ¹³ The fear of HA-SHEM is the hating of evil, pride and arrogance; and the evil way and the mouth of treacherous fickleness I

13. The essential foundation for the whole process of "sagacity" leading to close meditation on the moral law, leading in turn to the ideal of lucid knowledge, is, once again, the fear of the Holy One. Since there is no empirical evidence for the authority of the moral law, it is only through a prior emotional readiness, a relationship to the Almighty which attunes us to His will, in thought and act, that we can properly apprehend the authority of His law. Here the Teacher speaks of the particular evil of pride, which can infect our mind to such an extent that we become sealed off from all contact with wisdom. The conviction that our own desires and perspectives represent a valid morality can effectively prevent the true moral law from gaining a foothold in our heart. Only by infusing ourselves with a reverent fear of God can the infection of pride be removed and a realistic humility — an openness to His will — take its place.

Fear of the Almighty by itself, however, without the guiding principles of the moral law, is also insufficient to develop the human being to a proper level of Divine knowledge. With the best will in the world, a person may find the habits of false conceptions and feelings, of a relativistic morality, so ingrained in him that it is impossible for him to move out of their influence. Only the conjunction of a humble will to submit ourselves to God ("fear of HA-SHEM") and a knowledge of the principles of ethical living ("wisdom") can move us away from a "mouth of treacherous fickleness," the

יד שֶׁנָּאתִי: לִי־עֵצָה וְתוּשִׁיָּה אֲנִי בִינָה לִי גְבוּרָה: בִּי מְלָכִים
טו יִמְלֹכוּ וְרוֹזְנִים יְחֹקְקוּ צֶדֶק: בִּי שָׂרִים יָשֹׂרוּ וּנְדִיבִים כָּל־שֹׁפְטֵי
יז אֹהֲבַי יח אָרֶץ: אֲנִי אהביה אֵהָב וּמְשַׁחֲרַי יִמְצָאֻנְנִי: עֹשֶׁר־וְכָבוֹד אִתִּי
יט הוֹן עָתֵק וּצְדָקָה: טוֹב פִּרְיִי מֵחָרוּץ וּמִפָּז וּתְבוּאָתִי מִכֶּסֶף

result of a distorted moral vision, and lead us toward the lucid knowledge of a full moral being.

14. "Wise planning" is the choice made in a dilemma where more than one possibility confronts us. The resolution of such dilemmas is precisely the business of wisdom, the moral law: it deals in situations where free choice makes more than one mode of action possible, and principles of ethics teach a person "wise planning" to know which way to choose. "Providential action," as we explained previously (2:7), refers to acts of historic destiny that the Almighty allots to the great men of all generations. Wisdom, therefore, is the inspiration of both "wise planning" (the prudent resolution of dilemmas) and "providential action" (acts of historic import). "I am understanding," therefore, refers to the discernment of solutions, for which a deductive rationality is essential; while "power is mine" refers to acts of moral and historic significance, for which spiritual force is necessary. Both understanding and power, then, are the gifts of moral wisdom.

15–16. Two modes of justice are indicated here, of kings and rulers, on the one hand, and of princes and nobles on the other. Princes and nobles judge the people, render verdicts, and implement their decisions, strictly according to the codex of law, the directions of the Torah. The king and his counsellors, however, have much greater latitude in their decisions: the power of a king is greater and more flexible than the letter of the law; his edicts are properly and legitimately affected by particular needs and circumstances. They are, nevertheless,

hate. [14] Wise planning is mine, and providential action; I am understanding, power is mine. [15] By me do kings reign, and rulers decree justice. [16] By me do princes govern, and nobles, all the judges of the earth. [17] I love those who love me, and those who seek me eagerly shall find me. [18] Riches and honor are with me, timeless wealth and righteousness. [19] My fruit is better than gold, even than fine

guided by the higher law of moral wisdom. On these two systems of government hinges the future of political and social human life.

17. Those who have already come close enough to wisdom to cling to it in love, to expose their own innermost selves to it, will in return receive love and self-revelation through it; and as a lover protects the beloved, wisdom will also guard from sin those who cherish it. On a level of lesser achievement, even those who have not yet united themselves with wisdom, but earnestly and devoutly seek it, rising eagerly each morning in their quest (a play on the word *shachar*="morning" and *shachér*="seek earnestly"), are promised that by special grace they shall attain it.

18. This is an elaboration of 3:16 ("in its left hand are riches and honor"), showing how wisdom's bounty is superior to mere material prosperity. Wisdom's wealth lasts forever, accompanying a human being even into the world to come; while, unlike worldly honor, which is generally not based on righteousness, the prestige that wisdom brings is for good and righteous acts, and is therefore a true and meaningful honor.

19. The difference between "fruit" and "produce" is the difference between a possibly incomplete or unripe crop, and

PROVERBS 8:20-24

כ בְּאֹרַח־צְדָקָה אֲהַלֵּךְ בְּתוֹךְ נְתִיבוֹת מִשְׁפָּט: כא לְהַנְחִיל אֹהֲבַי ׀ יֵשׁ וְאֹצְרֹתֵיהֶם אֲמַלֵּא:
כב יְהֹוָה קָנָנִי רֵאשִׁית דַּרְכּוֹ קֶדֶם מִפְעָלָיו מֵאָז: כג מֵעוֹלָם נִסַּכְתִּי מֵרֹאשׁ מִקַּדְמֵי־אָרֶץ: כד בְּאֵין־תְּהֹמוֹת חוֹלָלְתִּי בְּאֵין מַעְיָנוֹת

the completed, ripened crop. Fruit is stored, just as gold is generally collected in treasuries, whereas produce is marketed, to be bartered, used as a form of currency for the acquisition of other goods. Wisdom is therefore described on these two levels of ripeness: For one whose wisdom is matured it becomes like a ripe harvest; he can handle it like "silver" and "market" it in an internal dialogue, applying all the systems of logic and deduction to it, so as to expand his "property" in wisdom. On the other hand, one whose wisdom is not yet matured to this degree can keep it in store, like fine gold.

20. The Almighty has two methods of dealing with humanity. One is the approach of strict justice, treating each person as he deserves; this is indicated here in the phrase "paths of justice": the modest term "paths" suggests the way of the individual, and the phrase implies that he is assessed and rewarded in exact accordance with his deeds. The other method is that of righteousness, of a bounteous goodness that does not scrutinize the exact value of each detail of human behavior, but responds more generally and more generously to the totality of human needs; the "*way* of righteousness" is the highroad on which *all* walk together.

21. This verse corresponds to the two approaches in the previous verse. Those who love the Creator will be rewarded with "substance" — with what already exists in reality, the fruit of their own virtue. This reward is, then, their own creation; it is mere justice, the yield of their own labor. In addition to this, however, Divine grace will also operate so as to "fill their

gold, and my produce than choice silver. [20] I walk in the way of righteousness, within the paths of justice, [21] to endow with substance those who love me, and that I may fill their treasuries.

[22] HA-SHEM made me as the beginning of His way, the first of His processes of old. [23] I was enthroned from primordial antiquity, from the start, before the very origins of the earth. [24] When there were no depths, I was brought forth; when there were

treasuries" with bounty, far beyond any calculation of what has been earned and deserved.

22. In accordance with the mystic insights of Kabbalah, the wisdom of the Torah is depicted as the blueprint, the ideal model of all creation. All the universes are described as fashioned after its pattern. Furthermore, wisdom was the initiatory principle inherent in the Creator's earliest manifestation of His being, in His providential relationship with the created world. That is what is meant here by "the beginning of His way": His "way" is His mode of relating to His world, His first descent from pure Being to the process of action in, and regulation of, a world separate from Himself. The beginning of this revelation of relationship was in wisdom, just as His very acts of regulating the creation — "His worlds of old" — were founded on the patterns of wisdom.

23. This alludes to the earliest stages of creation according to the cosmology of Midrash and Kabbalah, in which the hierarchy of angels was created, in the primordial light that preceded the formation of heaven and earth. Already then wisdom was "enthroned" as the ruling principle of all creation.

24. This refers to the first stages of the earth's emergence from

כה נִכְבַּדֵּי־מָיִם: בְּטֶרֶם הָרִים הָטְבָּעוּ לִפְנֵי גְבָעוֹת חוֹלָלְתִּי: עַד־
כו לֹא עָשָׂה אֶרֶץ וְחוּצוֹת וְרֹאשׁ עָפְרוֹת תֵּבֵל: בַּהֲכִינוֹ שָׁמַיִם
כז שָׁם אָנִי בְּחֻקוֹ חוּג עַל־פְּנֵי תְהוֹם: בְּאַמְּצוֹ שְׁחָקִים מִמָּעַל
כח בַּעֲזוֹז עִינוֹת תְּהוֹם: בְּשׂוּמוֹ לַיָּם ׀ חֻקּוֹ וּמַיִם לֹא יַעַבְרוּ־פִיו
כט
ל בְּחוּקוֹ מוֹסְדֵי אָרֶץ: וָאֶהְיֶה אֶצְלוֹ אָמוֹן וָאֶהְיֶה שַׁעֲשׁוּעִים
לא יוֹם ׀ יוֹם מְשַׂחֶקֶת לְפָנָיו בְּכָל־עֵת: מְשַׂחֶקֶת בְּתֵבֵל אַרְצוֹ
וְשַׁעֲשֻׁעַי אֶת־בְּנֵי אָדָם:
לב וְעַתָּה בָנִים שִׁמְעוּ־לִי וְאַשְׁרֵי דְּרָכַי יִשְׁמֹרוּ: שִׁמְעוּ מוּסָר וַחֲכָמוּ

the matrix of formlessness and void. It was the spirit of Divine wisdom that hovered over the abyss with the spirit of God, before the separation of the elements of creation.

25–26. After the elements began to separate out, water still covered all the earth. The division of the upper waters (the sky, mists, rain-clouds) from the lower left the dry land exposed; yet long before that, wisdom reigned and set out the guidelines for the whole structure of creation.

27–29. Creation meant in effect setting boundaries — establishing forms, limits and restraints — on the energies of the elements. Both earth and water were subject to the dictates of wisdom, filling their prescribed boundaries, so that a habitable world could emerge into existence.

30. This tender image depicts wisdom at first as an infant, nestling in the bosom of God, a source of constant delight to Him. Then, with the creation of time and the successive changes and innovations of the created world, wisdom is pictured as a child who exhibits all the variety and whimsy of play.

31. Once the earth has become habitable and all forms of

no fountains abounding with water. ²⁵ Before the mountains were hard-cast, before the hills, I was brought forth; ²⁶ while He had not yet made the earth, nor the fields, nor the first of the dust of the world. ²⁷ When He established the heavens, I was there; when He drew a circle upon the face of the deep, ²⁸ when He made firm the high heavens above, when the fountains of the deep grew mighty, ²⁹ when He set for the sea His decree, that the waters should not transgress His commandment, when He decreed the foundations of the earth, ³⁰ then I was beside Him as a nursling, and I was [His] delight day by day, playing before Him at all times, ³¹ playing in the habitable world of His earth, and [having] my delights with the sons of men.

³² And now, O children, listen to me; and happy are those who keep my ways. ³³ Hear moral

creation in water and on land have been completed, the metaphor of play is no longer appropriate; the irridescent, ever-changing activity of creation has ceased, and the previous image of delight returns, suggesting the joyful contemplation of wisdom. Now, however, the gift of delight is shared with "the sons of men" who can know and enjoy wisdom, meditate on it and act on it, in their earthly lives.

32. From the cosmic vastness of the previous section the Teacher returns to a direct personal appeal to his pupils. Since he has shown wisdom to be the foundation of universal creation, he calls on his "children" to accept his statements and retain them in their hearts.

לג וְאַל־תִּפְרָעוּ: אַשְׁרֵי אָדָם שֹׁמֵעַ לִי לִשְׁקֹד עַל־דַּלְתֹתַי יוֹם ׀ יוֹם
לד לִשְׁמֹר מְזוּזֹת פְּתָחָי: כִּי מֹצְאִי מצאי חַיִּים וַיָּפֶק רָצוֹן מֵיְהוָה:
לה וְחֹטְאִי חֹמֵס נַפְשׁוֹ כָּל־מְשַׂנְאַי אָהֲבוּ מָוֶת:

33. Again, the Teacher reverts to the basic concept of the difficulty of accepting and observing the moral law — both because it is not empirically demonstrable and because it cuts against human drives and desires. And once more he makes it clear that only through fear of God, through the "moral instruction" that controls and humbles the passions, can a person become wise and come to accept the moral law which is wisdom.

34. Wisdom is metaphorically pictured as hidden behind closed doors. The man who seeks it has to wait tirelessly at the gates, till the moment comes when the gates open and he can catch a glimpse of it.

instruction and become wise, and do not refuse it. ³⁴ Happy is the person who listens to me, watching at my doors day after day, waiting at the posts of my entrances: ³⁵ For whoever finds me finds life, and obtains favor of HA-SHEM; ³⁶ but he who sins against me does violence to his own soul; all who hate me love death."

35. When the gates do open, the vision of wisdom is such as to vitalize the seeker, imbuing him with new energy and grace in both body and spirit.

36. One who sins against the moral law, however, thereby does violence to his own spiritual being, whose entire life is nourished by wisdom. By extension, enemies of wisdom can be seen as the enemies of life, as allies of death.

ט א חָכְמוֹת בָּנְתָה בֵיתָהּ חָצְבָה עַמּוּדֶיהָ שִׁבְעָה: טָבְחָה טִבְחָהּ
ב מָסְכָה יֵינָהּ אַף עָרְכָה שֻׁלְחָנָהּ: שָׁלְחָה נַעֲרֹתֶיהָ תִקְרָא עַל־גַּפֵּי
ג מְרֹמֵי קָרֶת: מִי־פֶתִי יָסֻר הֵנָּה חֲסַר־לֵב אָמְרָה לּוֹ: לְכוּ לַחֲמוּ
ו בְלַחֲמִי וּשְׁתוּ בְּיַיִן מָסָכְתִּי: עִזְבוּ פְתָאיִם וִחְיוּ וְאִשְׁרוּ בְּדֶרֶךְ

1. The Teacher returns to the conception of wisdom as the basic Divine approach that was paramount in creation. The image of the construction of a house here elaborates on that conception. Inherently, in an ideal sense, in the first moment of creation the entire act of creation took place: the structure sprang into complete being out of the blankness of non-being that preceded creation. This was, however, only a potential state of existence; it had to be gradually realized in full detail with each successive day of the seven days of creation — and these are indicated in the "seven pillars" that wisdom hewed out, *after* (metaphorically speaking) she had already "built her house." These seven days gave full physical reality to each aspect of the universe, culminating in the Sabbath, when the central principle of the Almighty's miraculous relation to the world was established. This was the day when He reserved His right, as it were, to revert to miracles in the running of the world: He inserted within the natural law a clause of supernatural possibility.

2. We are told three things, in metaphor, about wisdom. The first is that she has constructed her house and hewn out its pillars. The second is that the banquet she has prepared for her guests is full of fine food and drink; and everything is set out in public, so that all may share in it.

3. The third thing is that wisdom does not issue her invitations personally, but sends out her maidens; this denotes that a man does not receive wisdom directly, but through the sages,

9 ¹ Wisdom has built her house, she has hewn out her seven pillars; ² she has prepared her meat, she has mixed her wine; she has also set her table. ³ She has sent out her maidens, [through whom] she calls on the summits of the city's heights: ⁴ "Whoever is simple, let him turn in here!" As for one who lacks a [self-disciplining] heart, she says to him: ⁵ "Come, eat of my bread, and drink of the wine which I have mixed. ⁶ Forsake the simpletons and live, and stride on the way of

prophets, and teachers, who invite him to the exalted banqueting-hall of wisdom.

4. The "simple" one here is a naïve, gullible person who has not grasped the principles of moral law, and can therefore be easily swayed. On the other hand, a person who "lacks a heart" may understand the moral law theoretically, but he lacks emotional control over his urges.

5. Wisdom first addresses the "simple" person, inviting him to accept its "bread," the basic principles of the moral law, which will give him awareness and discrimination and arm him against the guileful persuasions of evil. "Drink of the wine," on the other hand, is addressed to the person who has theoretical knowledge of moral law but has little control over his emotions: Through profound meditation, comparable to wine in its penetrating potency, he is urged to probe the depths of moral wisdom.

6. Again, the first part of this verse is addressed to the "simple" person who will be fortified by the "bread" of wisdom to grow out of his naïveté, while the second part is directed to the per-

ז בִּינָה: יֹסֵר לֵץ לֹקֵחַ לוֹ קָלוֹן וּמוֹכִיחַ לְרָשָׁע מוּמוֹ: אַל־תּוֹכַח
ח לֵץ פֶּן־יִשְׂנָאֶךָּ הוֹכַח לְחָכָם וְיֶאֱהָבֶךָּ: תֵּן לְחָכָם וְיֶחְכַּם־עוֹד
י הוֹדַע לְצַדִּיק וְיוֹסֶף לֶקַח: תְּחִלַּת חָכְמָה יִרְאַת יהוה וְדַעַת

son who lacks a "self-disciplining heart" and who is urged to contemplate the principles of moral wisdom till he reveals the essential happiness of a life of restraint and moral direction (the verb *v^e'ishru*, "and stride," also connotes *'osher*, happiness, good fortune).

7. Here, wisdom distinguishes between naïve and undisciplined, unrestrained persons on the one hand, whom it is good to try to redeem, and scorners and wicked men on the other hand, who will not respond to any moral appeal. The scorner requires empirical evidence before he will accept an idea; he therefore mocks the principles of morality, which cannot be demonstrated empirically but rather rest on "fear of HA-SHEM" — on a direct emotional apprehension of moral law and its sanctions as they operate in the world. This is the implication of "he who *corrects* a scorner": trying to impress such a skeptic through fear of retribution, for instance, will be worse than useless. The wicked man, however, is on a lower level of degradation: he is no longer open even to rational argument ("reproval"). He sins with open eyes, willfully, and simply heaps abuse and calumny on anyone who tries to argue with him.

8. With a further turn of the screw, wisdom advises against even trying rational argument with the scorner, the intellectual skeptic whose world-view is professedly entirely rational. Even if we try to fight him with his own weapons, the result will not be good: he may not mock us, but he will "hate" even the rational opponent who speaks for morality. Such skeptics, implies Scripture, instinctively recoil from any contact with an

understanding. ⁷ He who corrects a scorner gets himself shame, and he who reproves a wicked man [acquires] his blemish. ⁸ Do not reprove a scorner, lest he hate you; reprove a wise man, and he will love you. ⁹ Give to a wise man, and he will be yet wiser; teach a righteous man, and he will increase in learning. ¹⁰ The beginning of wisdom is the fear of HA-SHEM, and [the beginning of] holy

absolute morality, however rationally justified; the skeptic will keep his distance from moral wisdom and its arguments. As for the wise man, however, even though he has already accepted the principles of morality, he will always enjoy contact with moral wisdom, even if its arguments convey a criticism of his life; he, therefore, should be invited to the banquet, along with the "simple" and those who "lack a self-disciplining heart."

9. The wise man will always find scope for development in moral wisdom. He is never satisfied in full in his desire to know and to attune his life to his knowledge. The righteous man is in rather a different position: he may not be aware of all the moral laws in theory, but in practice he is so imbued with the habits of integrity that his life breathes righteousness. Of him Scripture says that it is worth while to teach him the theoretical principles of the moral law, since this is his deficiency, and since he will have no difficulty in integrating them into his life.

10. Wisdom invites a man to its feast, but sends maidens as messengers to issue the invitations. The metaphor suggests that wisdom is not immediately accessible to a person — he can arrive at it only through the agency of the prophets and teachers of the Tradition, and he will give respect and obedience to them only if he is filled with the prior emotions and attitudes of awe before the Holy One. Therefore the theme returns here that the

יא קְדֹשִׁים בִּינָה: כִּי־בִי יִרְבּוּ יָמֶיךָ וְיוֹסִיפוּ לְּךָ שְׁנוֹת חַיִּים: אִם־
יב חָכַמְתָּ חָכַמְתָּ לָּךְ וְלַצְתָּ לְבַדְּךָ תִשָּׂא: אֵשֶׁת כְּסִילוּת הֹמִיָּה
יד פְּתַיּוּת וּבַל־יָדְעָה מָּה: וְיָשְׁבָה לְפֶתַח בֵּיתָהּ עַל־כִּסֵּא
טו מְרֹמֵי קָרֶת: לִקְרֹא לְעֹבְרֵי־דָרֶךְ הַמְיַשְּׁרִים אֹרְחוֹתָם: מִי־

basis for an intellectual apprehension of the moral law is an emotional readiness and sensitivity. On that basis, a man can reflect and construct a complete mental model of all aspects of the sacred teachings.

Elsewhere in Scripture we find a similar text: "The beginning of wisdom is the fear of HA-SHEM" (Psalms 111:10). There is one significant difference between the two verses: here the word for "beginning" is *t*echilla*, and there it is *reshith*. Two differing concepts of fear are involved here. One type belongs to the sphere of wisdom, as it were: it is its *beginning*, in the sense of *reshith*, "the first part of" (as in Numbers 15:20 and Deuteronomy 18:4), already partaking of the nature of wisdom. This kind of fear is the recognition of God's sublimity, which impels man to awed obedience. The other kind bears only a relationship of *t*echilla* to wisdom: it is previous and external, but prerequisite to a grasp of the moral law. This is basically fear for oneself, the fear of punishment. It is not in itself a morally dignified stance, but it is *instrumental* in helping a man to accept and integrate the principles of moral wisdom. Through self-concern, a man can become sensitive to the appeal of wisdom and its messengers.

11. This is the appeal to the simple concern of a man for his own welfare. There is physical and material reward offered to those who adopt a morality of wisdom (note 3:2).

12. The verse expands on this theme: the life of wisdom is good, on purely ordinary, practical, utilitarian grounds. It brings benefits to a man that are obviously desirable. Conversely, to

men's knowledge is understanding. [11] For by me will your days be multiplied, and the years of your life will be increased. [12] If you are wise, you are wise for yourself; and if you scorn, you alone will bear it." [13] The woman of folly is turbulent, [a woman of] witlessness, and knows nothing; [14] and she sits at the entrance of her house, on a seat on the city's heights, [15] to call to those who pass by, who are going straight on their roads: [16] "Who-

reject the law of wisdom is to load oneself with the burden of inevitable punishment.

13. The woman of folly is contrasted here with the mellifluous teachings of wisdom. Again, there are two facets of folly: one is turbulence: it is volatile and clamorous with willful desire; and the other is "witlessness": folly is simple, naïve, unaware of the moral law, recklessly ignorant.

14. The image is contrasted at every point with the previous image of wisdom. Folly has no fixed abode, firm on the pillars of wisdom: she destroys the world, rather than builds it. She has prepared no meat, has mixed and decanted no wine, has set no table: for she is empty of all true delight. She sends no messengers, but herself sits at the door of her house, extending an obvious and crude invitation which can appeal to every man. Her elevated seat is the throne of physicality — all the bodily instincts are drawn toward her. And her call is not to the peaceful citizens, who remain intent on their pursuit of a hallowed life, but rather (verse 15) "to call to those who pass by," etc.

15. She tries to lure the wanderers, the transients, who have not yet found themselves spiritually. Like all men, they basically

יז פְּתִי יָסֻר הֵנָּה וַחֲסַר־לֵב וְאָמְרָה לּוֹ׃ מַיִם־גְּנוּבִים יִמְתָּקוּ
יח וְלֶחֶם סְתָרִים יִנְעָם׃ וְלֹא־יָדַע כִּי־רְפָאִים שָׁם בְּעִמְקֵי
שְׁאוֹל קְרֻאֶיהָ׃

want to find the right and the good; They "are going straight on their roads"; they are vulnerable, however, to distractions that seek to sway them off the straight path.

16–17. Folly offers a person bread and water, in place of wisdom's meat and wine. There is no question which fare is objectively more delicious and nourishing. But the great appeal of folly's sparse diet is precisely its illicitness: what is forbidden,

ever is simple, let him turn in here"; and as for him who lacks a [self-disciplining] heart, she says to him, ¹⁷ "Stolen waters are sweet, and bread eaten in secret is pleasant." ¹⁸ But he does not know that the shades of the dead are there, that her guests are in the depths of the netherworld.

what costs a great deal of effort to make our own, becomes dangerously attractive.

18. Spiritually, the victim is being lured to his death. Those who accept folly's invitation have already, in a spiritual sense, abandoned their hold on life.

PROVERBS 10:1–7

א מִשְׁלֵי שְׁלֹמֹה בֵּן חָכָם יְשַׂמַּח־אָב וּבֵן כְּסִיל תּוּגַת אִמּוֹ: לֹא־
ב יוֹעִילוּ אוֹצְרוֹת רֶשַׁע וּצְדָקָה תַּצִּיל מִמָּוֶת: לֹא־יַרְעִיב יְהוָה
ג נֶפֶשׁ צַדִּיק וְהַוַּת רְשָׁעִים יֶהְדֹּף: רָאשׁ עֹשֶׂה כַף־רְמִיָּה וְיַד
ד חָרוּצִים תַּעֲשִׁיר: אֹגֵר בַּקַּיִץ בֵּן מַשְׂכִּיל נִרְדָּם בַּקָּצִיר בֵּן
ה מֵבִישׁ: בְּרָכוֹת לְרֹאשׁ צַדִּיק וּפִי רְשָׁעִים יְכַסֶּה חָמָס: זֵכֶר
ו

1. A father is seen by his son as the source of discipline and moral instruction; if the son lives virtuously, then the credit goes to the father; that is his "gladness." The mother, on the other hand, expresses the grief of feeling personal responsibility and blame if the son chooses a life of vice, for evidently her loving relationship with him has served to protect her son from the discipline and wholesome rigors of the father's education.

2. Material wealth can sometimes be useful and effective, in a relative sense; even if it does not ultimately deserve the label "good," it can be said to be of benefit and avail to a man. Wealth gained through evil, however, is entirely ineffectual even on this utilitarian level; whereas righteousness has the ultimate potency to save a person from his mortal enemy, death.

3. Even in a time of famine, when all the wealth in the world is useless, as there is no food to buy — even then the Almighty will provide fully for the needs of the righteous.

4. The word *kaf* in the first part of the verse means only the palm of the hand, and graphically expresses the approach of a man who tries to earn a soft living, without using the full force or capability of his hands. This kind of wiliness will only lead to failure; while the man who works energetically will succeed in earning a good living.

10 ¹ The proverbs of Solomon: A wise son makes a father glad, but a foolish son is the grief of his mother. ² Treasures of wickedness avail nothing, but righteousness saves from death. ³ HA-SHEM will not let the soul of the righteous starve, but He thrusts away the desire of the wicked. ⁴ A palm of sly deceit impoverishes, but the hand of the diligent brings wealth. ⁵ An intelligent son gathers in the summer, while a shameful son sleeps at harvest-time. ⁶ Blessings devolve upon the head of the righteous, but the mouth of the wicked conceals violence. ⁷ The memory of the

5. The wise son continues the process of reaping the harvest even in summer, in the period *after* the spring harvest is actually over. The indolent son, however, lazes about and dozes off even when the harvest season is at its height and the field is bursting with grain. The image conveys the spiritual energy and activity of the wise man, who even in old age, when he can no longer be so very creative in his thought, will continue slowly accumulating nuggets of wisdom; and on the other hand, it depicts the sloth of the young man who is in the prime of creative and gainful ability, yet wastes the good years in lethargy.

6. The man who acts with justice, charity and loving-kindness receives universal gratitude, as if hands were laid in blessing on his head. Vicious behavior, on the other hand, has to be surreptitious, huddled away from the public eye, in a private world of shamefulness.

7. There is a distinction between "memory" and "name": "memory" refers to the reputation that a man's deeds create in

ח צַדִּיק לִבְרָכָה וְשֵׁם רְשָׁעִים יִרְקָב: חֲכַם־לֵב יִקַּח מִצְוֺת וֶאֱוִיל
ט שְׂפָתַיִם יִלָּבֵט: הוֹלֵךְ בַּתֹּם יֵלֶךְ בֶּטַח וּמְעַקֵּשׁ דְּרָכָיו יִוָּדֵעַ:
י קֹרֵץ עַיִן יִתֵּן עַצָּבֶת וֶאֱוִיל שְׂפָתַיִם יִלָּבֵט: מְקוֹר חַיִּים פִּי צַדִּיק
יא

the world, while "name" refers to the essential identity of a man. The verse sharply contrasts the righteous person with the wicked: Even the impression left by the mere deeds of a righteous man will be remembered for blessing; while not merely their deeds but the very name and essence of the wicked, the entire record of their being in the world, will rot away, leaving no trace.

8. The nature of the heart's impulses is rebelliously opposed to the moral discipline that wisdom imposes: natural human instinct often finds such a restraint irksome. Only someone who is "wise in heart," who has integrated his morality with his instincts and passions, will be able to relate to the commandments otherwise than in a strained, compelled way; to him they will come naturally, as the truest expression of *his* desires. He will "accept" (literally "take") them — and the verb is never used of any less spontaneous relationship with the commandments. The skeptic in the verse is normally a person who doubts the validity of the moral law. In this case, he is merely skeptical in his speech; in his heart he believes in the law of wisdom, but he feels compelled to express doubts. This kind of man is torn by inner conflict, never at peace with his own best instincts — the opposite of the "wise in heart," whose life is harmonious and serene.

9. Here again we find the two extremes. The wise man, who follows whole-heartedly, in sincerity, the route which he is told is the high road, is not only safe from external dangers, but is inwardly free of fear and anxiety. The fool, on the other hand,

righteous will be for a blessing, but the name of the wicked will rot. [8] The wise of heart will accept commandments, but a skeptic in his speech will weary in vain. [9] He who walks in steadfast sincerity walks securely, but he who perverts his ways will be found out. [10] He who winks an eye brings sorrow; and a skeptic in his speech will weary in vain. [11] A wellspring of life is the mouth of the righteous, but the mouth of the wicked

who wanders off on untried paths, will encounter danger and disaster.

10. Having depicted the two extreme positions, the master of Proverbs now describes two intermediate positions. There is the man who walks on the high road but cannot resist "winking an eye" and casting constant glances at the alternative path, so full of doubt is he about the right road. He will not encounter external danger, but his condition of doubt will in itself cause him sorrow and misery. There is also the man who does not really doubt the validity of the moral life, not even to the extent of glancing aside at alternative life-styles, but he cannot resist expressing himself like a skeptic. In his speech he maintains the pose of a doubting Thomas, in feigned uncertainty. The habit of verbal nihilism also carries its penalty in diminishing his integrity and inner harmony.

11. The way of wisdom is the road that leads to eternal life. The image used here is of a man who drinks from a magic fountain; and there are three groups of such people. First, there are those who arrive at truth by means of their intellect; of these the master of Proverbs states, "Intelligence is a wellspring of life to one who has it" (16:22). Then there are those who grasp truth through the Torah which they have learned, from sages

יב וּפִי רְשָׁעִים יְכַסֶּה חָמָס: שִׂנְאָה תְּעֹרֵר מְדָנִים וְעַל כָּל־פְּשָׁעִים
יג תְּכַסֶּה אַהֲבָה: בְּשִׂפְתֵי נָבוֹן תִּמָּצֵא חָכְמָה וְשֵׁבֶט לְגֵו חֲסַר־

and scholars well versed in it; of these the master of Proverbs states, "The teaching of the wise is a wellspring of life" (13:14). To this faith in tradition, an intense fear of God is essential — the "discipline of wisdom" referred to above (on 1:7); to this the master of Proverbs refers when he says, "The fear of HA-SHEM is a wellspring of life" (14:27). The third approach to wisdom is by imitation, by following in close detail the life-style and personal behavior of a *tzaddik*, a righteous man, learning from his lips his own approach to a life of wisdom. Concerning this the master of Proverbs states here, "A wellspring of life is the mouth of the righteous."

The *tzaddik* (the righteous man) is different from the sage in that he does not have a total grasp of all the complexities of the scope of ethics, nor a capacity to organize in systematic style the general principles of the moral law, to cover any hypothetical case. The *tzaddik* is simply imbued with the habits of moral virtue, so that for any individual problem of behavior he can respond with sound, practical advice. The wellspring of life that flows from him is therefore from his "mouth" and not from his knowledge of Torah. It is practical, immediate and personal, rather than theoretical and intellectual.

12. The strife referred to here is specifically the kind of issue that is open to two interpretations, so that the matter needs to be adjudicated; it is not a clear case where injustice is blatant — which is called "transgression" in the verse. The point the master of Proverbs is making is that on such controversial matters there is no objective need for anger and protest. It is only a subjective need or strong desire to hate that seizes hold of any petty pretext for strife. Hatred arises independently of any

conceals violence. ¹² Hatred stirs up strife, but love covers over all transgressions. ¹³ On the lips of the discerning one is wisdom found; but a rod for the back of one who lacks a [self-disciplining]

real cause, and proceeds to interpret events in the world in the light of its own hostility. A person's love, on the other hand, casts a forgiving cloud even over real acts of injury against him. Not the external fact but the internal attitude determines the nature and quality of human relations.

13. The "discerning one" denotes a person who has probed and fathomed the received principles of wisdom to such an extent that he has attained a complete grasp of their rationale. Unlike the "wise man," he no longer needs to consult his memory as each fresh case arises; he has so internalized and absorbed the ways of the ethical system that he can respond spontaneously to the contingencies of events; he can even extrapolate and postulate further structures of moral thought on the basis of the received principles. The image of the "*lips* of the discerning" therefore reinforces the idea of the spontaneous, direct quality of his responses: He no longer needs to mull over the solution to moral dilemmas.

The man who "lacks a self-disciplining heart" is one who has not set any kind of control-system in his emotional life. The "heart" is the directing force in the psyche. Ideally, it should have integrated the principles of wisdom so that the whole emotional life of the self runs smoothly in accordance with them. Some people, however, completely lack a regulating force in their lives. Their emotions are a matter of instinctive response, without consistency or direction. Such people need discipline imposed on them from without, to replace their own inadequate power of self-regulation. This is the symbolic sense of the "rod" in the verse.

יד לֵב חֲכָמִים יִצְפְּנוּ־דָעַת וּפִי־אֱוִיל מְחִתָּה קְרֹבָה: הוֹן עָשִׁיר
טו קִרְיַת עֻזּוֹ מְחִתַּת דַּלִּים רֵישָׁם: פְּעֻלַּת צַדִּיק לְחַיִּים תְּבוּאַת
טז רָשָׁע לְחַטָּאת: אֹרַח לְחַיִּים שׁוֹמֵר מוּסָר וְעֹזֵב תּוֹכַחַת מַתְעֶה:
יז מְכַסֶּה שִׂנְאָה שִׂפְתֵי־שָׁקֶר וּמוֹצִא דִבָּה הוּא כְסִיל: בְּרֹב דְּבָרִים

14. Discretion is a virtue, slyness is a vice. The fine line between the two is indicated here by the term "store up." Wise people are careful about revealing the secrets of their wisdom, but they exercise a *discrimination* in their reticence: those who are worthy are invited to share their secrets. The sly man, however, "conceals his knowledge" (12:23), from everyone; and it is a vice to entirely withhold knowledge from the world. Such intellectual retention is a very different matter from the discriminating approach of the wise. The skeptic in the verse denotes the doubter, whose skepticism is so deeply ingrained that he can never summon up real conviction about anything, however clearly evident. He cannot bring himself even to warn people of imminent disaster, so accustomed is he to doubt even the evidence of his senses. This is the discretion of folly, quite different from the discretion of wisdom, which is applied intelligently to valuable things, such as knowledge, so that they should not be cheapened or distorted.

15. Wealth acts as an insulation against disaster. It protects a person against the vicissitudes of life. If one loses his wealth, metaphorically his fortress has been conquered by the enemy, leaving him defenseless against disaster. Symbolically, the wealth mentioned here is the inner riches of wisdom which protect a man against his spiritual enemies — his desires and instinctive drives.

16. The term "activity" here refers to the labor that is invested in a specific undertaking, which culminates in a "finished product." With the righteous, even their preliminary and pre-

heart. [14] Wise men store up knowledge, but the mouth of the skeptic is an imminent ruin. [15] A rich man's wealth is his strong city; the ruin of the impoverished is their poverty. [16] The activity of the righteous makes for life, the product of the wicked, for failure. [17] He who heeds moral instruction is on the road to life, but he who forsakes reproof goes astray. [18] He who hides hatred has lying lips, and he who utters slander is a fool. [19] In a multitude of words transgression

paratory acts are filled with vital satisfaction, and all the more certainly their actual achievements; while for the wicked, even their final achievements savor of failure and disappointment.

17. The term "moral instruction" is related to the idea of correction or discipline, and denotes the deterrent power of punishment. Even such a negative motive, says the master of Proverbs, will have results that are more than simply negative: it will lead on to "the road to life." Reproof, on the other hand, produces a motivation to goodness, arising from an intellectual conviction of the utility of a moral life. Failure to heed this voice of good sense will not simply cut a person off from the good but will precipitate him into the way of death. The point made here is in effect, that in the area of ethics there are no half-measures: you orient yourself either toward life or toward death.

18–19. The theme here is the virtue and value of silence. In his commentary to *Avoth* (Ethics of the Fathers), Rambam (Maimonides) has written about its maxim (i, 17), "All my life I have grown among wise men and I have never found anything better for the constitution than silence." He notes that speech is of four kinds: forbidden, optional, virtuous, and permissible;

כ לֹא יֶחְדַּל־פֶּשַׁע וְחוֹשֵׂךְ שְׂפָתָיו מַשְׂכִּיל: כֶּסֶף נִבְחָר לְשׁוֹן צַדִּיק
כא לֵב רְשָׁעִים כִּמְעָט: שִׂפְתֵי צַדִּיק יִרְעוּ רַבִּים וֶאֱוִילִים בַּחֲסַר־לֵב
כב יָמוּתוּ: בִּרְכַּת יְהוָה הִיא תַעֲשִׁיר וְלֹא־יוֹסִף עֶצֶב עִמָּהּ: כִּשְׂחוֹק
כג לִכְסִיל עֲשׂוֹת זִמָּה וְחָכְמָה לְאִישׁ תְּבוּנָה: מְגוֹרַת רָשָׁע הִיא

and thus the wise man will speak only one quarter hat he has to say (the "virtuous" part). Forbidden speech is basically slander and calumny. Someone given to such talk disguises his hatred under a mask of friendliness. Such a person, who "hides hatred" with "lying lips" and thus "utters slander," is called a fool—the opposite of the wise man who is the model of the Book of Proverbs, to be emulated. Yet even one who does not actually indulge in the forbidden talk of slander but allows himself "optional" talk (for example, to praise someone) makes himself vulnerable to the sins that are all too easily committed in speech. The wise man will therefore refrain from any conversation that is not a positive contribution to the spiritual quality of life.

20. The "tongue" alludes to internal dialogue and reflection to achieve understanding. As the *tzaddik* (the righteous man) reflects on *tzedek*, righteousness and justice, he is like "choice silver," with no trace of dross, in his progress to true understanding. The wicked are far from *tzedek*, however, and their unruly hearts leap about from evil to another; and so their hearts are practically worthless for self-discipline.

21. The term "lips" alludes to external dialogue (with others) regarding externally acquired knowledge and information. Even the ordinary conversation of the *tzaddik*, not concerned with profound thought and understanding, is a source of mental nourishment for many. Skeptics, however, doubt the true norms and ways of wisdom, and so cannot nourish even their own minds, but die spiritually; for, lacking certainty, they

will not be lacking, but he who restrains his lips is wise. [20] Choice silver is the tongue of the righteous; the heart of the wicked is little worth. [21] The lips of the righteous feed many, but skeptics die for want of a [self-disciplining] heart. [22] The blessing of HA-SHEM, that makes rich, and He adds no sorrow with it. [23] It is like sport to a fool to carry out an evil scheme, and so is wisdom to a man of discernment. [24] What the wicked

achieve no effective self-control over their cravings and desires.

22. Wealth that is the result of hard work can never be enjoyed in full ease, since it carries with it the memory of the anxiety and labor that were invested in it. The true sensation of wealth comes only with the blessing of the Almighty God that gives a feeling of grace and ease to the enjoyment of what one has acquired.

23. The fool is a person who has rejected the rule of morality; the man of discernment has completely integrated the moral law into his personality. Both reach a point where they no longer act in conscious choice at each crisis, but respond spontaneously, each according to the rule or system of his being. This is the connotation of the phrase, "It is like sport"; each acts with an unconscious, instinctive expression of the self.

24. The word *m‘gorath*, "the dread of" — that which is dreaded — denotes something terrifying that a man does all in his power to avoid. The wicked will be punished in precisely those ways they most fear and most actively seek to prevent. The righteous, on the other hand, will be granted even those desires that are still buried in the subconscious, which they have taken no overt measures to achieve.

כה תְּבוֹאֵנוּ וְתַאֲוַת צַדִּיקִים יִתֵּן: כַּעֲבוֹר סוּפָה וְאֵין רָשָׁע וְצַדִּיק
כו יְסוֹד עוֹלָם: כַּחֹמֶץ ׀ לַשִּׁנַּיִם וְכֶעָשָׁן לָעֵינָיִם כֵּן הֶעָצֵל לְשֹׁלְחָיו:
כז יִרְאַת יְהוָה תּוֹסִיף יָמִים וּשְׁנוֹת רְשָׁעִים תִּקְצֹרְנָה: תּוֹחֶלֶת
כח צַדִּיקִים שִׂמְחָה וְתִקְוַת רְשָׁעִים תֹּאבֵד: מָעוֹז לַתֹּם דֶּרֶךְ יְהוָה
ל וּמְחִתָּה לְפֹעֲלֵי אָוֶן: צַדִּיק לְעוֹלָם בַּל־יִמּוֹט וּרְשָׁעִים לֹא

25. The wicked man essentially has no roots in reality. It is the nature of evil to lack true being: its substance evaporates, by a metaphysical law of nature. The righteous man, however, is the most concentrated focus of reality, his roots thrust deep into the essence of things. He *is*, and therefore what he is, what he creates and contributes to the world, cannot die.

26. Vinegar is meant to arouse the appetite before a meal [note Ruth 2:14]; but if it harms the teeth, although the appetite is aroused the food cannot be chewed and eaten properly. If a house is lit by smoky lamps, of what use is the illumination if the smoke dims one's sight? Similarly a sluggard (a lazy, indolent person) employed as a messenger may carry out his task, but his employer will have no satisfaction, as he is certain to do some damage. The point applies as well to a person who is indolent and lazy in carrying out the Divine purpose for which he was sent into this world. He too is bound to be unsatisfactory.

27. The paradox here is that fear, or anxiety, is usually thought to reduce energy and vitality. This particular kind of fear, however, part of our reverence and awe toward the Almighty, actually adds to our physical lifespan; while the lives of the wicked are shortened by Divine punishment.

28. Expectation and hope express different qualities of feeling.

dreads, that shall come upon him; but the desire of the righteous shall be granted. ²⁵ When the whirlwind passes, the wicked man is no more, but the righteous one is an everlasting foundation. ²⁶ As vinegar to the teeth and as smoke to the eyes, so is the sluggard to those who send him. ²⁷ The fear of HA-SHEM prolongs days, but the years of the wicked will be shortened. ²⁸ The expectation of the righteous is joy; but the hope of the wicked will perish. ²⁹ A stronghold to the steadfastly sincere is the way of HA-SHEM, but ruin is it to those who do iniquity. ³⁰ A righteous person shall not collapse forever, but the wicked

The righteous confidently anticipate the joy that is securely theirs in the future, while the wicked can merely *hope* to prosper; their future happiness is by no means certain; and it is indeed an illusory projection, doomed to failure.

29. Seeing how the Almighty cares for those who may falter or fail on life's journey, how His methods are imbued with kindness, compassion and truth, the man of steadfast sincerity and integrity adopts the same methods, taking courage in the fact that they are His ways. But people who "do iniquity" adopt methods and ways that are opposed to Him, and end disastrously.

30. Even if they should momentarily falter, the righteous are assured that they will regain their footing. The wicked, however, securely as they may seem to "inhabit the land," are destined to be swept away.

לא יִשְׁכְּנוּ־אָרֶץ: פִּי־צַדִּיק יָנוּב חָכְמָה וּלְשׁוֹן תַּהְפֻּכוֹת תִּכָּרֵת:
לב שִׂפְתֵי צַדִּיק יֵדְעוּן רָצוֹן וּפִי רְשָׁעִים תַּהְפֻּכוֹת:

31. As explained before (verse 11), the righteous man has not necessarily acquired a theoretical grasp of the complexities of ethics, but he has thoroughly integrated the principles of ethics into every facet of his practical experience. The *tzaddik* is a living example of what others preach, and therefore is ready at any moment with the practical answer to any particular moral problem. His mouth "buds with wisdom": it spontaneously bears the fruit of experience. In this, he even has an advantage over the wise man, whose theoretical knowledge can occasionally find itself unable to respond to the treacherously twisting tongue of the intellectually acute heretic. The *tzaddik* is armed with detailed practical experience of the virtuous life, and he can

shall not inhabit the land. [31] The mouth of the righteous buds with wisdom; but a tongue of treacherous fickleness will be cut off. [32] The lips of the righteous know what is acceptable, but the mouth of the wicked is treachery.

therefore destroy, point by point, the empirical arguments of the heretic.

32. The righteous man is practiced in goodness; it has become second nature to him; and it provides him clear solutions to dilemmas. The *tzaddik* knows instinctively what is gratifying and gracious in his relations with both man and God. The wicked live in a domain that is like a negative exposure of the world of wisdom: all its values are inverted, its perceptions distorted.

יא א מֹאזְנֵי מִרְמָה
ב תּוֹעֲבַת יהוה וְאֶבֶן שְׁלֵמָה רְצוֹנוֹ: בָּא־זָדוֹן וַיָּבֹא קָלוֹן וְאֶת־
ג יְשָׁרִים צְנוּעִים חָכְמָה: תֻּמַּת יְשָׁרִים תַּנְחֵם וְסֶלֶף בּוֹגְדִים וְשָׁדֵּם: לֹא־
ה יוֹעִיל הוֹן בְּיוֹם עֶבְרָה וּצְדָקָה תַּצִּיל מִמָּוֶת: צִדְקַת תָּמִים
ו תְּיַשֵּׁר דַּרְכּוֹ וּבְרִשְׁעָתוֹ יִפֹּל רָשָׁע: צִדְקַת יְשָׁרִים תַּצִּילֵם וּבְהַוַּת
ז בֹּגְדִים יִלָּכֵדוּ: בְּמוֹת אָדָם רָשָׁע תֹּאבַד תִּקְוָה וְתוֹחֶלֶת אוֹנִים

1. There is no middle ground, no neutral value between the moral and the immoral. By resisting the temptation to deceive others with false weights, for instance, one has not merely avoided an "abomination," but has done a positive good deed; the true weight is morally a "delight" to Him. To refuse to do evil is, in the ethical dimension, to do a mitzva, observe a Divine commandment.

2. The sophisticated skeptic who disputes the validity of the moral law willfully chooses a life without wisdom and without truth, hence a life of disgrace; while the modest man who humbly accepts the teachings of the Sages is embarked on the road of wisdom and moral dignity.

3. The upright man has no intellectual command of the ways of wisdom and righteousness, but they have become part of his nature. He can therefore yet be deterred from the right path by the physical demands of life. If he also has steadfast integrity, however, then his way in life will guide him. The "faithless" are the opposite of the upright: their sense of decency and fairness is distorted and perverted, and this will destroy them — like outlaws attacking their victims in a desolate, uninhabited site (as the verb for "destroy" connotes).

4. Riches are of considerable value in a time of peace (10:15), but in a period of prevailing "wrath" — for example, in

11 ¹ A deceiving balance-scale is an abomination to HA-SHEM, but a perfect weight is His delight. ² When arrogance comes, then comes disgrace, but with the modest is wisdom. ³ The steadfast integrity of the upright shall guide them, but the crookedness of the faithless will destroy them. ⁴ Riches avail nothing on the day of wrath; but righteousness saves from death. ⁵ The righteousness of the steadfastly sincere shall make straight his way, but a wicked man shall fall by his own wickedness. ⁶ The righteousness of the upright will save them; but the faithless shall be trapped in their own disaster. ⁷ When a wicked man dies, his hope will perish, and the expectation of his

pestilence or war — it cannot help. On the other hand, *tz*ᵉ*daka* (righteousness or charity) saves a person from death even at such a time (hence this does not duplicate the same phrase in 10:2, for that concerns natural death).

5. The singular characteristic of the *tamim* is his steadfastness and constancy. Even if he has not reached the level of the upright (*yashar*), this quality alone will keep him on a steady good course. The wicked man is the opposite of the *tamim*: he is steadfast in his wickedness — and thus finds his way full of pitfalls, into which he plummets.

6. While the upright go safely through evil times because righteousness has become their nature, the faithless come to grief.

7. The wicked live without the rock-like confidence with which the righteous can look forward to their ultimate reward: at best,

ח אָבָדָה: צַדִּיק מִצָּרָה נֶחֱלָץ וַיָּבֹא רָשָׁע תַּחְתָּיו: בְּפֶה חָנֵף
י יַשְׁחִת רֵעֵהוּ וּבְדַעַת צַדִּיקִים יֵחָלֵצוּ: בְּטוּב צַדִּיקִים תַּעֲלֹץ
יא קִרְיָה וּבַאֲבֹד רְשָׁעִים רִנָּה: בְּבִרְכַּת יְשָׁרִים תָּרוּם קָרֶת וּבְפִי
יב רְשָׁעִים תֵּהָרֵס: בָּז־לְרֵעֵהוּ חֲסַר־לֵב וְאִישׁ תְּבוּנוֹת יַחֲרִישׁ:
יג הוֹלֵךְ רָכִיל מְגַלֶּה־סּוֹד וְנֶאֱמַן־רוּחַ מְכַסֶּה דָבָר: בְּאֵין תַּחְבֻּלוֹת

the wicked live in "hope," a flickering prospect of success, which disappears as soon as they die. And even the one confident expectation that their heirs have — that they will inherit their property — is doomed to disappointment: All the life's work and wealth of the wicked will finally pass to strangers and be entirely lost.

8–9. Should a wicked man plot evil against a *tzaddik*, verse 8 depicts the outcome — as in the instance of Haman and Mordechai. Should a flatterer try to lead a *tzaddik* astray by his sycophancy, to destroy him, verse 9 foretells the outcome of that; here, too, the schemer will fall victim to his own plotting.

10–11. The righteous are actively benevolent: their relations with other human beings bring benefit and prosperity to the city. The upright represent a different type of goodness: Since they do good naturally, by their very being they constitute a blessing that operates irresistibly, like yeast in the dough, to elevate the whole environment. Conversely, the wicked have a destructive effect on their surroundings: the city suffers because of their actual destructive behavior and because of the spiritual negation that they represent. A curse from their lips, or a word of slander, can ruin the spiritual world built up by others.

12. Scripture refers here to a man who has had to suffer scorn and disparagement from his neighbor. Even when he is entitled to retort in kind, the "man of discernment" is obliged to keep silent and suppress his anger.

mourners is lost. ⁸ The righteous man is rescued out of trouble, and a wicked man comes in his stead. ⁹ With his mouth the flatterer would destroy his neighbor, but through knowledge shall the righteous be rescued. ¹⁰ When it goes well with the righteous, the city rejoices, and when the wicked perish, there is shouting for joy. ¹¹ By the blessing of the upright a city is exalted, but by the mouth of the wicked is it overthrown. ¹² He who despises his neighbor lacks a [self-disciplining] heart, but a man of discernment keeps silent. ¹³ He who goes about as a talebearer reveals secrets, but one who is trustworthy in spirit conceals a matter. ¹⁴ Where there are no reasoned strategies, a people falls; but in a

13. One who wanders around bearing tales is naturally constituted to betray his friend's secrets, which have been entrusted to him in the same way as money is placed in trust; talebearing stamps one as unreliable and unworthy of trust. Later we read, "He who goes about as a talebearer reveals secrets" (20:19). The logic works in reverse too. If we see someone revealing a secret, we should know that he is probably a habitual talebearer. On the other hand, the trustworthy person not only does not share a secret but does his best to keep it hidden.

14. "Reasoned strategies" here refers to the need in wartime for not one line of strategy but many: strategic plans that can instantly replace one tactical move with another, as soon as required. This kind of versatility means safety to a beleaguered nation — and, metaphorically, in the private battle against evil.

טו יֵרוֹעַ כִּי־עָרַב זָר וְשֹׂנֵא תֹקְעִים בּוֹטֵחַ: אֵשֶׁת־חֵן תִּתְמֹךְ כָּבוֹד וְעָרִיצִים יִתְמְכוּ־עֹשֶׁר:
טז יִפָּלֶם־עָם וּתְשׁוּעָה בְּרֹב יוֹעֵץ:
יז גֹּמֵל נַפְשׁוֹ אִישׁ חָסֶד וְעֹכֵר שְׁאֵרוֹ אַכְזָרִי: רָשָׁע עֹשֶׂה פְעֻלַּת־
יח שָׁקֶר וְזֹרֵעַ צְדָקָה שֶׂכֶר אֱמֶת: כֵּן־צְדָקָה לְחַיִּים וּמְרַדֵּף רָעָה
כ לְמוֹתוֹ: תּוֹעֲבַת יְהוָה עִקְּשֵׁי־לֵב וּרְצוֹנוֹ תְּמִימֵי דָרֶךְ: יָד לְיָד

15. It is folly to commit oneself to any kind of responsibility for a stranger's business affairs. When it comes to a friend, however, it is a good deed to help him in business, but even there, not to the extent of "clasping hands"—of accepting an absolute immediate responsibility for his financial commitments. "Hand-claspers" means those who accept such responsibility by a firm handshake.

16. Honor and riches, Divinely bestowed, go most happily together: wealth can be used to do good, and it thus brings honor to its possessor. When honor and riches are found separately, however, honor is valued above riches: it can be attained only by grace and goodness, not by sheer brute force of the kind that appropriates wealth.

17. A man of loving-kindness is one whose way of being and action is kindly, quite apart from any personal reward or even any emotional stimulus, such as pity. The cruel man, on the other hand, does not respond even when his emotions of pity over distress are aroused. The kindly person may seem to be doing himself a disservice on the social or communal level but certainly is doing good to the spiritual part of himself, which is, after all, his essence. The cruel person injures not only his spirit but even his material interests, since his callousness breeds callousness in others towards him.

18–19. Involved in worldly matters, accumulating material goods, the wicked man believes that his acts are all consum-

multitude of counsellors there is safety. [15] He who goes surety for a stranger will be broken by it, but one who hates hand-claspers [for surety] is secure. [16] A woman of grace sustains honor; and men of power sustain riches. [17] A man of loving-kindness does himself good, but a cruel person troubles his own flesh. [18] The wicked man carries out a deceitful act, but one who sows righteousness has a true reward. [19] Steadfast righteousness leads to life, but he who pursues evil does so to his own death. [20] The perverse of heart are an abomination to HA-SHEM; but those steadfastly sincere in their way are His delight. [21] Hand to hand [directly]

mated and complete, standing tangibly in the world; in his view he "carries out" his plans. From a spiritual perspective, however, material preoccupations are not ends in themselves, but means to larger spiritual ends, and the wicked man is therefore fooling himself when he sees his deeds as *achievements*: they are "deceitful acts" when we regard them as ends rather than means. One who deals in righteousness, however, may seem to be dealing in acts achieving nothing yet — merely sowing seed, with no visible fruit; but in due time he will reap his harvest, his "sure reward"; for righteousness is certain to lead to true life, both physical and spiritual. This is contrasted again with the wicked man, who is involved in activities of illusory worth: he is, in fact, hastening towards his demise — both physical and spiritual extinction.

20. Abomination and delight are two extremes. A person who regulates his life by the laws of wisdom is "wise in heart" and steadfastly sincere in his life-road; he is constant. The "perverse in heart" is his opposite. Disputing the laws of wisdom, he is an

כב לֹא־יִנָּקֶה רָע וְזֶרַע צַדִּיקִים נִמְלָט: נֶזֶם זָהָב בְּאַף חֲזִיר אִשָּׁה
כג יָפָה וְסָרַת טָעַם: תַּאֲוַת צַדִּיקִים אַךְ־טוֹב תִּקְוַת רְשָׁעִים
כד עֶבְרָה: יֵשׁ מְפַזֵּר וְנוֹסָף עוֹד וְחוֹשֵׂךְ מִיֹּשֶׁר אַךְ־לְמַחְסוֹר: נֶפֶשׁ־
כה
כו בְּרָכָה תְדֻשָּׁן וּמַרְוֶה גַּם־הוּא יוֹרֶא: מֹנֵעַ בָּר יִקְּבֻהוּ לְאוֹם

abomination in God's sight. In between is a person who does not dispute the laws of wisdom, yet neither is he constant in his way; yielding to his impulses, he sometimes swerves from the proper path. He is still engaged in an inner struggle, to finally conquer or be conquered.

21. The punishment of the wicked will occur by the Almighty's individual attention; it will hit its target, and its target alone, when providence acts directly, without natural intermediaries — as when a person transmits something from his hand to another's. No one else suffers. Should natural catastrophes become the instrument of punishment, however, many will suffer indiscriminately—even the righteous—while some of the wicked may escape scot-free. Furthermore, God promises immunity even to the family of the righteous. Thus "God remembered Abraham and delivered Lot [Abraham's nephew] from the holocaust" (Genesis 19:29).

22. Not only does a gold ring add no beauty to a swine, but it even becomes repulsive in the context of the ugliness and filth of its wearer. Similarly, a beautiful woman is affected even in her physical charm by ugly traits of personality: all that is conveyed by the term, *ta'am* ("taste, flavor"), to express the "aura" of personality, behavior, mannerisms and conversation, which reflect the inner quality of the soul. In the context of an unpleasant character, even beauty is distorted and vulgar. Metaphorically, this suggests the way in which intellectual grace and vigor is spoiled—becomes ugly—when it is coupled with a corrupt character.

shall the evil man not go unpunished, but the progeny of the righteous shall escape. ²² As a ring of gold in a swine's snout, so is a beautiful woman of ugly personality. ²³ The yearning of the righteous is only good; the hope of the wicked is wrath. ²⁴ There is one who scatters and is yet given more, and one who withholds unduly, only to suffer want. ²⁵ The beneficent soul shall be made rich, and one who gives refreshment shall himself too be refreshed. ²⁶ He who withholds grain, the people shall curse him; but a blessing on

23. Yearning and hope denote different degrees of probability. Even the mere yearning desire of the righteous man, his inner longing that has no guarantee of fulfillment, will be "good": because it is for good and pure ends, it will be blessed and gratified. On the other hand, even the "hope" of the wicked, apparently accessible and rationally within their grasp, is doomed to frustration.

24. As the Sages taught, it is best to strike a balance between extravagance and miserliness: The middle way is the recommended ethical path. If a person is to tend to one extreme, however, worldly wisdom usually considers it better to tend towards miserliness and at least conserve his resources. Here, on the contrary, the master of Proverbs declares extravagance better. It can at least give a person a good reputation and may ultimately even attract business; whereas miserliness repels people, isolates an individual and may even reduce his opportunities in business.

25-26. The second verse illustrates the first. If a person refuses to sell needed food till the price rises, people may starve

כז וּבְרָכָה לְרֹאשׁ מַשְׁבִּיר׃ שֹׁחֵר טוֹב יְבַקֵּשׁ רָצוֹן וְדֹרֵשׁ רָעָה
כח תְבוֹאֶנּוּ׃ בּוֹטֵחַ בְּעָשְׁרוֹ הוּא יִפֹּל וְכֶעָלֶה צַדִּיקִים יִפְרָחוּ׃ עֹכֵר
ל בֵּיתוֹ יִנְחַל־רוּחַ וְעֶבֶד אֱוִיל לַחֲכַם־לֵב׃ פְּרִי־צַדִּיק עֵץ חַיִּים
לא וְלֹקֵחַ נְפָשׁוֹת חָכָם׃ הֵן צַדִּיק בָּאָרֶץ יְשֻׁלָּם אַף כִּי־רָשָׁע וְחוֹטֵא׃

meanwhile, and he will feel their curse. Metaphorically, the text refers to withholding or sharing and spreading knowledge of the Torah. One who "hoards" it for himself alone is castigated, while one who is generous and creative with his learning will find himself blessed — spiritually enriched, and mentally rewarded by increased knowledge and understanding.

27. Evidently good is more foreign to human nature than evil: we have to seek it "diligently," repeatedly, with special attention; for from childhood, a person's nature tends instinctively to evil. It is enough, however, to merely "search" for evil: it is always accessible. One who earnestly desires good has to set his mind first on turning his will to goodness. This desire is not a natural gift but has to be cultivated. As for evil, however, "it shall come to him," quite spontaneously, since instinct and physical desire provide the fuel and the fire.

28. A fruit-bearing tree also produces leaves, which protect the fruit. The rich think their money the main thing, but it is only leaves without fruit, and when it withers there is nothing. The material gain of the righteous person, however, serves as a protection from the distractions of life, so that he can produce the durable "fruit" of his Torah study and Divine worship.

29. Metaphorically, this refers to the house of wisdom and prudent spiritual understanding, which will fall into ruins if its

the head of him who sells it. **27** He who diligently seeks good seeks favor, but if one searches for evil, it shall come to him. **28** He who relies on his riches shall fall, but the righteous shall flourish like a leaf. **29** He who troubles his own house shall inherit the wind, and the skeptic shall be servant to the wise of heart. **30** The fruit of the righteous is [from] a tree of life, and a wise man wins souls. **31** Behold, the righteous will be requited on earth; how much more the wicked and the sinner!

spiritually profligate owner lacks ethical discipline and moral control. The stormwind of his unrestrained desires will bring disaster. He will then be like a penniless slave fit to serve the man who has conducted his affairs wisely and ethically.

30. Righteousness applies all the laws of wisdom to practical life, and is therefore compared to a fruit-bearing tree. The *tzaddik* and his friends can enjoy this fruit, which is their own deeds, and through it gain eternal life. The wise man wins souls and attracts disciples, through the power of his teaching, while the righteous man vitalizes others through his acts; he stimulates them to behave like him and also gain eternal life.

31. Since the righteous man, the *tzaddik*, has the transcendent reward of eternal life reserved for him, it is to his benefit that his sins—for every man sins—be punished in this world. He pays his debt in the small coin of life on earth, so that his capital may remain for eternity. The wicked man, however, pays in the hard currency of his eternal life, for he has no righteous deeds, no fruit of eternal life, to sustain him.

יב א אֹהֵב מוּסָר אֹהֵב דָּעַת וְשׂוֹנֵא תוֹכַחַת בָּעַר: טוֹב יָפִיק רָצוֹן
ב מֵיהוָה וְאִישׁ מְזִמּוֹת יַרְשִׁיעַ: לֹא־יִכּוֹן אָדָם בְּרֶשַׁע וְשֹׁרֶשׁ
ג צַדִּיקִים בַּל־יִמּוֹט: אֵשֶׁת־חַיִל עֲטֶרֶת בַּעְלָהּ וּכְרָקָב בְּעַצְמוֹתָיו
ד מְבִישָׁה: מַחְשְׁבוֹת צַדִּיקִים מִשְׁפָּט תַּחְבֻּלוֹת רְשָׁעִים מִרְמָה:

1. The intellectual, who loves knowledge, is obviously open to a reproach based on a logical demonstration of good and evil — referred to here as "reproof"; but even moral discipline, making a person aware of punishment for evil, is based on a reverent cognition of the providential relations of God and man, confirmed by knowledge, and it speaks therefore to the intellectual, the one who "loves knowledge." On the other hand, it is obviously "brutish" to be unresponsive to the immediate stimulus of fear of punishment. Yet, says the master of Proverbs, a man worthy of the name will be sensitive also to the logical, reasoned approach of reproof. It is only a brute who is entirely deaf to the truth of ethics.

2. Without deep thought or subtle planning, the good man obtains Divine good will, because his simple thoughts and deeds are for good and right ends. In contrast, a man of evil, with no reliance on the Almighty, invests deep thought to devise plans to harm his neighbor; and the verb *yarshi'a* ("He will condemn") connotes that his wicked plans become a strong source of evil deeds.

3. The concept of "establishment" has at its core the sense of a "stable base," the physical foundation on which an object rests. A "root," on the other hand, is organically connected with the plant, with the branches and leaves; it is the plant's source of vital nourishment. The wicked have no root in this sense, since a man is like an inverted tree, with its root above, in the spiritual world which infuses him with his essential humanity; and the wicked are cut off from their root of spiritual intellect,

12 ¹ He who loves moral discipline loves knowledge, but one who hates reproof is brutish. ² A good man shall obtain favor of HA-SHEM, but a man of evil devices He will condemn. ³ A man will not be established by wickedness, but the root of the righteous shall never falter. ⁴ A woman of valor is her husband's crown, but one who acts shamefully is like rottenness in his bones. ⁵ The thoughts of the righteous are just, but the strategies of the

depending for stability on the physical basis of material possessions. Even this basis will prove illusory, however; because their wealth is the product of evil, it will be lost in the end. The righteous, however, being rooted in purity, are assured of a real and lasting stability, however precarious their physical existence may seem to be.

4. The good wife not only integrally strengthens her husband, but like a crown becomes a symbol of pride and conscious dignity for her husband: because of her, his social status is enhanced. The bad wife, however, not only fails to be a source of pride to her husband, but, inherently, he feels her as "bone of his bones," as a part of himself, and he thus experiences a corruption, a debility in his own being.

5. Even the "thoughts" of the righteous — their simplest, most provisional notions — will be inspired by a sense of justice; while even the most complex and deliberate strategies of the wicked are still geared to deceit and robbery. The righteous, therefore, have no need of complex strategies; for them, the simple intention to do right suffices; while the wicked need a devious and distorted chain of projects in order to plot their career of crookedness.

ו דִּבְרֵי רְשָׁעִים אֱרָב־דָּם וּפִי יְשָׁרִים יַצִּילֵם: הָפוֹךְ רְשָׁעִים וְאֵינָם
ז
ח וּבֵית צַדִּיקִים יַעֲמֹד: לְפִי־שִׂכְלוֹ יְהֻלַּל־אִישׁ וְנַעֲוֵה־לֵב יִהְיֶה
ט לָבוּז: טוֹב נִקְלֶה וְעֶבֶד לוֹ מִמִּתְכַּבֵּד וַחֲסַר־לָחֶם: יוֹדֵעַ צַדִּיק
י
יא נֶפֶשׁ בְּהֶמְתּוֹ וְרַחֲמֵי רְשָׁעִים אַכְזָרִי: עֹבֵד אַדְמָתוֹ יִשְׂבַּע־לָחֶם
יב וּמְרַדֵּף רֵיקִים חֲסַר־לֵב: חָמַד רָשָׁע מְצוֹד רָעִים וְשֹׁרֶשׁ

6. The term *divrey* (words) connotes lengthy talk. The wicked go on and on, speaking evil gossip and slander, to destroy their fellow-humans. The upright, however, are by nature honest and decent; far from "lurking for blood," they do good beyond the letter of the law. In verse 11:6 they are assured of safety from natural misfortunes; here the assurance is extended to man-made troubles.

7. "Overthrown" signifies an utter catastrophe, a reversal of all the hopes and achievements of the wicked, a fitting punishment, when his time comes, for one whose whole value system is, in fact, an inversion of truth; and then he vanishes from existence. The righteous, even if they should deserve punishment, will suffer in relatively superficial ways: their solid basis in existence will be untouched.

8. The "heart" is the dominant force of desire in the personality; where it tends to evil, even the intellect — potentially the source of the loftiest conceptions and insights — is corrupted. It becomes a handmaiden to the distorted heart, and it too becomes despicable. Where the heart is pure, however, man's intellect becomes his chief glory, his distinctive faculty, that can learn the laws of wisdom to impose mastery over the self, and can reveal supernal concepts unknown to the senses or the empirical mind.

9. Society generally considers physical, menial labor a disgrace;

wicked are deceit. ⁶ The words of the wicked are to lurk for blood, but the words of the upright shall save them. ⁷ Let the wicked be overthrown, and they are no more; but the house of the righteous shall stand. ⁸ A man shall be praised according to his intelligence, but one with a distorted heart shall be despised. ⁹ Better is one who is lightly esteemed and is his own servant, than one who is pompous while lacking bread. ¹⁰ A righteous man has regard for the life of his beast, but the tender mercies of the wicked are cruel. ¹¹ He who tills his land will have his fill of bread, but one who pursues after phantoms lacks a [self-disciplining] heart. ¹² A wicked person

but it is true, inherent shame and disgrace to suffer hunger for the sake of pretended prestige. Figuratively, this also refers to one who pretends to learning and will not toil to acquire the "bread" of Torah knowledge.

10. Aside from the literal meaning — the importance of kindness to animals — there is a metaphorical sense: The "bestial" side of man, his instinctive drives, may be placed in perspective by the *tzaddik* who "knows the soul (literal meaning of the Hebrew) of his beast," i.e. of his body, that supports his life-spirit here on earth. He gives the body its due, and learns to control the demands of the flesh. The wicked, however, respond with "tender mercies" to the needs of the flesh, but thereby act cruelly to their true selves, to the spiritual faculty in them.

11–12. Here again we have both a literal and a metaphorical plane of meaning. The righteous labor for their livelihood, putting hard physical work into the tasks of farming, etc. — and

PROVERBS 12:12-19

יג צַדִּיקִים יִתֵּן: בְּפֶשַׁע שְׂפָתַיִם מוֹקֵשׁ רָע וַיֵּצֵא מִצָּרָה צַדִּיק:
יד יָשִׁיב מִפְּרִי פִי־אִישׁ יִשְׂבַּע־טוֹב וּגְמוּל יְדֵי־אָדָם יָשׁוּב לוֹ: דֶּרֶךְ אֱוִיל
טו יָשָׁר בְּעֵינָיו וְשֹׁמֵעַ לְעֵצָה חָכָם: אֱוִיל בַּיּוֹם יִוָּדַע כַּעְסוֹ וְכֹסֶה
יח קָלוֹן עָרוּם: יָפִיחַ אֱמוּנָה יַגִּיד צֶדֶק וְעֵד שְׁקָרִים מִרְמָה: יֵשׁ
יט בּוֹטֶה כְּמַדְקְרוֹת חָרֶב וּלְשׁוֹן חֲכָמִים מַרְפֵּא: שְׂפַת־אֱמֶת תִּכּוֹן

"the root of the righteous will yield fruit" and sustain life. He lives with self-discipline. The wicked prefer to sit idly and plot the ruin of their colleagues which will bring wealth to themselves. Spiritually too, the righteous invest much loving effort into the care and training of their souls—uprooting weeds, planting good seed, and finally culling wisdom as the fruit of their labor. The wicked, however, pursue their fantasies, their lust for "empty things"; and they reap nothing in the end.

13. "Lips" symbolize superficial, thoughtless talk, and this can indeed be a "crime" that ensnares a person—for example, if he says something disastrously stupid to a king. The righteous man has trained himself to avoid this, and even when in trouble he can speak with sense to extricate himself.

14. A man's words are likened to a tree's fruit, its choice product, as they reveal his basic nature. In *Mishley*, "mouth" symbolizes wisdom, which can indeed produce choice "fruit" in nourishing and satisfying thoughts. In addition, a man reaches perfection with his hands as well, by good deeds, which have reciprocal effect on his character, making him a better person.

15. Doubting the laws of wisdom, the skeptic is deceived by the apparent smoothness and ease of a sensual life and refuses to be warned of the decay and death that is its consequence. The wise man, however, listens to the advice of his experienced teachers and chooses the initially difficult road of abstinence and spiritual concentration which leads to life and happiness.

desires the prey of evil men, but the root of the righteous will yield [fruit]. ¹³ In the crime of the lips is a snare for the evil man, but the righteous one comes out of trouble. ¹⁴ By the fruit of a man's mouth shall he be satisfied with good, and the reward of a man's handiwork shall be rendered him. ¹⁵ The way of a skeptic is straight in his eyes, but a wise man listens to counsel. ¹⁶ A skeptic's anger is known within the day, but a sagacious man conceals disgrace. ¹⁷ He who breathes truth utters righteousness, but a false witness, deceit. ¹⁸ There is one who speaks like the stabs of a sword, but the tongue of the wise brings healing. ¹⁹ The lip of truth will stand solid forever, while a

16. Since anger is a shameful trait, it is the way of wisdom and intelligence to suppress it and show patience. The skeptic, however, accepts and learns nothing from the laws of wisdom, and develops no control of his temper. He is prone to rage and vengeance on the instant. If a sagacious man needs to retaliate, he chooses his time and his means so that he brings no disgrace upon himself.

17-18. This is a guideline for discriminating the voice of truth from that of falsehood, for a judge who has to decide between conflicting testimonies, for example. The true witness speaks quietly, simply; he merely "breathes" his testimony; while the false witness, in spite of all his rhetorical sophistication, will betray his own deceit. He may swear oaths to ruin his opponent—like sword-stabs—but the calm wisdom of the true witness heals all wounds.

19. Even his "lip," denoting the most superficial, external kind

PROVERBS 12:20-25

כ לָעַד וְעַד־אַרְגִּיעָה לְשׁוֹן שָׁקֶר: מִרְמָה בְּלֶב־חֹרְשֵׁי רָע וּלְיֹעֲצֵי
כא שָׁלוֹם שִׂמְחָה: לֹא־יְאֻנֶּה לַצַּדִּיק כָּל־אָוֶן וּרְשָׁעִים מָלְאוּ רָע:
כב תּוֹעֲבַת יְהוָה שִׂפְתֵי־שָׁקֶר וְעֹשֵׂי אֱמוּנָה רְצוֹנוֹ: אָדָם עָרוּם
כג כֹּסֶה דָּעַת וְלֵב כְּסִילִים יִקְרָא אִוֶּלֶת: יַד־חָרוּצִים תִּמְשׁוֹל
כה וּרְמִיָּה תִּהְיֶה לָמַס: דְּאָגָה בְלֶב־אִישׁ יַשְׁחֶנָּה וְדָבָר טוֹב

of self-expression, is sufficient for the true witness: he has no need of elaborate rhetoric to establish his sincerity. The false witness however, may employ his "tongue" — his logical and rhetorical faculties — but to no end, since his lies will be recognized directly, in spite of all his cleverness.

20. "Plowing up evil" is contrasted with "counselling peace": for peace means the survival of the world, while evil is the destruction of the world. "Counsellors of peace" are those who desire well-being and life in every sphere, domestic or political. Those who "plow up evil," on the contrary, intend to undermine the state of things; they work insidiously, so as not to arouse suspicion, and are therefore constantly tense nd anxious, while those who work for peace are relaxed and confident, filled with the joy of open beneficence.

21. The term "wrong" here denotes the natural result of the crimes of the wicked: one crime leads to another in natural succession, till they are "filled with evil." The righteous have no reason to sin, even unintentionally, since they have no "precedent" for crime, no previous wrongdoing to lead to more: All their "precedents" are virtuous acts which bring more virtuous acts in their train.

22. "Those who act faithfully" are persons who keep their word, be it to God or to their fellow-man. The opposite of "lying lips," they evoke an opposite response from Heaven.

lying tongue is but for a moment. ²⁰ Deceit is in the heart of those who plow up evil, but for the counsellors of peace there is joy. ²¹ No wrong shall be caused for the righteous, but the wicked are filled with evil. ²² Lying lips are an abomination to HA-SHEM, but those who act faithfully are His delight. ²³ A sagacious man conceals knowledge, but the heart of fools proclaims skepticism. ²⁴ The hand of the diligent will rule, but swindle shall lead to payment of tribute. ²⁵ Care in a man's heart bows it down, but

23. Unlike the wise man, the sagacious (or guileful) man does not know the laws of wisdom; yet, left in doubt, he chooses the right path. Whatever knowledge he does gain, by his own search, he keeps strictly to himself. Unlike the skeptic, the fool knows the laws of wisdom, but overcome by his strong desires, in his fear of punishment he professes skepticism and doubt about them, as a defense and camouflage.

24. No idler, the diligent person works steadily, seeking no sudden riches through trickery or deceit. Eventually such people amass their wealth and gain the upper hand in society. The swindler is a lazy wretch, ultimately reduced to "paying tribute" and serving a wealthy master, like a slave.

25. Anxiety is one of the most destructive feelings a man can experience. The wise man will take one of two courses when he feels anxiety welling up: he will either "bow it down"—suppress it (this renders the text: Care in a man's heart?—let him bow it down)—or else make himself cheerful by deliberately evoking some positive image of hope and optimism to counteract his anxiety.

כו יְשַׂמְּחֶנָּה: יָתֵר מֵרֵעֵהוּ צַדִּיק וְדֶרֶךְ רְשָׁעִים תַּתְעֵם: לֹא־יַחֲרֹךְ
כח רְמִיָּה צֵידוֹ וְהוֹן־אָדָם יָקָר חָרוּץ: בְּאֹרַח־צְדָקָה חַיִּים וְדֶרֶךְ
נְתִיבָה אַל־מָוֶת:

26. The righteous man, the *tzaddik*, does not depend on his own wisdom alone but draws his sense of right from his observation of role-models; while the wicked are guided only by their own judgment, which often proves faulty.

27. The swindler refuses to exert himself to earn a livelihood, hoping to make his fortune easily by crooked methods; but then even if he succeeds he has to conceal his ill-gotten wealth; while the possessions of a hard-working person are a true source of pleasure and value.

a good word makes it cheerful. [26] The righteous man is guided by observing his neighbor, but the way of the wicked leads them astray. [27] The swindler shall not glimpse his prey, but precious is the wealth of a diligent man. [28] On the road of righteousness is life, and in the way of its path there is no death.

28. *Derech* (way) denotes an inter-urban highway; *orach* (road), the branch of a highway, a side-road leading off to villages; while *nethiv* (path) designates a private path or lane. The mitzvoth (commandments) between a man and his Maker are *orach*, a road, taken by the religious person, leading him to everlasting life. Certain rare individuals, however, like Moses and Elijah, are so extremely devout, on their own "private" path of life, that they do not experience the usual physical death, and are transferred into immortality.

יג א בֵּן חָכָם מוּסַר אָב וְלֵץ לֹא־שָׁמַע גְּעָרָה: מִפְּרִי פִי־אִישׁ יֹאכַל
ג טוֹב וְנֶפֶשׁ בֹּגְדִים חָמָס: נֹצֵר פִּיו שֹׁמֵר נַפְשׁוֹ פֹּשֵׂק שְׂפָתָיו
ד מְחִתָּה־לוֹ: מִתְאַוָּה וָאַיִן נַפְשׁוֹ עָצֵל וְנֶפֶשׁ חָרֻצִים תְּדֻשָּׁן:

1. The wise son acts according to the laws of moral wisdom, which run counter to natural instinct. They can therefore be inculcated only on a foundation of moral instruction, discipline and training, by which the child's imagination can be educated to understand the evil consequences of wayward behavior. Only by deliberate moral training, therefore, does the child become a moral being, a "wise son," who demonstrates the success of his father's "moral instruction." If a person never hears rebuke from his father, however, and never experiences the need to restrain his will, not only is he not "wise," but in fact he becomes a scorner, who mocks the moral law.

2. The apparently synonymous terms mouth, lips, tongue, which are used in parallel stanzas throughout Proverbs, refer respectively to the three different kinds of intellectual apprehension: wisdom, knowledge, and understanding (*chochma, da'ath, bina*). Thus here, "mouth" denotes *chochma*, moral wisdom; and like the tree of knowledge of good and evil, its "fruit" may be consumed either for benefit or for destruction. In the realm of morality there is always an open choice between two possibilities—pride and humility, for instance, or cruelty and compassion—and it is the task of the moral faculty, *chochma*, wisdom, to work within these possibilities to good ends. Then man's experience is wholesome and nourishing. One who betrays the true purpose of his being, however, and violates the faculties and qualities entrusted to him, loses control over his whole personality and his relations with the world. He eats "fruit of violence."

3. The term "lips" denotes external superficial speech, while

13

¹ A wise son [receives] a father's moral instruction, but a mocking person has not heard rebuke. ² From the fruit of his mouth shall a man eat good, but the soul of the faithless, violence. ³ He who guards his mouth preserves his life; for one who opens wide his lips, there is ruin. ⁴ The soul of the sluggard craves, but has nothing; but the

"mouth" symbolizes reflective inward expression. Both are pictured as a fortified wall around the soul, defending it against attackers; and the master of Proverbs urges restraint not only at the outer wall, to guard our lips from superficial talk and idle chatter, but even at the inner wall: even the expression of wise meditation should be done sparingly and with great discrimination, for "God is in Heaven and you are on the earth; therefore, let your words be few" (Ecclesiastes 5:1). A profound and deliberate reticence is the sign of moral strength: in this way, spiritual vitality is preserved: he "preserves his life." The babbler, gossiper and slanderer, however, dissipate their strength and leave themselves wide open even for physical destruction.

4. In his laziness, the sluggard has no wish to call on his limbs and faculties to work to any end. This does not mean that he has no desires and cravings, however; quite the contrary. The pity of it is that the less effectively and diligently a person is prepared to work to satisfy his appetite, the sharper and more voracious his appetite grows. Diligent and industrious people, on the other hand, who do physical work, find their appetites fully satisfied. On a spiritual level, the reference here is to spiritual labors: The lazing soul of the sluggard may hunger for spiritual perfection, but if his will and faculties do not work industriously toward this goal, then the soul hungers in eternal frustration.

ה דְּבַר־שֶׁקֶר יִשְׂנָא צַדִּיק וְרָשָׁע יַבְאִישׁ וְיַחְפִּיר: צְדָקָה תִּצֹּר תָּם־
ו דֶּרֶךְ וְרִשְׁעָה תְּסַלֵּף חַטָּאת: יֵשׁ מִתְעַשֵּׁר וְאֵין כֹּל מִתְרוֹשֵׁשׁ
ז וְהוֹן רָב: כֹּפֶר נֶפֶשׁ־אִישׁ עָשְׁרוֹ וְרָשׁ לֹא־שָׁמַע גְּעָרָה: אוֹר־
ח צַדִּיקִים יִשְׂמָח וְנֵר רְשָׁעִים יִדְעָךְ: רַק־בְּזָדוֹן יִתֵּן מַצָּה וְאֶת־

5. Righteousness must be based on truth. If the heart turns to falsehood, it perverts justice, listens to evil gossip and slander, and sees the worst in others, besmirching and disgracing them behind their backs by evil, calumnious talk.

6. A person who is "steadfast in his way" is unswervingly and innately pure, without violent needs and desires that tempt him away from the straight path. Such a person can guide his life by the conventions of correct behavior, but in his relations with the Almighty even he needs the guidance of *tz^edaka*, "righteousness"; here, the ordinary conventions of decency are not sufficient. Steadfast innocence and wholesomeness, therefore, need the buttressing of righteousness, to create the fully integrated spiritual personality. On the other hand, the man who has "sin," needs and desires that distort his vision, falls easy prey to "wickedness."

7-8. These verses concern apparent wealth, which on closer inspection proves to be nothing; and apparent poverty, which in fact is great wealth. The acquisition of goods is, in the deepest sense, no acquisition at all. Seen with the clear, rational mind, there is no real link between the goods and their owner; experience shows how easily the two are separated: fortunes are lost, or at best inherited by others. In reality, the materially wealthy man *has* nothing, in the sense of spiritual gain and development. A person who dispenses his money in charity and good deeds, however, is *acquiring* spiritual wealth that will endure and stand by him to all eternity. Then verse 8 continues: The main value of riches is that they should "ransom a man's

soul of the diligent shall be gratified. [5] A righteous man hates lying, but a wicked man imparts foulness and disgrace. [6] Righteousness guards him who is steadfast in his way, but wickedness perverts the sinner. [7] There is one who thinks himself rich, yet has nothing; one who thinks himself poor, yet has great wealth. [8] The ransom of a man's life are his riches; the poor man hears no angry retort. [9] The light of the righteous rejoices, but the lamp of the wicked will ebb out. [10] By arrogant dispute comes only contention, but

life": They should be used to creative ends, so that his spiritual self is enhanced. When the needy come to him for aid, they hear no angry retort, and get no niggardly response, but are given their aid gladly and eagerly.

9. "Light" denotes here an innate luminosity — sunlight, for instance — while "lamp" means an artefact requiring material means, such as wicks and oil, to produce light. The righteous radiate with a constant, essential light, to which the body (the "wick") is irrelevant. This radiance is true joy, as only something timeless can know true joy. Transience is inherently sadness. For the wicked, however, the light of their material success is only provisional, remaining as long as they are alive in this world, as long as the wick lasts. Thereafter the light is extinguished. This continues the theme of the previous verse, the need to keep alive the soul, which has the capacity for eternal life.

10. The word *zadon* ("arrogant dispute") denotes a deliberate will to openly reject the laws of wisdom and the truth. When controversies break out among people, they will not reach the

יא נוֹעָצִים חָכְמָה: הוֹן מֵהֶבֶל יִמְעָט וְקֹבֵץ עַל־יָד יַרְבֶּה: תּוֹחֶלֶת
יג מְמֻשָּׁכָה מַחֲלָה־לֵב וְעֵץ חַיִּים תַּאֲוָה בָאָה: בָּז לְדָבָר יֵחָבֶל לוֹ
יד וִירֵא מִצְוָה הוּא יְשֻׁלָּם: תּוֹרַת חָכָם מְקוֹר חַיִּים לָסוּר מִמֹּקְשֵׁי

point of violence or even war if the people are able to communicate with one another, all expressing their views in an open forum, and decide according to the traditional laws of moral wisdom. If arrogance prevails, however, and there is an attitude of cynical rejection of moral law, no amount of discussion will help to resolve the problem, and the controversy will escalate to *matsa* (contention), to rancorous discord close to blows and physical conflict. Korach (Numbers 16–17) is an example. With the "well-advised," however, informed by the laws of wisdom, this cannot happen.

11. Even a very wealthy man will lose his fortune if he fritters it away on vanities; constant attention is necessary to increase a person's property, or else it gradually diminishes. On the other hand, even someone without much capital can accumulate a fortune, by careful and gradual saving. All this is a metaphor for Torah-learning: The greatest scholar will ultimately forget his Torah if he spends his energies on useless things, while the man who persistently applies himself to study will gradually become a substantial scholar.

12. The word *tocheleth* (hope) denotes a sure expectation, while *ta'ava* (desire) is a mere yearning, unsupported by any objective guarantee of fulfillment. Even a well-based expectation will cause sickening frustration if its fulfillment is delayed too long: however confident we may be in our calculation and anticipation, human nature does not easily bear continued suspense. In the case of a desire without any real hope, the frustration is of course even more sickening — so intense, indeed, that if the yearning should unexpectedly be fulfilled, it is experienced like a sudden revival, an infusion of returning life.

with the well-advised is wisdom. ¹¹ Wealth from vanity will dwindle, but he who gathers by diligence will increase. ¹² Hope deferred makes the heart sick, but a desire fulfilled is a tree of life. ¹³ He who despises a word will suffer by it; but he who reveres a commandment will be rewarded. ¹⁴ The teaching of the wise is a wellspring of life,

13. It is an old controversy (Talmud, *Sanhedrin* 111a) whether all six hundred and thirteen commandments of the Torah must be fulfilled, or even one is sufficient to save a person from hell and gain him eternal life. This verse indicates the truth of both positions. We must have faith in the validity of *all* the commandments, and be committed to fulfilling all of them. If we reject even one of them, we are called "one who despises God's word," as though we rejected the whole Torah; and "he who despises a [Divine] word will suffer by it": he will be rigorously punished. On the other hand, if we believe in the Torah and all its commandments, then even if we have the opportunity to actually fulfill only one commandment, we receive reward as though we fulfilled the entire Torah, since *commitment* to the Torah is the essential thing. This is the import of the second part of the verse: "he who reveres a commandment" and is committed to its fulfillment — even if he has in fact performed only the one commandment, he will be rewarded for his dedication to the entire Torah.

14. The way of moral wisdom is called the way of life; the opposite, the way of foolishness, is the road to spiritual death. To draw and drink the water of eternal life, and avoid evil cravings and characteristics, "the snares of death" — we need to learn from a sage who can impart all the rules and details of the moral law, or from the actions and behavior of a *tzaddik*.

טו שֵׂכֶל־טוֹב יִתֶּן־חֵן וְדֶרֶךְ בֹּגְדִים אֵיתָן: כָּל־עָרוּם יַעֲשֶׂה
יז בְדָעַת וּכְסִיל יִפְרֹשׂ אִוֶּלֶת: מַלְאָךְ רָשָׁע יִפֹּל בְּרָע וְצִיר אֱמוּנִים
יח מַרְפֵּא: רֵישׁ וְקָלוֹן פּוֹרֵעַ מוּסָר וְשֹׁמֵר תּוֹכַחַת יְכֻבָּד: תַּאֲוָה

15. The term *séchel* (intelligence) denotes the intuitive power of a person of intellect to reach to the heart of abstruse concepts that ordinary wisdom and understanding cannot grasp. "Good intelligence" denotes an additional dimension of Divine inspiration that guides a man to mystic apprehensions beyond human intelligence. This is a special grace, a gift of the Almighty, that helps a man to avoid the snares of death (verse 14). In contrast, faithless traitors to the Almighty take the way of death; *eithan* (harsh) connotes stony barren soil (cf. Deuteronomy 21:4); and they will receive no relieving "water" from the sources of life.

16. As explained previously (12:23) *'orma* (sagacity, shrewdness) signifies the capacity to cover up knowledge and not reveal what one knows. Nevertheless, a sagacious man acts only on a basis of solid knowledge: where he is in doubt about the rightness or effectiveness of an act, he will await clarification. This is the very nature of *'orma*—to act in the light of knowledge, and yet to hide that knowledge from others. The "fool" (*k^esil*) is one who, for the sake of his desires, perfidiously evades the laws of wisdom; even if he has grasped them he will cast doubt on them, in order to gratify his cravings freely. Hence "the heart of fools proclaims skepticism" (12:23); indeed he "unfolds" all the aspects of his so-called skepticism, like a garment spread out to conceal in darkness his sinful deeds.

17. An emissary carries messages in both directions; he brings back a response to the original dispatch. The wicked messenger, however, brings back no reply; he betrays his original trust,

to turn away from the snares of death. ¹⁵ Good intelligence gives grace, but the way of the faithless is harsh. ¹⁶ Every shrewd man acts with clear forethought, but a fool unfolds skepticism. ¹⁷ A wicked messenger falls into evil, but a faithful emissary brings health. ¹⁸ Poverty and shame shall come to him who refuses moral instruction, but one who heeds reproof will be honored. ¹⁹ A

making mischief instead of bridging gaps. Ten of the twelve spies whom Moses sent to explore the Holy Land (Numbers 13) are an example of this kind of messenger: they distorted their report and did their best to make their mission fail. The two exceptions were Caleb and Joshua, who brought back a true report, and thus brought health to the sickly situation that the wicked messengers had created.

On the metaphorical level this applies to the soul, which has been sent on a mission by the Almighty, to make his way here in this lowly world and bring back word to Him who sent it. The evil messenger who betrays his trust, making mischief here below and bringing back no word to the Creator, meets an evil end, being fated to suffer the punishments of hell. As for the "faithful emissary," following a straight course in truth and trust, for him "the sun of righteousness shall shine, with healing in its wings" (Malachi 3:20).

18. The difference between "instruction" and "reproof" is that moral instruction and discipline work through fear of punishment, while "reproof" rests on argument and reason. A person who responds to rational, reasoned reproof is worthy of honor: he is sensitive enough to intelligent rebuke not to need grosser methods of spiritual correction. At the other extreme is one who will not respond even to the fiercest threats of retribution; he is a lost soul, and poverty and shame will be his lot.

כ נֶהְיָה תֶעֱרַב לְנָפֶשׁ וְתוֹעֲבַת כְּסִילִים סוּר מֵרָע: הָלוֹךְ אֶת־
כא חֲכָמִים וחכם וְרֹעֶה כְסִילִים יֵרוֹעַ: חַטָּאִים תְּרַדֵּף רָעָה וְאֶת־
כב צַדִּיקִים יְשַׁלֶּם־טוֹב: טוֹב יַנְחִיל בְּנֵי־בָנִים וְצָפוּן לַצַּדִּיק חֵיל
כג חוֹטֵא: רָב־אֹכֶל נִיר רָאשִׁים וְיֵשׁ נִסְפֶּה בְּלֹא מִשְׁפָּט: חוֹשֵׂךְ

19. The fool is not stupid; he knows the truth of moral law; but so compelled by desire is he, so sweet does his animal self find its gratification, that he develops no resistance but continues to yield, knowing that this does him no good.

20. A person learns from his companions, be they wise or foolish. If they are wise, at first he will not be accepted as a companion, an equal or peer of theirs. He will merely be one who walks humbly in their footsteps. With fools, though, he may call himself a companion right away. For wisdom is hard to learn, but folly not at all. Moreover, the difficult word *ro'eh* (companion) also means "shepherd": with fools, he may step at once even into a position of leadership, but in the end he will suffer for his chosen society. As our Sages taught, "Better be a tail to lions, and not a head to foxes" (*Avoth* iv, 20).

21. Evil comes by no miraculous intervention of Heaven but from the very nature of sin itself. Sin generates punishment, as a natural consequence. For the righteous, however, even where their virtue does not generate reward as a natural consequence, Heaven will especially intervene to repay them. This can be illustrated by the instance of a king who ordered his servants not to eat of a certain tree, because it was poisonous, but to eat of another tree, whose fruit was wholesome. The servants who disobeyed would receive their punishment of death by poison—a natural consequence of their act. The servants who ate of the wholesome fruit would not only benefit from the fruit itself but would also receive a reward from the king for their obedience.

desire attained is sweet to the senses, and to turn away from evil is an abomination to fools. [20] He who walks with wise men becomes wise, but a companion of fools will suffer harm. [21] Evil pursues sinners, but good rewards the righteous. [22] A good man leaves an inheritance to his children's children, but the wealth of the sinner is stored away for the righteous. [23] Abundant food is in the tillage of the poor, but one may be swept away without justice. [24] He who spares his rod

22. Despite verse 21, we sometimes see righteous persons suffering, while wicked people live at ease. Hence the assurance that if we do not see a *tzaddik* properly rewarded, it is because the Almighty will give his recompense to his children and future generations. Conversely, the apparent success of the sinner is only temporary; his fortune is destined finally for the righteous.

23. Yet why (verse 22) does the Almighty not reward a *tzaddik* himself? The whole world may be sustained for his sake, while he does not obtain proper sustenance for his own sake. Thus the Talmud states that the Almighty said of Rabbi Chanina ben Dosa, "The whole world is nourished for the sake of Chanina My son, and Chanina My son makes do with a measure of carobs from one Friday to the next." For answer we are reminded that an abundance of food comes from the hard labor of the poor, tilling the soil, pulling the weeds, etc. Not only are they paid a pittance, however, but some of them may even be swept away by adversity, dying of famine—although they supply so much of the world's food. Similarly, the great merit of the *tzaddik* removes the barriers to the flow of Heaven's bounty, yet he himself may live a life of privation: for the Almighty knows that should he become affluent, his merit would become insuffi-

כה שֶׁבֶט שׂוֹנֵא בְנוֹ וְאֹהֲבוֹ שִׁחֲרוֹ מוּסָר: צַדִּיק אֹכֵל לְשֹׂבַע נַפְשׁוֹ וּבֶטֶן רְשָׁעִים תֶּחְסָר:

cient to effect the flow of Divine beneficence — just as the poor would no longer work the land if they had enough to live on. This is a paradox of Divine providence, whose indisputable justice remains beyond our understanding.

24. The father who cannot bear to discipline his son actually cares more for himself — his own tender feelings — than for his son's ultimate good. Indulgence is not love. Taken metaphorically, this applies to the problem of the previous verse: The Almighty's apparent harshness with His righteous

hates his son, but he who loves him disciplines him alertly. ²⁵ A righteous person eats to satisfy his soul, but the belly of the wicked shall feel want.

ones is actually the discipline of a loving father who intends their ultimate bliss.

25. A righteous person eats only enough for his needs, while the wicked glut themselves, and yet cannot have enough; they always want more. Thus a measure of carobs was truly enough for Rabbi Chanina ben Dosa for a week: it satisfied his need, and he wanted no more. Worldly pleasure meant nothing to him; for him true pleasure meant the spiritual delight of the world to come.

PROVERBS 14:1-5

יד א חַכְמוֹת נָשִׁים בָּנְתָה בֵיתָהּ וְאִוֶּלֶת בְּיָדֶיהָ תֶהֶרְסֶנּוּ:
ב הוֹלֵךְ בְּיָשְׁרוֹ יְרֵא יְהֹוָה וּנְלוֹז דְּרָכָיו בּוֹזֵהוּ:
ג בְּפִי־אֱוִיל חֹטֶר גַּאֲוָה וְשִׂפְתֵי חֲכָמִים תִּשְׁמוּרֵם:
ד בְּאֵין אֲלָפִים אֵבוּס בָּר וְרָב־תְּבוּאוֹת בְּכֹחַ שׁוֹר:
ה עֵד אֱמוּנִים לֹא יְכַזֵּב וְיָפִיחַ כְּזָבִים עֵד

1. Moral wisdom is symbolized as a woman, ready to learn from and obey her lord, the higher intellect, which bestows insight and truth. Folly and skepticism are akin to immoral women who perversely seek fatal escapades. Wisdom includes many elements, which like building materials can construct a royal Sanctuary; and symbolically, all souls blessed with wisdom will work together as one to build it, with a totality of moral enlightenment. But skepticism, casting doubt on the laws of wisdom, cannot build but only pull down and demolish what wisdom constructs.

2. By his nature, the upright man's mind takes a straight, direct road of integrity; and in his straightforward way he gains details of understanding, to arrive at the truth about the Almighty and His relations with the world. Those who have not this honesty and "straightness" of intellect, however, veer onto irrelevant philosophical tangents, and end up by denying God's providence, ultimately despising Him.

3. The laws of wisdom are incapable of proof. Without an overweening pride and insistence on his own intellectual grasp, a person submits to Divine wisdom without dispute. The skeptic, however, arrogantly poses his doubt as a wisdom, and his arrogance projects from his mouth like a deformity. On the other hand, the "lips" of the wise, denoting their external, surface talk, express the wisdom of the moral law, that has become firm knowledge for them; and thus they will be protected from pride.

14

¹ The wisdom of women builds her house, but skepticism with her own hands tears it down. ² He who walks in his uprightness fears HA-SHEM, but one who is perfidious in his ways despises Him. ³ In the mouth of the skeptic is a rod of pride; but the lips of the wise will preserve them. ⁴ Where there are no oxen, the manger is clean, but an abundance of crops comes by the strength of the ox. ⁵ A faithful witness will not lie; but a false witness breathes out lies. ⁶ A mocking person seeks wisdom, and there is none; but knowledge

4. The word *alafim* (oxen) is from a root denoting training. Oxen trained to the plow need not be kept in the manger, where they only consume, for they can produce crops. Similarly, a man should train himself to plow the fields of wisdom, and then he will produce great things, both intellectually and spiritually. Otherwise, he will be like the stalled ox that does nothing but fatten itself all day: so far from increasing the spiritual treasure of the world, he then injures it by sensuality.

5. The verb *yᵉchazév* (lie) denotes the use of lies that become apparent only in the course of time; they have a specious credibility at first. A false witness obviously needs such deceptions, while a truthful witness will have no need of them, and his words will ring true first and last. The false witness can only "breathe out" his statement: he cunningly avoids clarity and finality in his testimony, so as not to incriminate himself. Metaphorically, this applies to one who is loyal to the moral law and attests to it: his words remain valid beyond the changes of time and fashion. The skeptic, with all his plausible analogies and distinctions, will find that his arguments ultimately do not stand up to examination.

PROVERBS 14:6-11

ו שָׁקֵר: בִּקֶּשׁ־לֵץ חָכְמָה וָאָיִן וְדַעַת לְנָבוֹן נָקָל: לֵךְ מִנֶּגֶד לְאִישׁ
ח כְּסִיל וּבַל־יָדַעְתָּ שִׂפְתֵי־דָעַת: חָכְמַת עָרוּם הָבִין דַּרְכּוֹ וְאִוֶּלֶת
ט כְּסִילִים מִרְמָה: אֱוִלִים יָלִיץ אָשָׁם וּבֵין יְשָׁרִים רָצוֹן: לֵב יוֹדֵעַ
יא מָרַּת נַפְשׁוֹ וּבְשִׂמְחָתוֹ לֹא־יִתְעָרַב זָר: בֵּית רְשָׁעִים יִשָּׁמֵד

6. A mocking person scorns moral law because there is no empirical evidence for its validity and it can be accepted only in humility and faith. By his mockery, he cuts off any chance of acquiring moral wisdom; and without a basis in faith, he can gain no further understanding. On the other hand, having accepted the moral law on a basis of faith, the "man of understanding" has the creative intelligence to build on that basis a whole structure of clear personal knowledge.

7. While the "mocking person" of the previous verse scoffs at the moral law because there is no objective, empirical proof for its validity, the foolish man accepts the moral law as binding, but he finds it too oppressive to his rebellious drives and desires. He therefore detests the clear conclusions to which moral wisdom leads him, and dishonestly casts doubt on the moral law in order to escape from his dilemma. Hence if a man has reached clear moral knowledge (*da'ath*) on the basis of faith in the moral law, the master of Proverbs instructs him to stay well away from the "foolish man" whose strong sensual desires vitiate such clear knowledge that he has. The dishonest doubter of this kind may corrupt his companions so that in the grip of desire they will forget all their *da'ath*, the clear moral knowledge they once possessed.

8. Since the "fool" of the previous verse is not a real skeptic, because he does not doubt the truth of the moral law but simply will not yield to it, so as to be "free" to yield to his cravings—his skepticism is deceit: mere pretense. On the other hand, the "shrewd man" of our verse is not himself wise; he has

is easy for the man of understanding. **7** Go away from the presence of a foolish man, or you will not know the lips of knowledge. **8** The wisdom of a shrewd man is to understand his way, but the skepticism of fools is deceit. **9** Guilt communicates between skeptics, but between the upright — Divine good will. **10** The heart knows its own bitterness, and in its joy no stranger can meddle. **11** The house of the wicked will be overthrown,

not learned the moral law thoroughly. Yet he is no naïve simpleton; with his shrewdness he can discern right from wrong, truth from falsehood. Hence he will not follow a dubious road blindly but will strive first to understand its nature; and thus in some details he will attain wisdom.

9. The skeptics are people genuinely in doubt about the validity of the moral law. Even they, however, in their heart of hearts, are conscious of guilt for their distorted ideas and actions: somewhere they know that their lives do not ring true. And it is this semi-conscious guilt that acts as a common language and bond between them: They can sense it in each other, and pick up the signals of broken moral functioning in others. On the other hand, the upright, who live in integrity and harmonious obedience to the moral tradition, communicate to each other their joy and confidence in the knowledge that their lives are pleasing to the Creator.

10. Literally "its soul's bitterness": the skeptic's inmost soul experiences bitterness and finds no rest, because it senses its guilt. This feeling, like the joy in an upright man's heart, are too deep and concealed in the heart for others to share or know.

11. The innermost feelings ("heart") of the skeptic and of the

יב וְאֹהֶל יְשָׁרִים יַפְרִיחַ: יֵשׁ דֶּרֶךְ יָשָׁר לִפְנֵי־אִישׁ וְאַחֲרִיתָהּ דַּרְכֵי־
יג מָוֶת: גַּם־בִּשְׂחֹק יִכְאַב־לֵב וְאַחֲרִיתָהּ שִׂמְחָה תוּגָה: מִדְּרָכָיו
יד יִשְׂבַּע סוּג לֵב וּמֵעָלָיו אִישׁ טוֹב: פֶּתִי יַאֲמִין לְכָל־דָּבָר וְעָרוּם
טו יָבִין לַאֲשֻׁרוֹ: חָכָם יָרֵא וְסָר מֵרָע וּכְסִיל מִתְעַבֵּר וּבוֹטֵחַ: קָצַר־

upright man, alluded to in verse 10, anticipate the respective futures of the two types. The guilty heart knows that its "house," however strong apparently, shall fall; while the joyful heart of an upright man looks forward to the prosperity of *its* "house," even if what he has now can be symbolically described as but a temporary, makeshift "tent."

12. This is the way of the skeptic, who doubts the laws of wisdom and accepts no moral discipline. He starts out by "feeling right," living in accord with his instincts and desires, with no spiritual conflicts; but, in the end, his road proves fatal. The way of moral wisdom, on the other hand, seems thorny and difficult at first, involving a constant struggle against nature, but it leads to harmony and achievement.

13. Laugh as the skeptic may, as fortune seems to smile on him in his life without moral discipline and restraint, his heart aches with its inward bitterness (verse 10), ultimately knowing that its joy is really sorrow, for it is going the way of death (verse 12).

14. The "recoiling of heart" is one whose heart cannot reconcile itself to his actions, because it senses that his way is bad. Nevertheless, he will earn his true deserts for walking in the ways of death. The good man, however, will certainly recoil from him and veer away from the company and example of such a man.

15. Thus far the master of Proverbs has spoken of the *kᵉsil* (fool,

but the tent of the upright shall flourish. **12** There is a way which seems right to a man, yet the end of it is the ways of death. **13** Even in laughter the heart aches, and its end is that joy becomes sorrow. **14** The recoiling of heart shall have his fill from his own ways, and from him shall a good man [veer off]. **15** The naïve man believes every word, but a shrewd man looks well to his going. **16** A wise man fears, and turns away from evil, but a fool oversteps the bounds, and is

who yields to his desires and ignores the moral law) and the *e'vil* (skeptic, who doubts the moral law and imposes no self-discipline). Their hearts trouble them: they are uncertain about their way in life. On the other hand, the *pethi* (naïve man, simpleton) lacks sense and believes both the *k^{e}sil* and the *e'vil*, indiscriminately; and his heart does not trouble him. He suffers from no pangs of doubt or self-accusation. The *'arum* (shrewd man) is his opposite. He tests every statement, assesses every idea shrewdly, to see if it will benefit him spiritually or harm him, and acts only on the basis of this thorough assessment. Thus "the wisdom of a shrewd man is to understand his way" (verse 8); and "every shrewd man acts with clear forethought" (13:16).

16. To learn to be moral, a person needs a framework of disciplining, since all his natural instincts draw him away from morality. This discipline is fear of HA-SHEM: the awareness that a great King stands over him observing his deeds; thus he will be ashamed to do anything against his Maker's will. The beginning of moral wisdom, therefore, is fear of HA-SHEM. This is the condition and the means to wisdom. So, since the wise man fears the Almighty, he turns away from evil. His natural

יח אַפַּיִם יַעֲשֶׂה אִוֶּלֶת וְאִישׁ מְזִמּוֹת יִשָּׂנֵא: נָחֲלוּ פְתָאיִם אִוֶּלֶת
יט וַעֲרוּמִים יַכְתִּרוּ דָעַת: שַׁחוּ רָעִים לִפְנֵי טוֹבִים וּרְשָׁעִים עַל־
כ שַׁעֲרֵי צַדִּיק: גַּם־לְרֵעֵהוּ יִשָּׂנֵא רָשׁ וְאֹהֲבֵי עָשִׁיר רַבִּים: בָּז־
כב לְרֵעֵהוּ חוֹטֵא וּמְחוֹנֵן עֲנָיִים אַשְׁרָיו: הֲלוֹא־יִתְעוּ חֹרְשֵׁי רָע עֲנָוִים

inclinations are disciplined so they cannot run wild. The fool, on the other hand, overreaches himself and oversteps the proper bounds; he runs wild past all restraints of discipline and wisdom. Having no fear of the Almighty, he has instead a foolhardy confidence.

17. An understanding person is patient and slow to anger; even intelligent self-interest indicates this, since anger breeds anger, and a vengeful attitude induces a similar attitude in others. Hence "a man of discernment keeps silent" (11:12). A quick-tempered man, however, expresses his anger instantly (at the root of *apayim*, "temper," is the word *af*, "nose," indicating external expression) and he "acts in skepticism," as one who doubts and dismisses the intelligent ways of understanding. Should he be patient and forbearing on the surface, but seethe with resentment within, imagining and planning revenge, in violation of the laws of wisdom, he does not "act in skepticism," but he "elevates" it (verse 29) from the depths of his mind to occupy his thoughts. And if he then foments "wicked devices," schemes and plans to harm someone, he will be hated by all.

18. The naïve person accepts unthinkingly all that the skeptics and cynics tell him; it is as though he "inherited" their opinions without working for them. A shrewd person, on the other hand, will do nothing without first assessing and judging the reasons and methods for his actions. Knowledge is the crown on his head.

confident. [17] A quick-tempered man acts in skepticism, while a man of wicked devices is hated. [18] The naïve inherit folly; but the shrewd are crowned with knowledge. [19] The evil bow down before the good, and the wicked at the gates of the righteous man. [20] Even by his own neighbor the poor man is hated, while many are the friends of the rich. [21] He who despises his neighbor sins, but one who is gracious to the lowly, happy is he. [22] Will they who plow evil not go astray, and will there not be loving-kindness and

19. Although evil is opposed to good, and wickedness to righteousness, when evil comes face to face with good it is compelled to yield before it; and so too "the wicked at the gates of the righteous man." It is the nature of evil to give way to good, as darkness gives way to light.

20-21. Although it is natural for people to love their own kind, the poor are hated even by their poor neighbors, who give their affection to the rich. This is against the laws of moral wisdom, which tell us to love humility, to be gracious to the poor, and to hate arrogance. This hatred of a poor neighbor, therefore, is a sin — a deviation from the moral law; while love of the poor is a source of spiritual happiness, as it inculcates love of humility and hatred of pride.

22. "Plowing" denotes scheming or planning to act in secret. Those who thus plot evil cannot be helped by others to return to the right road: they will stray from it in the darkness of their own secrecy. People who are modestly secretive about their good actions, however, are inspired by love and truth, not hoping for any public reward or recognition. That is the

כג וְחֶסֶד וֶאֱמֶת חֹרְשֵׁי טוֹב: בְּכָל־עֶצֶב יִהְיֶה מוֹתָר וּדְבַר־שְׂפָתַיִם
כד אַךְ־לְמַחְסוֹר: עֲטֶרֶת חֲכָמִים עָשְׁרָם אִוֶּלֶת כְּסִילִים אִוֶּלֶת:
כה מַצִּיל נְפָשׁוֹת עֵד אֱמֶת וְיָפִחַ כְּזָבִים מִרְמָה: בְּיִרְאַת יְהוָה
כו מִבְטַח־עֹז וּלְבָנָיו יִהְיֶה מַחְסֶה: יִרְאַת יְהוָה מְקוֹר חַיִּים לָסוּר

meaning of loving-kindness (*chesed*): an act that is done without hope of reward.

23. Whenever sorrow comes upon a person, he should ponder it deeply and silently in his heart, till he realizes that his sins are the cause of it, and he repents. This is the reason for the mourning period after a death; and it is therefore good to go to a house of mourning (Ecclesiastes 7:2) and contemplate, and return to God. In this way, out of every grief, silently and actively endured, comes spiritual profit. If the sufferer, however, merely complains and bewails his fate, then the result is spiritual loss. Thus after his sons were killed, "Aaron was silent" (Leviticus 10:3), and he was rewarded for his silence.

24. The true wealth of the wise is in their minds, for material wealth is illusory and ephemeral; their wisdom is their diadem of glory. Again, they are crowned by wisdom's rejection of the physical cravings of this world. Satisfaction with their lot is riches indeed. Now, unlike the skeptic, the fool generally does not doubt the moral law; only, swayed by his desires, he rejects it, and then claims skepticism as his excuse (13:16). Hence, says the verse, it is at best highly uncertain if the fool has any true skepticism about the moral laws of wisdom.

25. By testifying to the truth, witnesses can save the lives of persons facing death on account of false testimony. If, however, a witness comes to save the defendant with false testimony that speciously sounds true ("breathes out" connotes incomplete,

truth for those who plow good? [23] In all sorrow there is profit, but the talk of the lips only brings lack. [24] The crown of the wise is their riches, but the skepticism of fools is uncertainty. [25] A truthful witness saves lives, but one who breathes out lies is all deceit. [26] In the fear of HA-SHEM, a man has strong confidence, and his children will have a place of refuge. [27] The fear of HA-SHEM is a wellspring of life, to veer from the snares of death.

vague or unclear statements whose falsehood can only be verified later), this is not called "saving lives" in any sound, lasting sense; it is simply deceit. Only truth can be described as saving lives.

26. Wisdom without fear of the Almighty cannot survive. All kinds of psychological pitfalls, fantasies and desires can endanger our commitment to a life of moral wisdom. Only fear of God can restrain improper natural drives, and can even provide some kind of inherited immunity to our children: The experienced reality of the Divine presence in the home is absorbed by the children, as no theoretical ethical principles can be.

27. This continues the same theme as the previous verse: The way of moral wisdom is the way of life, but fear of God is necessary for safety from pitfalls and snares of death. On the other hand, without moral wisdom and knowledge of the Torah, fear of the Creator is equally insufficient: "Where there is no wisdom, there is no fear" (*Avoth* iii, 21). Thus we read elsewhere, "The teaching of the wise is a wellspring of life, to turn away from the snares of death" (13:14).

כח מְֽמַקְשֵׁי־מָ֑וֶת׃ בְּרָב־עָ֥ם הַדְרַת־מֶ֑לֶךְ וּבְאֶ֥פֶס לְ֝אֹ֗ם מְחִתַּ֥ת
כט רָזֽוֹן׃ אֶ֣רֶךְ אַ֭פַּיִם רַב־תְּבוּנָ֑ה וּקְצַר־ר֝֗וּחַ מֵרִ֥ים אִוֶּֽלֶת׃ חַיֵּ֣י
ל בְ֭שָׂרִים לֵ֣ב מַרְפֵּ֑א וּרְקַ֖ב עֲצָמ֣וֹת קִנְאָֽה׃ עֹ֣שֵֽׁק־דָּ֭ל חֵרֵ֣ף עֹשֵׂ֑הוּ
לא וּ֝מְכַבְּד֗וֹ חֹנֵ֥ן אֶבְיֽוֹן׃ בְּ֭רָעָתוֹ יִדָּחֶ֣ה רָשָׁ֑ע וְחֹסֶ֖ה בְמוֹת֣וֹ צַדִּֽיק׃
לב בְּלֵ֣ב נָ֭בוֹן תָּנ֣וּחַ חָכְמָ֑ה וּבְקֶ֥רֶב כְּ֝סִילִ֗ים תִּוָּדֵֽעַ׃ צְדָקָ֥ה תְרֽוֹמֵם־

28. The first "people" (*'am*) refers to a nation united in loyalty to the king. The second line, "people" (*le'om*) denotes a population united by a spiritual belief. Even where there is an impressive display of numbers, the minister, in charge of legislating and regulating religion, will find himself helpless if there is a lack of people of religious faith and understanding.

29. Intelligence and prudence dictate that one should restrain his temper or his impulse to avenge every slight (see verse 17). A person may, however, be apparently slow to anger, while in his heart he is easily aroused to long for revenge (*ruach*, "spirit," denotes the inner temper, rather than its outward display; see verse 17). This is against the laws of moral wisdom, which direct us to cultivate impulses of mercy and forgiveness in our hearts.

30. When a person "elevates skepticism" of the moral law to his conscious mind (verse 29) as he churns with inner resentment and vengefulness, this is not only against the moral law but destructive to the hater himself. The heart that is distorted with suppressed anger cannot function properly and will not allow the whole body to function smoothly and well; flesh and bones are only as healthy as the spirit they encase.

31. The Almighty created man for his own good, and intended human beings to help one another, if some were more successful than others in the effort to earn a living. Thus, a

28 In a multitude of people is a king's majesty, but in the lack of people is a minister's ruin. **29** He who is slow to anger has great understanding, but a short-tempered man elevates skepticism. **30** A tranquil heart is the life of the flesh; but envy is the rot of the bones. **31** He who oppresses a poor man blasphemes his Maker, but one who is gracious to the needy honors Him. **32** A wicked man is thrust down by his own evil, but a righteous person [even] at his death has hope. **33** In the heart of an understanding man, wisdom reposes, but within fools it makes itself known. **34** Righteous-

wealthy man in need of workers should employ the poor, and there should be charity where needed. The wealth of the rich was given them partly in order to help the poor, and if the rich evade this duty, it is as though they cast aspersions on the justice and beneficence of the Almighty's creation. For the poor may then see only an evil purpose to their existence.

32. The wicked is hurled down to destruction by his own evil, even in the height of fortune. In contrast, the righteous man has trust in merciful Divine protection not merely during his lifetime but even in the throes of death.

33. Moral wisdom, which depends on the received traditions of morality, has a difficult struggle against the temptations of natural impulses and desires. Only if it is reinforced by a personal intellectual vitality ("understanding"), which can construct a private moral vision, will it be able to "repose" serenely in one's heart. The fool, however, though he knows the moral law, has displaced it in his heart, the center of his being, by his desires and lawless passions. It still exists somewhere

לה גּוֹי וְחֶסֶד לְאֻמִּים חַטָּאת: רְצוֹן־מֶלֶךְ לְעֶבֶד מַשְׂכִּיל וְעֶבְרָתוֹ תִּהְיֶה מֵבִישׁ:

"within" him; in some part of his consciousness it merely "makes itself known," and he uses it for evil ends, against wisdom's ways.

34. The word *goy* (nation) represents the lowest form of national group, a mere mass of people without leader or religious faith to unite them. Even such a group is exalted by a righteous way of life. On the other hand, even *l'om* (a people), the highest type of a collective population, united by religious faith, is corrupted in the most shameful way if it deviates from the way of moral wisdom and righteousness.

35. The term *maskil* ("who deals wisely") denotes doing one's

ness exalts a nation, but sin is a reproach to any people. **35** A king's favor is given a servant who deals wisely, but his wrath shall fall on one who acts shamefully.

work alertly and intelligently, keeping its end purpose in sight. The contrasting term *mévish* (who acts shamefully) indicates tardiness, with no concern for consequences or end purpose. The tasks of a king's servants (employees) are for the public welfare, and he will therefore be well pleased with the first kind, while the second will move him to a general wrath, even at the innocent. Hence, as the Sages taught, a person should always see the world as exactly half meritorious, half guilty. One good deed of his can sway the balance in the world's favor, by evoking Divine good will for all; and one bad deed can have the opposite effect on the welfare of the world.

PROVERBS 15:1-6

טו א מַעֲנֶה־רַּךְ יָשִׁיב חֵמָה וּדְבַר־עֶצֶב יַעֲלֶה־אָף:
ב לְשׁוֹן חֲכָמִים תֵּיטִיב דָּעַת וּפִי כְסִילִים יַבִּיעַ אִוֶּלֶת: בְּכָל־מָקוֹם
ג עֵינֵי יְהוָה צֹפוֹת רָעִים וְטוֹבִים: מַרְפֵּא לָשׁוֹן עֵץ חַיִּים וְסֶלֶף
ד בָּהּ שֶׁבֶר בְּרוּחַ: אֱוִיל יִנְאַץ מוּסַר אָבִיו וְשֹׁמֵר תּוֹכַחַת יַעְרִם:
ה בֵּית צַדִּיק חֹסֶן רָב וּבִתְבוּאַת רָשָׁע נֶעְכָּרֶת: שִׂפְתֵי חֲכָמִים
ו
ז

1. The term *chéma* (wrath) denotes intense inner anger, concealed from others, while *af* (anger) means a superficial rage, quickly expressed and dissipated. Even intense inner anger can be dispelled by a gentle word, while a provocative remark that inflicts pain will stir up the desire for immediate revenge.

2. The tongue denotes words of understanding, spoken with discernment. When the wise speak to people of understanding, their "tongue" makes abstract ideas as clear and palpable as *da'ath* (knowledge), matters known as certainly as if sensed physically. Now the fool knows the laws of moral wisdom, but yielding to his desires, he ignores them, claiming to be skeptical of them, in order to rationalize his morally undisciplined life. His "mouth," denoting wise speech, expresses only a spuriously wise skepticism. There is no heart's wisdom in it, for he is totally insincere.

3. Although we say, metaphorically, that the Almighty regards only the righteous and His sight is turned away from the wicked, this denotes that His special providential good will falls only on the righteous. In actuality He perceives *all* that is done in the world, good and bad; His whole creation is in His sight, and the Divine providence acts accordingly. Nothing escapes Him; and thus He "keeps watch," regulating the future according to human action, whether good or bad, however hidden it may be.

4. The tongue that is perverted, speaking slander or idle evil

15 ¹ A soft answer turns away wrath, but a distressing word stirs up anger. ² The tongue of the wise uses knowledge well, but the mouth of fools pours out skepticism. ³ The eyes of HA-SHEM are in every place, keeping watch on the evil and the good. ⁴ The tongue's medicine is the tree of life, but perverseness in it is a wound to the spirit. ⁵ A skeptic despises his father's moral discipline, but one who heeds reproof is sagacious. ⁶ The house of a righteous man is of great durability, but with the revenue of a wicked man, it is troubled. ⁷ The

gossip, is the symptom of a sick human being, since speech is so integrally an expression of the man. This kind of serious inner disease is curable by the study of Torah and its moral wisdom, the "tree of life for those who hold fast to it" (3:18).

5. Moral discipline is based on fear—fear of the consequences of evil—which in turn is based on knowledge—the knowledge that there exists a Creator who rewards and punishes. The *kᵉsil* (fool) knows and acknowledges the moral law, but is swayed by his desires to assume a skeptical position. The *e'vil* (skeptic) is genuinely skeptical and hostile to moral authority. He despises moral correction and discipline, because he does not believe in its premise: Divine providence. Now *tochacha* (reproof) denotes an appeal to good sense, showing the actual benefits of moral wisdom. This, only the most unintelligent boor will reject; even the skeptic will listen, as long as he is open to reason. A shrewd, sagacious man, who is beginning to distinguish between good and evil, can gain in shrewdness by "heeding reproof" well.

6. The spiritual house of a *tzaddik* is built on the structured ways of righteousness. It will endure in the strength of his

ח שִׂפְתֵי חֲכָמִים יְזָרוּ דָעַת וְלֵב כְּסִילִים לֹא־כֵן׃ זֶבַח רְשָׁעִים תּוֹעֲבַת יְהוָה
ט וּתְפִלַּת יְשָׁרִים רְצוֹנוֹ׃ תּוֹעֲבַת יְהוָה דֶּרֶךְ רָשָׁע וּמְרַדֵּף צְדָקָה
י יֶאֱהָב׃ מוּסָר רָע לְעֹזֵב אֹרַח שׂוֹנֵא תוֹכַחַת יָמוּת׃ שְׁאוֹל
יב וַאֲבַדּוֹן נֶגֶד יְהוָה אַף כִּי־לִבּוֹת בְּנֵי־אָדָם׃ לֹא־יֶאֱהַב־לֵץ הוֹכֵחַ

faculties. But if he would share the "revenue of the wicked," bringing the gains of robbery and violence into his house — or, taken metaphorically, cultivating corrupt and sensual desires — then he will trouble and disrupt the peace of his spiritual house.

7. The truly wise place a "hedge" (*zér*) 'round their wisdom, keeping it from the *k^esil* (fool) who spouts a skepticism that refutes knowledge. In his heart the *k^esil* acknowledges the moral law, but he is swayed and blinded by his desires. Hence his heart is as steadfast as foam on water.

8. What the Almighty primarily desires is the honest outpouring of the heart yearning for Him. Without this, the most lavish sacrifice is abominable; with it, simple prayer is sufficient, even without sacrifice.

9. The *way* to his wickedness, a bad man's evil feelings of arrogance, vengeance and cruelty, are more hateful to the Almighty than the evil actions they lead to, for his actions are only the outcome of the evil within. Conversely, even if a person but pursues righteousness, without attaining it, the Almighty bears him affection; the psychological intent is the main thing.

10. In discipline there is good correction and painful correction. The good kind is a warning of the punishment that will befall the wicked; this motivates a person to keep to the right path. It is painful correction when a person is made to suffer bitterly — and this happens when he has already forsaken

lips of the wise hedge knowledge about, but the heart of the foolish is not steadfast. [8] The sacrifice of the wicked is an abomination to HA-SHEM; but the prayer of the upright is His delight. [9] An abomination to HA-SHEM is the way of a wicked man, but He loves one who pursues righteousness. [10] There is dire moral discipline for one who forsakes the road; he who hates reproof will die. [11] The netherworld and perdition are before HA-SHEM; how much more, then, the hearts of the children of men! [12] A mocking person does not like being reproved; he will not go to the wise.

the right path, after having followed it. Through this pain he can come to realize its cause, repent, and be healed. Otherwise, if a person resists this reproof given through suffering, death is the ultimate consequence.

11. This is an answer to those philosophers who maintain that it is impossible for God to know the thoughts of man: either because they are hidden so deep in the human heart, or because they are in constant flux, changing from moment to moment. The netherworld is far deeper, far more beyond sight and ken than the human heart; and *avaddon* (perdition) is the primordial volatile substance that constantly assumes different forms — and both of these the Almighty knows. Then He certainly knows the hearts of the human beings.

12. The scorner mocks at the moral law because it is not rationally demonstrable. When he is faced, however, with rational moral arguments and reproof, he cannot mock them; but he is simply repelled by them. He will therefore keep away from teachers of moral wisdom.

PROVERBS 15:13-19

יג \ לֵב שָׂמֵחַ יֵיטִב פָּנִים וּבְעַצְּבַת־לֵב רוּחַ נְכֵאָה: לֵב נָבוֹן יְבַקֶּשׁ־דָּעַת וּפְנֵי כְסִילִים יִרְעֶה אִוֶּלֶת: כָּל־יְמֵי עָנִי רָעִים וְטוֹב־לֵב מִשְׁתֶּה תָמִיד: טוֹב־מְעַט בְּיִרְאַת יְהוָה מֵאוֹצָר רָב וּמְהוּמָה בוֹ: טוֹב אֲרֻחַת יָרָק וְאַהֲבָה־שָׁם מִשּׁוֹר אָבוּס וְשִׂנְאָה־בוֹ: אִישׁ חֵמָה יְגָרֶה מָדוֹן וְאֶרֶךְ אַפַּיִם יַשְׁקִיט רִיב: דֶּרֶךְ עָצֵל כִּמְשֻׂכַת חָדֶק וְאֹרַח יְשָׁרִים סְלֻלָה:

13. The heart that is complacently involved in worldly success, untroubled by its sins or its lack of spiritual achievement, makes for a cheerful face (appearance), but not for a healthy spiritual life and development. All one's spiritual faculties may then be in a miserable, wretched state, concerned only with earthly pleasures. If a person is concerned and troubled, however, over his spiritual condition, his spirit is elevated, and that is far better than a cheerful face.

14. An understanding person can draw inferences, and thus after a long and conscientious process of mental enquiry and reflection he can gain a knowledge of the moral laws and their reasons; for the ruling heart, imposing these laws on the self, wishes to know their reasons and inner meanings. The k^esil (fool), however, ignoring the moral laws (which he knows) in favor of unbridled desires, sets his face to "feed skepticism"; he becomes the shepherd ($ro'eh$) of skepticism, as it were, to make a mask out of intellectual doubt of the moral laws, behind which he will feel free to gratify his desires without restraint. [The word pi, "mouth of," is written as p^enei, "face of"; and thus it bears this meaning too.]

15. This verse is the argument of the fool (k^esil) who prates skepticism, assuming an attitude of doubt about moral law to cover up lawless desires: People who are strictly obedient to the Torah, they say, nevertheless lead hard lives, in poverty and

13 A merry heart makes a cheerful face, but by sorrow of heart the spirit is broken. **14** The heart of an understanding person seeks knowledge, but the face of fools feeds skepticism. **15** All the days of a poor person are wretched, but one who has a continual feast has a merry heart. **16** Better is a little with the fear of HA-SHEM, than great treasure and turmoil with it. **17** Better a dinner of herbs where love is, than a fatted ox and hatred with it. **18** A wrathful man stirs up a quarrel, but one who is slow to anger abates strife. **19** The way of a sluggard is as a hedge of thorns, but the road of the upright is even.

affliction, while persons who enjoy constant pleasure have a cheerful heart. Thus the skeptic concludes that the moral life does not pay. To this "the heart of an understanding person," having sought out knowledge (verse 14), replies with verse 16.

16. The little that remains to the God-fearing man after he has invested all his time and energy in spiritual perfection is better than the treasure of one whose spiritual life is impoverished.

17. Affection makes a small meal sweet, while hatred turns the most sumptuous feast bitter. Only inner peace and love and trust in HA-SHEM constitute true happiness and good fortune, and not the apparent, illusory delights of this world.

18. A man of *chéma*, inner seething wrath, stirs up a quarrel: he will find something over which to disagree violently with another person; for he seeks an outlet for his rage in arousing general contention and strife. But a person slow to anger can soothe his rancor with a soft answer, a gentle word (verse 1).

כ ‏בֵּן חָכָם יְשַׂמַּח־אָב וּכְסִיל אָדָם בּוֹזֶה אִמּוֹ: אִוֶּלֶת שִׂמְחָה
כב ‏לַחֲסַר־לֵב וְאִישׁ תְּבוּנָה יְיַשֶּׁר־לָכֶת: הָפֵר מַחֲשָׁבוֹת בְּאֵין סוֹד
כג ‏וּבְרֹב יוֹעֲצִים תָּקוּם: שִׂמְחָה לָאִישׁ בְּמַעֲנֵה־פִיו וְדָבָר בְּעִתּוֹ
כד ‏מַה־טּוֹב: אֹרַח חַיִּים לְמַעְלָה לְמַשְׂכִּיל לְמַעַן סוּר מִשְּׁאוֹל

19. The term *derech* (way) means the highroad, and the *orach* (road) signifies a branch road, leading to a particular destination, such as a village. The sluggard finds even the well-paved public highroad too difficult and thorny to traverse, while an upright man finds even a small private road sufficiently smooth for him. Metaphorically, this suggests that a lazy, slothful person finds the moral law, even in its clearest and most generally valid guidelines, too difficult for him, since he cannot overcome his passions and instincts; while the upright person finds even the private special paths of voluntary piety quite straightforward, since his heart offers no resistance out of cravings and desires.

20. This is reminiscent of 10:1, "A wise son makes a father glad, but a foolish son is the grief of his mother." There the import is that the son's wisdom itself gives joy to his father, and his folly gives sorrow to his mother. Here the intent is rather that when the son grows up and lives according to the laws of moral wisdom, he will endeavor to give pleasure to his father by his virtuous way of life; this itself is one of the moral laws. The fool, on the other hand, who is bound by his desires, will actively scorn his mother when she rebukes him for his deplorable ways.

21. Without a heart that imposes self-discipline, a person cannot attain adequate self-control and self-management. Unable to govern himself, he depends on external authority (like an animal that must be led with a rod). Such a person takes happily to a foolish skepticism. The man of discernment is just

²⁰ A wise son makes a father glad, but a foolish person despises his mother. ²¹ Skepticism is joy to him who lacks a [self-disciplining] heart; but a man of discernment walks aright. ²² Without secret consideration, thoughts are frustrated; but in a multitude of counsellors they are established. ²³ A man has joy in the answer of his mouth, and a word at its right time, how good it is! ²⁴ The road of life goes upward for the intelligent one, that he

the opposite of this: he has wisdom and understanding to guide him from within along the right road, and needs no external signposts and guidelines.

22. "Thoughts" denote random, possible ideas; a plan is one thought chosen to act on. Thoughts leading to plans should not be disclosed; otherwise enemies will frustrate them, and alternative plans will be needed, requiring the advice of many counsellors.

23. "Mouth" alludes to wisdom. One who is conditioned by moral wisdom can respond instantly to any moral question, and this brings him joy. Even better is the feeling of bringing benefit with his wisdom in a time of need; that is the essence of goodness—to be effectively helpful at the right moment.

24. The morally intelligent man will realize that the path to life is upward, and the path to death leads down; and even though it is much harder to go up than down—the law of gravity (resistance) applies here too—he will exert all his intellectual and spiritual energy to go up toward spiritual life, and away from the physical degradation of the downward road that ends in timeless death.

כה מָטָּה: בֵּית גֵּאִים יִסַּח יְהוָה וְיַצֵּב גְּבוּל אַלְמָנָה: תּוֹעֲבַת יְהוָה
כו מַחְשְׁבוֹת רָע וּטְהֹרִים אִמְרֵי־נֹעַם: עֹכֵר בֵּיתוֹ בּוֹצֵעַ בָּצַע
כז וְשׂוֹנֵא מַתָּנֹת יִחְיֶה: לֵב צַדִּיק יֶהְגֶּה לַעֲנוֹת וּפִי רְשָׁעִים יַבִּיעַ
כח רָעוֹת: רָחוֹק יְהוָה מֵרְשָׁעִים וּתְפִלַּת צַדִּיקִים יִשְׁמָע: מְאוֹר־
כט עֵינַיִם יְשַׂמַּח־לֵב שְׁמוּעָה טוֹבָה תְּדַשֶּׁן־עָצֶם: אֹזֶן שֹׁמַעַת
לא

25. If you see some proud man's opulent house built on the property of a poor widow, who has no one to fight for her rights, know that there is One to defend her, to demolish that house and restore her rights. Divine providence works to achieve justice where no mundane force of justice seems able to intervene.

26. The Almighty detests the hypocrisy of a person who speaks pure words of pleasantness and harbors wicked thoughts.

27. The Hebrew for "greedy of gain" denotes earning wealth crookedly or dishonestly. If a person does so, let him not think he will bring honor to his house; on the contrary, he will bring only trouble. On the other hand, when one earns his own living honestly and wants nothing unearned from others, he will not die of hunger or sicken from overwork. By Divine protection he will live.

28. The way of righteousness includes due deliberation before speaking; it includes even a careful decision *whether* to speak at all, whether to answer a question or a taunt. There are many cases where silence is the best answer. As for the wicked, however, their mouths let loose slander and heresy, without any heart's control.

29. Providence responds to human activity: If a person

may depart from the netherworld beneath. [25] HA-SHEM will demolish the house of the proud, but he will establish the border of the widow. [26] The thoughts of a wicked person are an abomination to HA-SHEM; while words of pleasantness are pure. [27] He who is greedy of gain troubles his own house, but one who hates gifts shall live. [28] The heart of the righteous ponders how to answer, but the mouth of the wicked pours out evils. [29] HA-SHEM is far from the wicked, but He hears the prayer of the righteous. [30] The light of the eyes rejoices the heart; good news makes the bones fat. [31] The ear that listens to the reproof of life will

---

estranges himself from the Almighty, then He is in fact distant from him; and if one moves closer to Him, then He is there, near to him, as He is with a *tzaddik*, heeding his prayer. This is the meaning of "HA-SHEM is close to all who call on Him" — not that God changes His mind, as it were, in response to human prayer, but that He simply allows a man to place Him at whatever distance he desires.

30–31. If a person sees something good, the sight rejoices his heart, where all his spiritual resources lie. Simply hearing of something good at a distance (not in sight) merely "makes the bones fat": it has a physical effect, which is less central than the spiritual impact of the sense of sight. Therefore, simply hearing reproof is not sufficient. We should live among the wise, observe them, with that faculty of vision that is more powerful than hearing, since personal experience is more vivid than theoretical knowledge.

לב פּוֹרֵעַ מוּסָר מוֹאֵס נַפְשׁוֹ וְשׁוֹמֵעַ תוֹכַחַת קוֹנֶה לֵּב׃
לג יִרְאַת יְהוָה מוּסַר חָכְמָה וְלִפְנֵי כָבוֹד עֲנָוָה׃

32. Moral correction involves the threat of punishment, primarily spiritual punishment in the Hereafter. If a person dismisses and ignores that, he has no concern for his own soul; he despises it. Now, if one lacks a heart to impose self-control, he yields to desire like an animal. Not knowing right from wrong, he will respond not to threats but only to direct pain. Should he pay heed, however, to reasoned reproof, he can gain the heart of understanding and self-discipline that he lacks.

abide among the wise. [32] He who dismisses moral correction despises his own soul, but one who listens to reproof gains a [self-disciplining] heart. [33] The fear of HA-SHEM is the moral instruction of wisdom, and before honor goes humility.

33. Honor is accorded a person who listens to rational reproof, since his resulting repentance is based not on fear of the consequences of sin but on an intelligent recognition of the validity of moral law. Such rationality, however, is based on humility; the arrogant man hardens himself against the rational appeals of morality and will never, therefore, gain this honor.

PROVERBS 16:1–7

טז א לְאָדָ֥ם מַֽעַרְכֵי־לֵ֑ב וּ֝מֵיְהוָ֗ה מַעֲנֵ֥ה לָשֽׁוֹן׃
ג כָּֽל־דַּרְכֵי־אִ֭ישׁ זַ֣ךְ בְּעֵינָ֑יו וְתֹכֵ֖ן רוּח֣וֹת יְהוָֽה׃ גֹּ֣ל אֶל־יְהוָ֣ה מַעֲשֶׂ֑יךָ
ד וְ֝יִכֹּ֗נוּ מַחְשְׁבֹתֶֽיךָ׃ כֹּ֤ל פָּעַ֣ל יְ֭הוָה לַֽמַּעֲנֵ֑הוּ וְגַם־רָ֝שָׁ֗ע לְי֣וֹם רָעָֽה׃
ה תּוֹעֲבַ֣ת יְ֭הוָה כָּל־גְּבַהּ־לֵ֑ב יָ֥ד לְ֝יָ֗ד לֹ֣א יִנָּקֶֽה׃ בְּחֶ֣סֶד וֶ֭אֱמֶת

1. The heart organizes what to say, and since a man has free will, he prepares many alternative arrangements of ideas. Nevertheless, the final formulation in language is a gift from Heaven; we require Divine aid. Hence, "So I prayed to the God of heaven; and said to the king…" (Nehemiah 2:4-5): the prayer was for proper, felicitous expression.

2. The ways of the spirit are complex, and it is impossible for a man alone to discriminate which way is absolutely pure. Only the Almighty can discern ulterior motives which may lie behind apparently virtuous behavior. A man may be kind, honest, compassionate, even humble, and all inspired by a desire for recognition and praise. Only the Creator sees the psychological complexities of men in true perspective.

3. Since human thoughts are multiple and ever in flux, only if we orient our minds toward the fulfillment of His will can our mental life acquire a stability and consistency it would not otherwise have.

4. The Almighty is the fitting center for our purposes in life, since all of creation was brought into being for His glory. By His wish, all human acts should lead to the sanctification of His name. Even the wicked who profane His name with apparent impunity, who seem to flourish in this world, were also created for His glory, since the day of retribution awaits them — and this too sanctifies the Divine name.

5. In general, the Almighty does not punish a person for evil

16 ¹ The preparations of the heart are man's, but the answer of the tongue is from HA-SHEM. ² All the ways of a man are pure in his own eyes, but HA-SHEM examines the spirits. ³ Commit your actions to HA-SHEM, and your thoughts will be established. ⁴ HA-SHEM has made everything for His own purpose, and even the wicked for the day of evil. ⁵ Everyone proud in heart is an abomination to HA-SHEM; hand to hand, he shall not go unpunished. ⁶ By loving-kindness and truth is iniquity expiated, and by the fear of HA-SHEM one departs from evil. ⁷ When a man's ways please HA-

thoughts or character-traits, until they surface in evil actions; and even then He may not punish the sinner directly, but rather leave him to the vicissitudes of time. The one exception is the sin of pride that sets a man posing above ordinary mortals and ordinary morality. This is so hateful to the Almighty that He punishes the person immediately, "hand to hand"—by direct transmission of the penalty, not leaving him to the vicissitudes of nature, which may be long in coming. With arrogance there is no hope of repentance, and therefore no point in delay.

6. Even after deliberate sin a person can find rectification if he commits himself to unconditional loving acts of kindness for his fellow-men, and to the study of Torah. As our Sages taught, "loving-kindness means altruistic kind deeds, and truth means Torah" (*B⁽ᵉ⁾rachoth* 5b). Nevertheless, better than rectification and expiation is never to have sinned at all: to walk firmly in the fear of God which is a deterrent from evil.

7. The Almighty is pleased by those who are steadfast in their wholehearted way toward Him so that no foreign impulse or

ז יְכֻפַּר עָוֹן וּבְיִרְאַת יְהוָֹה סוּר מֵרָע: בִּרְצוֹת יְהוָה דַּרְכֵי־אִישׁ
ח גַּם־אוֹיְבָיו יַשְׁלִם אִתּוֹ: טוֹב מְעַט בִּצְדָקָה מֵרֹב תְּבוּאוֹת בְּלֹא
ט מִשְׁפָּט: לֵב אָדָם יְחַשֵּׁב דַּרְכּוֹ וַיהוָֹה יָכִין צַעֲדוֹ: קֶסֶם ׀ עַל־
יא שִׂפְתֵי־מֶלֶךְ בְּמִשְׁפָּט לֹא יִמְעַל־פִּיו: פֶּלֶס וּמֹאזְנֵי מִשְׁפָּט לַיהוָה
יב מַעֲשֵׂהוּ כָּל־אַבְנֵי־כִיס: תּוֹעֲבַת מְלָכִים עֲשׂוֹת רֶשַׁע כִּי בִצְדָקָה
יג יִכּוֹן כִּסֵּא: רְצוֹן מְלָכִים שִׂפְתֵי־צֶדֶק וְדֹבֵר יְשָׁרִים יֶאֱהָב: חֲמַת־

desire arises in them. Then He is steadfast and constant in granting them His favor. Since they have achieved peace with the inner enemies of sinful urges, He rewards them by giving them peace with any external, physical enemies they may have.

8. The modest possessions of a *tzaddik*, a righteous person, are under Divine protection and will endure. All the great profits and possessions that are acquired unjustly, however, will be ultimately lost. (Verse 15:16 above dealt with inner satisfaction and pleasure from what one has; hence this is not a duplication.)

9. Even though man has free will to decide on his course of action, it still remains in Heaven's power to let him carry out his projects (actually take the physical steps along the route he has planned) or to prevent him. Just as felicitous oral expression is a Divine gift (verse 1), so do physical movement and achievement depend on His will. In the transitive, the Hebrew for "calculates" denotes peculiar, improper plans; hence the Almighty impedes him.

10. Whatever issues from the lips of a king, even in superficial talk, is regarded as magic or wizardry: Conclusions and decisions are derived from his words. Hence he must speak clearly and truly; his mouth must never betray him.

SHEM, He makes even his enemies be at peace with him. ⁸ Better is a little with righteousness than great revenues with injustice. ⁹ A man's heart calculates his way, but HA-SHEM directs his steps. ¹⁰ A magic rests on the lips of the king; let his mouth not betray him in judgment. ¹¹ A just compass and balance scale are HA-SHEM's; all the weights in the bag are His work. ¹² It is an abomination to kings to commit wickedness, for the throne is established by righteousness. ¹³ Righteous lips are the delight of kings, and they love him who speaks in decency. ¹⁴ The wrath of a

11. The compass measures distance, to determine the shortest route to a destination. Thus the Almighty can measure a person's ways and behavior, and guide him aright. And He can weigh his deeds in the pans of a balance-scale, as it were, to reward him as he deserves, good or evil. The "weights in the bag" are His (Divine) deeds, against which He measures human deeds, to make a correspondence. Thus "if you obey My commandments ... I will give you the rain of your land ... Take heed lest your heart be deceived ... and He will shut up the heaven and there will be no rain" (Deuteronomy 11:13-17).

12. Kingdoms are set up on a basis of social justice, but they become stabilized and durable through righteousness—good deeds. Hence the opposite, wickedness, is self-destructive for a sovereign.

13. "Righteous lips" refers to strict justice in civil life; "speaking in decency" is a higher level of personal integrity, going beyond the strict demands of the law, with a straightforward, honest mind.

יד חֲמַת־מֶלֶךְ מַלְאֲכֵי־מָוֶת וְאִישׁ חָכָם יְכַפְּרֶנָּה: בְּאוֹר־פְּנֵי־מֶלֶךְ חַיִּים
טו וּרְצוֹנוֹ כְּעָב מַלְקוֹשׁ: קְנֹה־חָכְמָה מַה־טּוֹב מֵחָרוּץ וּקְנוֹת בִּינָה
טז נִבְחָר מִכָּסֶף: מְסִלַּת יְשָׁרִים סוּר מֵרָע שֹׁמֵר נַפְשׁוֹ נֹצֵר דַּרְכּוֹ:
יז
יח לִפְנֵי־שֶׁבֶר גָּאוֹן וְלִפְנֵי כִשָּׁלוֹן גֹּבַהּ רוּחַ: טוֹב שְׁפַל־רוּחַ אֶת־
יט ענוים
כ עֲנָוִים מֵחַלֵּק שָׁלָל אֶת־גֵּאִים: מַשְׂכִּיל עַל־דָּבָר יִמְצָא־טוֹב

14. The term *chéma* (wrath) denotes an intense inner (unexpressed) anger. In an ordinary man it need have no dire effects. The wrath of a king, however, can wreak destruction. A wise man must be found, who will know how to appease his fury. Metaphorically, this refers also to Divine wrath, which can arouse angels of destruction. Someone like Pin*e*chas can turn His wrath away (Numbers 25:7–11).

15. After a wise man appeases the king's rage (verse 14), the ruler's face is bright with good will, which means life to his subjects, instead of the threatened death. This restoration of grace is like the rains that come after a long dry period, as it bestows his good will and blessing.

16. Wisdom, the received teaching on moral matters, is compared to gold, which is stored in treasure-houses and valued as a precious substance in itself. Understanding, the deductive capacity that leads a man to his own rational conclusions about truth and falsehood, is compared to silver, whose value and function are defined in market terms. Silver is used actively to exchange and acquire goods, as understanding operates in the world to acquire ever new and more valuable insights.

17. The upright have no inner struggle with their lower nature; all is like a paved highway for them, and they can easily keep evil at bay. One whose instincts do not work so harmoniously and who is obliged to walk along an unpaved "way" is in a

king is as messengers of death, but a wise man will pacify it. [15] In the light of a king's countenance is life, and his favor is like a cloud of the spring rain. [16] How much better it is to get wisdom than gold, and to get understanding, more choice than silver. [17] The highway of the upright is to depart from evil, he who guards his way preserves his soul. [18] Pride goes before a calamity, and haughtiness of spirit before a fall. [19] Better to be of a lowly spirit with the humble than to divide the spoil with the proud. [20] With intelligence about a matter one

position of constant danger and has to maintain alertness, in his effort to guard his soul.

18-19. "Haughtiness of spirit" is a stage before pride: a tendency to superiority that has not yet stamped itself on the character. At this stage it is easy to fall into real arrogance, which Heaven detests and punishes severely (verse 5). The humble person, on the other hand, recognizes human limitations and sees no reason for pride. There are two forms of humility, however: in one, the "lowly spirit," there is no self-esteem at all, and the person is so undemanding that he does not even feel insults or mockery; the other, "humility," is a rational realization of human limitation, imposed on a basic sense of personal worth. Even though humility is the one trait in which we are advised to go to extremes (and not to keep to the "golden mean" generally prescribed), the extreme of the "lowly spirit" should be tempered by "humility," by a rational and healthy concept of oneself. Ultimately humility does bring honor (15:33).

20. Without an intelligent choice of means to achieve his

כא וּבוֹטֵחַ בַּיהוָה אַשְׁרָיו: לַחֲכַם־לֵב יִקָּרֵא נָבוֹן וּמֶתֶק שְׂפָתַיִם
כב יֹסִיף לֶקַח: מְקוֹר חַיִּים שֵׂכֶל בְּעָלָיו וּמוּסַר אֱוִלִים אִוֶּלֶת: לֵב
כג חָכָם יַשְׂכִּיל פִּיהוּ וְעַל־שְׂפָתָיו יֹסִיף לֶקַח: צוּף־דְּבַשׁ אִמְרֵי־
כד נֹעַם מָתוֹק לַנֶּפֶשׁ וּמַרְפֵּא לָעָצֶם: יֵשׁ דֶּרֶךְ יָשָׁר לִפְנֵי־אִישׁ
כה
כו וְאַחֲרִיתָהּ דַּרְכֵי־מָוֶת: נֶפֶשׁ עָמֵל עָמְלָה לּוֹ כִּי־אָכַף עָלָיו פִּיהוּ:

purpose, a person will not find the good he seeks. If he uses his mind he will, like anyone seeking and finding his objective. There is another way in life, however: to trust in HA-SHEM, believing implicitly that He will do everything necessary. This brings not some chance success by good fortune, but basic spiritual happiness.

21. By habituation and study, the "wise in heart" has more fully absorbed the principles of ethics into his emotional and instinctive life than the mere "wise man," who still has to struggle to impose a received morality on his rebellious nature. The "man of discernment" too has easy control of his instincts, since he understands the moral laws with such clarity that they become objects of rational knowledge for him. The "wise in heart" does not have his considered understanding of moral wisdom, but he accepts it equally in his nature; and by making it fluent on his lips (familiar) he can increase his knowledge of moral wisdom that he receives from others, though without inner understanding.

22. If the "wise in heart" does not achieve an understanding of moral wisdom (verse 21), he can grasp it by his intelligence, a fine sense of perception of hidden truths and supernal concepts, which even imbues him at times with flashes of Divine inspiration. This intelligence is his "fountain of life." Though skeptics flout moral wisdom and discipline, casting philosophical doubt on it all, including its roots in the fear of God, the

will find good; and one who trusts in HA-SHEM, happy is he. **21** The wise in heart shall be called a man of discernment, and the sweetness of lips increases learning received. **22** Intelligence is a wellspring of life to one who has it, and the moral correction of skeptics [in their] skepticism. **23** The heart of a wise man gives his mouth intelligence, and adds received learning to his lips. **24** Pleasant words are like a honeycomb, sweet to the soul and health to the bones. **25** There is a way which seems right to a man, yet its end are the ways of death. **26** A toiling soul toils for him, for his mouth

same faculty of intelligence chastises them, dissipating their doubts and obfuscations.

23. The "wise in heart" of the previous verses will find his mouth informed or inspired with the ability to express the truth of moral wisdom, thus to increase awareness and knowledge by clear thought.

24. When the "wise in heart" speaks with the harmony and illumination of clear knowledge, he will impart the sweetness of reason to the apparently arbitrary dogmas of morality. His words carry the total pleasure that comes with spiritual concepts: they are sweet to the soul, but also bring physical health, so that one's whole being is filled with strength.

25–26. This is what the "wise in heart" says: The pursuit of materialistic pleasures is doomed to end in death: physical death, the end of every man, and spiritual death, for the waste of spiritual energies in physical pursuits. Nothing could be more irrational than to put all our spiritual energies to work to satisfy

שְׂפָתוֹ כח אִישׁ בְּלִיַּעַל כֹּרֶה רָעָה וְעַל־שְׂפָתָיו כְּאֵשׁ צָרָבֶת: אִישׁ תַּהְפֻּכוֹת
כט יְשַׁלַּח מָדוֹן וְנִרְגָּן מַפְרִיד אַלּוּף: אִישׁ חָמָס יְפַתֶּה רֵעֵהוּ וְהוֹלִיכוֹ
ל בְּדֶרֶךְ לֹא־טוֹב: עֹצֶה עֵינָיו לַחְשֹׁב תַּהְפֻּכוֹת קֹרֵץ שְׂפָתָיו כִּלָּה
לא רָעָה: עֲטֶרֶת תִּפְאֶרֶת שֵׂיבָה בְּדֶרֶךְ צְדָקָה תִּמָּצֵא: טוֹב אֶרֶךְ
לג אַפַּיִם מִגִּבּוֹר וּמֹשֵׁל בְּרוּחוֹ מִלֹּכֵד עִיר: בַּחֵיק יוּטַל אֶת־הַגּוֹרָל
וּמֵיְהוָה כָּל־מִשְׁפָּטוֹ:

the cravings of the "mouth" — the appetite. Since a man's essential part is his soul, he should obviously invest all his energy in developing this element, even at the cost of his physical satisfaction. This seems an arduous way of life at first, but finally we reap the fruits of true achievement, that remains with us for all eternity.

27. Now the master of Proverbs turns to the diametric opposite of the "wise of heart": the ungodly and unprincipled man, who entirely rejects moral obligations and works clandestinely to undermine his neighbor ("digs up evil"), while speaking words of burning love.

28. The "treacherously fickle man" does a turnabout with the truth and takes pleasure in provoking quarrels. The grumbler constantly complains and criticizes, keeping true friends apart by sowing suspicion and promoting hostilities.

29. This is another in the list of destructive types of character.

30. The evil man makes malicious plans with ease and speed: A slight gesture of the eye, and an entire project of destruction is worked out. A gesture of the lips, and it is executed.

31. The respect due an old man for the experience and achievement of his years is conditional on his life having been a

compels him. ²⁷ An ungodly man digs up evil, and in his lips there is a kind of searing fire. ²⁸ A treacherously fickle man sows a quarrel, and a grumbler separates good friends. ²⁹ A man of violence entices his neighbor, and leads him on a way that is not good. ³⁰ He winks his eyes, to devise treacherous things; he purses his lips— brings evil to pass. ³¹ A hoary head is a crown of glory; it is found in the way of righteousness. ³² He who is slow to anger is better than a mighty man, and one who rules his spirit than one who captures a city. ³³ The lot is cast into the lap; but its whole decision is from HA-SHEM.

righteous one. Only the righteous aged have accumulated not simply years but good deeds and an estimable relationship with their Maker. They alone deserve the crown of glory, universal honor and respect.

32. "A mighty man" (*gibbor*) means a person quick to take revenge on his enemies: his "might" is in his physical conquest of external foes. Should he obey the moral laws, however, and overcome his instincts of jealousy and revenge, then he will be better than the "mighty," for he will have conquered his most formidable enemy—his inner urges. There is, moreover, another level of self-conquest, where not merely *af*, anger in its outward physical expression, is suppressed, but even *ruach*, the spirit of anger, the inner desire for vengeance, is eliminated. That is the ultimate moral achievement.

33. There are times when a matter seems entirely up to fate or chance, as when people cast lots to decide something. Till the lot falls, the outcome apparently is hidden in the lap of fate, of

יז א טוֹב פַּת חֲרֵבָה וְשַׁלְוָה־בָהּ מִבַּיִת מָלֵא
ב זִבְחֵי־רִיב: עֶבֶד־מַשְׂכִּיל יִמְשֹׁל בְּבֵן מֵבִישׁ וּבְתוֹךְ אַחִים יַחֲלֹק
ג נַחֲלָה: מַצְרֵף לַכֶּסֶף וְכוּר לַזָּהָב וּבֹחֵן לִבּוֹת יהוה: מֵרַע מַקְשִׁיב
ד עַל־שְׂפַת־אָוֶן שֶׁקֶר מֵזִין עַל־לָשׁוֹן הַוֹּת: לֹעֵג לָרָשׁ חֵרֵף עֹשֵׂהוּ
ה
ו שָׂמֵחַ לְאֵיד לֹא יִנָּקֶה: עֲטֶרֶת זְקֵנִים בְּנֵי בָנִים וְתִפְאֶרֶת בָּנִים

mere chance. But in reality, the outcome is the Almighty's deliberate decision.

---

1. The prosperity and success of the wicked, however impressive, is only illusion. Far better is the fortune of the *tzaddik*, even if he has only a crust of bread, because he has peace in his home, while a wicked man is in a state of discord, either with his family or with other people. Inner serenity, undisturbed tranquility, are the essence of true success in life, and this can be attained even with a piece of dry bread.

2. Wealth and power are not hereditary: they go to the ambitious and hard-working. Eventually, therefore, an intelligent and industrious slave or servant will rise above a spoiled, lazy son. Symbolically this means that a serious, intelligent proselyte will succeed more than a Jew born into the fold, if the native son is lazy and irresponsible. Not birth but personal effort ultimately counts.

3–4. The impurities of silver are removed in a refining pot, while gold, in which impurities are more ingrained, requires the full blast of a furnace. Thus Heaven cleanses the hearts of men, each with the force of purging that it requires. Some sins are easily removed, being obvious matters of temptation and desire that bring a simple confusion between good and evil. Other sins require stronger fires of purification, as they involve distortion of the conception of truth and falsehood. The first kind of sinner

17 ¹ Better a piece of dry bread and tranquility with it, than a house full of feasting with strife. ² A servant who acts wisely will rule over a son who acts shamefully, and will share in the inheritance among the brothers. ³ The refining pot is for silver, and the furnace for gold; but HA-SHEM tries the hearts. ⁴ An evil-doer pays attention to wicked lips, and a liar gives ear to an injurious tongue. ⁵ One who mocks the poor blasphemes his Maker; a person glad at calamity will not go unpunished. ⁶ Children's children are the crown of

is described as "paying attention to wicked lips" (lips connoting the superficial expression of evil): he is an "evil-doer," a sinner on account of sensual temptation. The second kind of sinner "gives ear to an injurious tongue," symbolizing the faculty of reason and understanding (*bina*). This, if corrupted, radically subverts our whole perception of reality. Sins of wrong belief are therefore more destructive than mere wrong acts, as they involve elements of heresy and need more intensive cleansing.

5. "He who oppresses a poor man blasphemes his Maker" (14:31) because, as we explained there, his Creator certainly prepared his sustenance for him, and if you withhold part of it from him, it is as if you blaspheme Him, since you make it appear that the poor man was created merely to suffer, to no good purpose. But even if you merely mock and sneer at him for his misfortune, this too is blasphemy, for the same reason. And if you exult at his plight, because he was your enemy, you will pay for it. "When your enemy falls, do not rejoice" etc. (24:17).

6. A man is both a biological and a spiritual being. As a

PROVERBS 17:7-12

ז אֱוִלְתָּם: לֹא־נָאוָה לְנָבָל שְׂפַת־יֶתֶר אַף כִּי־לְנָדִיב שְׂפַת־שָׁקֶר:
ח אֶבֶן־חֵן הַשֹּׁחַד בְּעֵינֵי בְעָלָיו אֶל־כָּל־אֲשֶׁר יִפְנֶה יַשְׂכִּיל:
ט מְכַסֶּה־פֶּשַׁע מְבַקֵּשׁ אַהֲבָה וְשֹׁנֶה בְדָבָר מַפְרִיד אַלּוּף: תַּחַת
יא גְּעָרָה בְמֵבִין מֵהַכּוֹת כְּסִיל מֵאָה: אַךְ־מְרִי יְבַקֶּשׁ־רָע וּמַלְאָךְ
יב אַכְזָרִי יְשֻׁלַּח־בּוֹ: פָּגוֹשׁ דֹּב שַׁכּוּל בְּאִישׁ וְאַל־כְּסִיל בְּאִוַּלְתּוֹ:

biological entity, he is comforted in his old age, when death approaches, by his own physical descendants, who will exist in his stead when he is gone. As a human and spiritual being, he takes pride and credit in the righteousness of his fathers, whose spiritual heritage he bears.

7. The opposite of generous, the churl (*naval*) is niggardly, and as a rule does not even promise any kindness or charity. Should he make a promise, however, and not keep his word, such "extravagant speech" is shameful. Miserly though he be, he should keep his word. If a generous man makes a vain promise, it is trebly blameworthy: (1) he is normally open-handed; (2) he has not kept his promise; (3) he lied.

8. "For a bribe blinds the eyes of the wise" (Deuteronomy 16:19): Even judges who think themselves incorruptible will find their perceptions influenced by the gift of a claimant. And having given a bribe, a man will no longer bother preparing seriously for his appearance in court. He feels like a person wearing a charming jewel which must win him favor with everyone: The bribe is certain to decide the judge's verdict. He will succeed.

9. "Love covers over all transgressions" (10:12). The converse is also true: If someone covers up a transgression, he elicits love from the wrongdoer. Should he "harp on the matter," however, reproaching a friend repeatedly about a misdeed, he will even turn him into an enemy (see e.g. II Samuel 3:6-11). Or it

the aged, and the glory of children are their fathers. ⁷ Extravagant speech is not becoming to a churl; much less lying lips to a generous man. ⁸ A bribe is a charming jewel in the eyes of him who has it; wherever he turns, he prospers. ⁹ He who covers up a transgression seeks love, but one who harps on a matter estranges a familiar friend. ¹⁰ A rebuke goes deeper into a man of understanding, than a hundred blows into a fool. ¹¹ [He is] only rebellion seeking wickedness, even if a cruel messenger be sent against him. ¹² Let a bear robbed of her whelps meet a man, rather than a

means that if the transgressor repeats his offense, he will ultimately "estrange his friend": the other will no longer pardon him. This applies also to the relations of a man and his Maker: if a person persists in his sin the Almighty will no longer forgive him.

10-11. A "fool" gains nothing from being beaten: his mind's rebellion against the moral law is inspired by his desires, although originally he recognizes the validity of moral teaching. Such a deliberate sinner cannot be corrected, even by a hundred stripes or by a "cruel messenger." On the other hand, a "man of understanding," whose acknowledgment of the moral law is not distorted by his personal needs, responds to a mere rebuke.

12. The bereft bear is a physical danger. The skeptic, able to inject into the heart of the fool his own philosophical doubts and dispute of moral law and wisdom, is a far worse peril—spiritually fatal. As a hunter, a man may prevail against the bear; or the bear may simply let him go. The fool will never prevail against skepticism, and never relinquish it.

יג	מֵשִׁיב רָעָה תַּחַת טוֹבָה לֹא־תָמִישׁ רָעָה מִבֵּיתוֹ: פּוֹטֵר מַיִם **תָּמוּשׁ**
יד	רֵאשִׁית מָדוֹן וְלִפְנֵי הִתְגַּלַּע הָרִיב נְטוֹשׁ: מַצְדִּיק רָשָׁע וּמַרְשִׁיעַ
טו	צַדִּיק תּוֹעֲבַת יְהֹוָה גַּם־שְׁנֵיהֶם: לָמָּה־זֶּה מְחִיר בְּיַד־כְּסִיל
טז	לִקְנוֹת חָכְמָה וְלֶב־אָיִן: בְּכָל־עֵת אֹהֵב הָרֵעַ וְאָח לְצָרָה יִוָּלֵד:
יז	
יח	אָדָם חֲסַר־לֵב תּוֹקֵעַ כָּף עֹרֵב עֲרֻבָּה לִפְנֵי רֵעֵהוּ: אֹהֵב פֶּשַׁע
יט	
כ	אֹהֵב מַצָּה מַגְבִּיהַּ פִּתְחוֹ מְבַקֶּשׁ־שָׁבֶר: עִקֶּשׁ־לֵב לֹא יִמְצָא־

13. The Almighty repays measure for measure. If a person merely does evil, he can correct his way and all will be well. If he returns evil for good, however, he is repaid in kind: should he even repent and do good, "evil will not depart from his house" at the time.

14–15. Once one has opened up a hole in a reservoir, there is no holding back the flood. Similarly, once a controversy really gets going, there is no controlling its fury or its destructiveness. It is better therefore for a judge to try to make peace between litigants, before he delivers the verdict and bad feeling can no longer be restrained. This is laudable, however, only in the early stages of the case — before the judge has arrived at his assessment, or even before the case has been heard. Once the judge has reached his verdict, then to try to urge a compromise would be unjust to both litigants: It would "justify the wicked and condemn the righteous."

16. The term *m^echir* (price) denotes a valued object bartered for something desired. Unable to restrain forbidden cravings, the fool wants to acquire the moral wisdom that will control him, and imagines that he can offer up his uninhibited cravings and desires in a fair barter; but he lacks the heart.

17–18. The definition of a true friend is that he loves a person constantly — even more in time of trouble, when he should be

fool [someone] with his skepticism. [13] If one returns evil for good, evil will not depart from his house. [14] The beginning of strife is like letting out water; then before discord breaks out, withdraw. [15] He who justifies the wicked and he who condemns the righteous, both of them are an abomination to HA-SHEM. [16] Why is there a price in the hand of a fool to buy wisdom, when he has no [self-disciplining] heart? [17] A friend loves at all times, and a brother is born for adversity. [18] A man without a [self-disciplining] heart clasps hands, becoming surety in the presence of his neighbor. [19] He who loves strife loves transgression; one who makes his entrance high seeks disaster. [20] He who has a perverse heart will find

like a brother, ready for any sacrifice. Yet it is improvident and senseless even for such a loving friend to "clasp hands," give a firm handshake to go surety and become immediately responsible for his friend's business debts and commitments. This is to act "without a heart," without foreseeing the future.

19. If a person loves strife and rancorous discord to the point of physical blows, it is either because he "loves transgression" and criminal wrongdoing, or because he is haughty, thinking himself superior to the common folk. If metaphorically he is a lowly small house with only the entrance raised high—he enters society displaying hauteur—he will meet disaster.

20. If a person's heart (denoting his faculty of self-control) follows perverse ways of unwisdom, even if his mind seeks the good way he will not find it. That can be gained only through

כא טוֹב וְנֶהְפָּךְ בִּלְשׁוֹנוֹ יִפּוֹל בְּרָעָה: יֹלֵד כְּסִיל לְתוּגָה לוֹ וְלֹא־
כב יִשְׂמַח אֲבִי נָבָל: לֵב שָׂמֵחַ יֵיטִב גֵּהָה וְרוּחַ נְכֵאָה תְּיַבֶּשׁ־גָּרֶם:
כג שֹׁחַד מֵחֵיק רָשָׁע יִקָּח לְהַטּוֹת אָרְחוֹת מִשְׁפָּט:
כד אֶת־פְּנֵי מֵבִין חָכְמָה וְעֵינֵי כְסִיל בִּקְצֵה־אָרֶץ: כַּעַס לְאָבִיו בֵּן
כה כְּסִיל וּמֶמֶר לְיוֹלַדְתּוֹ: גַּם עֲנוֹשׁ לַצַּדִּיק לֹא־טוֹב לְהַכּוֹת נְדִיבִים

the wisdom of tradition. Yet he may avoid doing evil. Should he develop a fickle, treacherous tongue, however ("tongue" denotes speech informed by understanding), with false equations and philosophical inquiries into other faiths and beliefs, leading to heresy, not only will he fail to find any good, but he will fall into evil.

21. A fool from birth, overpowered from the start by his passions and cravings, no matter what he may learn, brings his father the deepest sorrow, since he is evidently beyond hope. On the other hand, a churl (the opposite of a generous person) generally becomes so by conditioning and habit. It may well be his father, churlish himself, who has trained him in this direction, and is happy with the result. In the end, however, he will have no joy: his happiness will turn to grief.

22. One who is cheerfully at home in this world, prospering, may bring well-being to his body. But if his spiritual being is "broken" within (not prospering at all in its growth), then his very essence ("bones") is dried up and decays.

23. Other bribes, e.g. to favor one side, a judge might take openly, but this a wicked judge takes stealthily, "out of the bosom" of the giver, with the express purpose of undermining the system of justice.

24. Moral wisdom is close to a man's spiritual nature, so long

no good, and one with a fickle tongue falls into evil. [21] He who sires a fool does so to his sorrow, and the father of a churl has no joy. [22] A merry heart enhances the body, but a wretched spirit dries the bones. [23] A wicked man takes a bribe out of the bosom, to pervert the ways of justice. [24] Wisdom is before him who has understanding, but the eyes of a fool are on the ends of the earth. [25] A foolish son is vexation to his father, and bitterness to her that bore him. [26] It is also not good to punish a righteous man, nor to smite the

as he has not defiled his nature with lawless desires. One can indeed look at wisdom through the reflection of his own self, as it were: it is like looking in a mirror and seeing our own true nature looking back at us; for the essence of our spiritual being is stamped with moral wisdom. One who has corrupted his nature with forbidden passions, however, has a mirror that has rusted, as it were: it is encrusted with dirt, and can no longer reflect truly. He will see wisdom as something alien and inaccessible, at "the ends of the earth."

25. Apart from grieving his father with his degraded way of life, a foolish son also angers him because his wife suffers, or because he is forever quarreling with her over the son (see 19:13).

26–28. It seems obviously "not good" that the Almighty should "punish a righteous man" or "smite the generously noble"; this is the age-old complaint and problem of the suffering of the righteous. To this our text replies that "he who has knowledge restrains his words" and asks nothing, for he knows the Almighty bestows His providential care in absolute

יָקָר־ כז עֲלֵי־יֹשֶׁר: חוֹשֵׂךְ אֲמָרָיו יוֹדֵעַ דָּעַת וְקַר־רוּחַ אִישׁ תְּבוּנָה: גַּם
אֱוִיל מַחֲרִישׁ חָכָם יֵחָשֵׁב אֹטֵם שְׂפָתָיו נָבוֹן:

perfection, without any injustice. Hence he will neither probe nor speak out [though it be beyond his ken]. A man of understanding indeed comprehends it: It is to punish the righteous in this world for some sin, so that they may receive their reward unalloyed in the hereafter. Hence he calms the inner spirit, to raise no storm about it. Should, however, even a skeptic, who doubts and disputes everything, keep his tongue from wagging about this question, he "will be reckoned wise" — for he is thus

generously noble for their uprightness. ²⁷ He who has knowledge restrains his words; a man of discernment will calm his spirit. ²⁸ Even a skeptic when he keeps silent will be reckoned wise; one who shuts his lips is deemed a man of understanding.

acting according to the laws of moral wisdom, whatever his inner doubts. And if he "shuts his lips" completely, uttering not a murmur even in his superficial talk (symbolized by "lips"), he will be thought the "man of discernment" of the previous verse.

יח א לְתַאֲוָה יְבַקֵּשׁ
ב נִפְרָד בְּכָל־תּוּשִׁיָּה יִתְגַּלָּע: לֹא־יַחְפֹּץ כְּסִיל בִּתְבוּנָה כִּי אִם־
ג בְּהִתְגַּלּוֹת לִבּוֹ: בְּבוֹא־רָשָׁע בָּא גַם־בּוּז וְעִם־קָלוֹן חֶרְפָּה: מַיִם
ד / ה עֲמֻקִּים דִּבְרֵי פִי־אִישׁ נַחַל נֹבֵעַ מְקוֹר חָכְמָה: שְׂאֵת פְּנֵי־רָשָׁע
ו לֹא־טוֹב לְהַטּוֹת צַדִּיק בַּמִּשְׁפָּט: שִׂפְתֵי כְסִיל יָבֹאוּ בְרִיב וּפִיו
ז לְמַהֲלֻמוֹת יִקְרָא: פִּי־כְסִיל מְחִתָּה־לוֹ וּשְׂפָתָיו מוֹקֵשׁ נַפְשׁוֹ:

1. If a person has become detached from immoral cravings, for example by old age or illness, and he seeks to rearouse them, the result will be physical debility, enfeeblement. Alternatively, the text can mean that if someone removes himself from human contact, for example by becoming a hermit in the desert, he will find lust raging only the more fiercely, "breaking out in all its strength (*tushiya*)," when opportunity occurs after long deprivation.

2. The skeptic, for all his doubts and objections, seeks to gain understanding. The fool knows moral wisdom, but ignores it in favor of gratifying his cravings. He has no delight in or wish for understanding, wanting only the images of desire that disclose themselves in his heart.

3. The righteous behave with respect towards all men. The wicked have the habit of contempt for all, even for those deserving of respect, and certainly they behave insultingly to the less respectable of their friends, in whom they find "ignominy" or a lack of worth.

4. When a person speaks of matters of moral wisdom, it is like drawing water from a deep well, for wisdom is hidden deep in the psyche and requires much labor to bring it to the surface. At the same time, it flows constantly and effortlessly, for it rises from the very nature of the soul and would burst forth

18 ¹ If a person detached seeks his own desire, he breaks out in all debility. ² A fool has no delight in understanding, but only in the disclosure of his heart. ³ When a wicked man comes, there comes also contempt, and with ignominy disgrace. ⁴ The words of a man's mouth are deep waters, a welling brook, a fountainhead of wisdom. ⁵ "It is not good to show favor to a wicked man, nor to subvert the justice of a righteous person." ⁶ [Thus] a fool's lips enter into contention, and his mouth calls for strong clouts. ⁷ A fool's mouth is his

spontaneously, were it not for a man's physical drives that block its passage, and make strong effort necessary to draw it up to the surface.

5–6. With his uncertainties and doubts about the laws of moral wisdom, the skeptic may keep silent about the inscrutable ways of Divine providence (17:26–28). The fool knows the validity of moral wisdom, but prefers to indulge his cravings and desires. His "lips enter into contention," querulously protesting that it is the Almighty's way "to show favor to a wicked man" and to "subvert the justice of a righteous person": evil men prosper, and a *tzaddik* suffers. The fool's outer, superficial talk ("lips") is already in conflict with Divine providence; and when he speaks with his "wisdom" (symbolized by "mouth"), he becomes more strident and hostile, to the point of physical blows, as it were.

7. His outer, superficial talk ("lips" in verse 6) against Divine providence (verse 5) prepares a snare for his soul, in which he is trapped by his serious, thoughtful talk ("mouth"). Then comes calamity, involving Divine physical punishment as well.

ח דִּבְרֵי נִרְגָּן כְּמִתְלַהֲמִים וְהֵם יָרְדוּ חַדְרֵי־בָטֶן: גַּם מִתְרַפֶּה
י בִּמְלַאכְתּוֹ אָח הוּא לְבַעַל מַשְׁחִית: מִגְדַּל־עֹז שֵׁם יהוה בּוֹ־
יא יָרוּץ צַדִּיק וְנִשְׂגָּב: הוֹן עָשִׁיר קִרְיַת עֻזּוֹ וּכְחוֹמָה נִשְׂגָּבָה
יב בְּמַשְׂכִּתוֹ: לִפְנֵי־שֶׁבֶר יִגְבַּהּ לֵב־אִישׁ וְלִפְנֵי כָבוֹד עֲנָוָה: מֵשִׁיב
יג דָּבָר בְּטֶרֶם יִשְׁמָע אִוֶּלֶת הִיא־לּוֹ וּכְלִמָּה: רוּחַ־אִישׁ יְכַלְכֵּל

8. The "grumbler" constantly complains that the Almighty created him for a miserable life, evil being more prevalent than good; would that he had never been born. The Almighty (says he) has abandoned him to a chance fate. His words are like blows, as though HA-SHEM were always striking him down. The truth is, however, that the clouts and blows are all within, from his own perverse vision of things. He forever broods and fumes, imagining that others have everything he lacks, and all Heaven's favors to him seem evil. God made man upright and whole, but he distorts his life with his perceptions.

9. Workers employed to build a palace for the king are obviously expected to build. If one worker builds and pulls down what he has done, and another sits idle and does nothing, both will be punished equally, for in either case the building is not completed. Similarly, there is in effect no real difference between one who does a mitzva (a positive act commanded by the Almighty) and then "extinguishes" it, as it were, by committing a sin, and one who sits still, neither sinning nor doing any good; both have not fulfilled their duty. Their task was to build the "name of HA-SHEM," which "is a strong tower" (verse 10), and in this, both have failed equally.

10–11. By his righteousness, a *tzaddik* establishes the "strong tower" of verse 10, as everything he does is for His name's sake and for His glory; and this becomes a refuge to which he can run, to be elevated to spiritual and physical safety. A rich man,

calamity, and his lips are a snare to his soul. [8] The words of a grumbler are like blows, and they go down into the very vitals of the stomach. [9] Also, he who is slack in his work is brother to one who is a destroyer. [10] The name of HA-SHEM is a strong tower: a righteous person shall run within and be raised on high. [11] A rich man's wealth is his strong city, and like a high wall in his imagination. [12] Before a calamity a man's heart is haughty, but before honor goes humility. [13] He who answers a matter before he hears [it], it is confusion and disgrace for him. [14] The spirit of a man will

however, who regards his wealth as a fortress against trouble, is deceiving himself, for material possessions provide only an imaginary refuge, not a real one.

12. "Everyone proud in heart is an abomination to HA-SHEM," directly punished by Him (16:5). Hence a haughty, arrogant heart presages the calamity that must follow — even for a rich man who thinks to find refuge in his wealth (verse 11). A humble man, however, trusts in the "strong tower" (verse 10), the name of HA-SHEM who abides "with him that is of a contrite and humble spirit" (Isaiah 57:15). He will attain honor.

13. It is the way of wisdom to give only a clear and lucid answer. Therefore, obviously we should listen carefully to a question in all its ramifications, in order to arrive at a clear view, and thus earn the respect of the listener. If we rush into a reply before hearing the questioner out, we will give a confused answer and earn only disgrace.

14. If a person's spirit is strong, it will sustain even a sick body

טו מַחֲלֵהוּ וְרוּחַ נְכֵאָה מִי יִשָּׂאֶנָּה: לֵב נָבוֹן יִקְנֶה־דָּעַת וְאֹזֶן
טז חֲכָמִים תְּבַקֶּשׁ־דָּעַת: מַתָּן אָדָם יַרְחִיב לוֹ וְלִפְנֵי גְדֹלִים יַנְחֶנּוּ:
יז וּבָא־ צַדִּיק הָרִאשׁוֹן בְּרִיבוֹ יָבֹא־רֵעֵהוּ וַחֲקָרוֹ: מִדְיָנִים יַשְׁבִּית הַגּוֹרָל
יט וּמִדְיָנִים וּבֵין עֲצוּמִים יַפְרִיד: אָח נִפְשָׁע מִקִּרְיַת־עֹז ומדונים כִּבְרִיחַ
כ אַרְמוֹן: מִפְּרִי פִי־אִישׁ תִּשְׂבַּע בִּטְנוֹ תְּבוּאַת שְׂפָתָיו יִשְׂבָּע:
כא מָוֶת וְחַיִּים בְּיַד־לָשׁוֹן וְאֹהֲבֶיהָ יֹאכַל פִּרְיָהּ: מָצָא אִשָּׁה מָצָא

with its courage and patience. If the spirit is sick, however, then a person's case is much graver, as the sickness may even affect the body (see 17:22).

15. The "discerning man" is one who gains understanding for himself by inference and deduction. The "wise" man, on the other hand, receives traditional wisdom on faith, and in his search for clear knowledge he is obliged to listen (with "the ear of the wise") to the words of the discerning, who have acquired such knowledge for themselves.

16. The term *mattan* (gift) denotes presents given to both rich and poor alike. A man bestowing them may feel as though there is no point to granting gifts to the rich. Yet it sometimes turns out that such gifts help him later on when he needs assistance: the wealthy remember what he has done for them.

17–19. In a business or property dispute, it is better to come to an agreement than to insist on going to court, where the loss is certain to outweigh the gain. If the matter is too doubt-ridden for a clear settlement, it is ultimately best to cast lots, leaving the decision to Divine providence (see 16:33). A person may be certain of winning once he tells his side to the judge ("He who pleads his case first seems just"), yet he does not know what the other party will argue in refutation. Hence the outcome is never certain. A man's expectancy of his inheritance may be as mighty

sustain his illness, but a broken spirit who can bear? [15] The heart of a discerning man acquires knowledge, and the ear of the wise seeks knowledge. [16] A man's gift makes room for him, and brings him before great men. [17] He who pleads his case first seems just, but his neighbor comes and searches him out. [18] The lot [cast] makes legal judgments cease, and separates the contentious. [19] A brother may be defrauded out of a strong city, as judgments at law are like the bolt of a castle. [20] With the fruit of his mouth shall a man's belly be satisfied; by the produce of his lips will he be satisfied. [21] Death and life are in the power of the tongue, and those who love it will eat its fruit. [22] He who finds a wife has found

as a strong city, yet his brothers may criminally defraud him. Judgments in law can bar a person from his property or his rights like the powerful bolt of a castle. Hence casting lots is, in the end, far preferable.

20. The "mouth" refers to the inner wisdom of the moral law, and the "lips" to the external expression of clear knowledge. When a man attains "produce," a clear matured knowledge of wisdom, his superficial talk too gives full satisfaction, leaving nothing more to be desired.

21. The "tongue" connotes the lofty faculty of discernment and understanding that can differentiate truth from falsehood. And these two are issues of life and death: With a true perception of the principles of our faith we will live, while with perverse negative conclusions about Divine existence and

כג טוֹב וַיָּפֶק רָצוֹן מֵיהוָה: תַּחֲנוּנִים יְדַבֶּר־רָשׁ וְעָשִׁיר יַעֲנֶה עַזּוֹת:
כד אִישׁ רֵעִים לְהִתְרֹעֵעַ וְיֵשׁ אֹהֵב דָּבֵק מֵאָח:

providence, reward and punishment, etc., one will die. Those who love rational thought and understanding will never reach final satisfaction, for it has no end, so that they will be happily occupied ("will eat") in their mental and spiritual development as long as they live.

22. If a man finds a woman whom he sees as good (who appeals to him) and from whom he obtains favor and goodness (he appeals to her), this relationship is "from HA-SHEM," by His special providence and goodness.

23. This should rather be rendered: "When a poor man utters

> goodness and obtained favor from HA-SHEM. [23] The poor man utters entreaties, but the rich man answers with impudence. [24] A man [has] friends pretending friendship, but there is a true friend who sticks closer than a brother.

entreaties" and begs for help, "the rich man should answer his own impudence" and subdue it. Even if arrogant by nature, let him control himself and grant the poor man his entreaty.

24. One who cultivates many friends has no true friend, for love is a special rare feeling that becomes dissipated when widespread. So if a person has many friends (popularity), he has pretended friendship. If he has one friend, that one is closer than a brother: for this is the nature of love, that it creates bonds closer than ties of blood.

PROVERBS 19:1-8

יט א טוֹב רָשׁ הוֹלֵךְ
ב בְּתֻמּוֹ מֵעִקֵּשׁ שְׂפָתָיו וְהוּא כְסִיל: גַּם בְּלֹא־דַעַת נֶפֶשׁ לֹא־
ג טוֹב וְאָץ בְּרַגְלַיִם חוֹטֵא: אִוֶּלֶת אָדָם תְּסַלֵּף דַּרְכּוֹ וְעַל־יְהוָה
ד יִזְעַף לִבּוֹ: הוֹן יֹסִיף רֵעִים רַבִּים וְדָל מֵרֵעֵהוּ יִפָּרֵד: עֵד שְׁקָרִים
ה
ו לֹא יִנָּקֶה וְיָפִיחַ כְּזָבִים לֹא יִמָּלֵט: רַבִּים יְחַלּוּ פְנֵי־נָדִיב וְכָל־
ז הָרֵעַ לְאִישׁ מַתָּן: כָּל אֲחֵי־רָשׁ ׀ שְׂנֵאֻהוּ אַף כִּי מְרֵעֵהוּ
ח רָחֲקוּ מִמֶּנּוּ מְרַדֵּף אֲמָרִים לֹא־הֵמָּה: קֹנֶה־לֵּב אֹהֵב נַפְשׁוֹ

1. It is better to have all the world see your poverty while you maintain inner integrity, without ever coming to grief, than to be foolishly dominated by crude passions, while making a show of moral wisdom, your lips hiding what is in your heart.

2. If a person veers from the proper path not through foolishness but for mere lack of knowledge, that too is not good. And even if he veers only because he is hasty, he is also sinning.

3. God gave a man all the equipment he needs in order to walk on a straight, purposeful road, by His revealed laws of wisdom. All he needs is implicit faith. Skepticism and doubt, however, make a person fume at the Creator for supposedly leaving him without guidance in life.

4. The friends of the wealthy are really friends of wealth: they attach themselves to such a man for the sake of his possessions. If he loses his wealth, by the same token he loses his friends. Unfortunately, friendship is often really only love of one's own self, given only for the sake of potential personal benefit.

5. The term *sheker* (falsehood, false) denotes obvious lying; *kazav* (a lie) denotes falsehood disguised as truth. If a person gives obviously false testimony, he will certainly be punished; but even if someone merely "breathes out" lies that sound true,

19 ¹ Better is a poor man who walks in his steadfastness, than one who is perverse in his lips, and is a fool. ² It is also not good that a soul be without knowledge; and he who hastens with his feet sins. ³ The skepticism of a man distorts his way, and his heart fumes against HA-SHEM. ⁴ Wealth brings many new friends, but a poor man becomes sundered from his friend. ⁵ A false witness will not go unpunished, and one who breathes out lies shall not escape. ⁶ Many will entreat the favor of a generous man, and everyone is a friend to a man who gives gifts. ⁷ All the brothers of a poor man hate him; how much more do his friends draw far away from him! [Yet] he pursues words, saying they are still his. ⁸ He who

producing plausible vague insinuations in ordinary conversation, he too will be unmasked in the end, and receive his punishment.

6. A generous man (*nadiv*) gives judiciously to those who need, in the time of their need: he will therefore receive entreaties from many poor people — but not true friendship. On the other hand, the man who gives gifts (*ish mattan*) is profuse with gifts to all and sundry, rich and poor alike: he will attract every man's pretended friendship.

7. When a man loses his wealth, the good-time friends desert him. If he becomes a *rash*, abjectly poor, even his close kin desert him. Yet he desperately continues to boast that they are all still his friends.

8. "Gaining a heart" means mastering the emotional center of

PROVERBS 19:9–14

ט שֹׁמֵר תְּבוּנָה לִמְצֹא־טוֹב: עֵד שְׁקָרִים לֹא יִנָּקֶה וְיָפִיחַ כְּזָבִים יֹאבֵד:

י לֹא־נָאוֶה לִכְסִיל תַּעֲנוּג אַף כִּי־לְעֶבֶד ׀ מְשֹׁל בְּשָׂרִים: שֵׂכֶל

יא אָדָם הֶאֱרִיךְ אַפּוֹ וְתִפְאַרְתּוֹ עֲבֹר עַל־פָּשַׁע: נַהַם כַּכְּפִיר זַעַף

יב מֶלֶךְ וּכְטַל עַל־עֵשֶׂב רְצוֹנוֹ: הַוֹּת לְאָבִיו בֵּן כְּסִיל וְדֶלֶף טֹרֵד

יד מִדְיְנֵי אִשָּׁה: בַּיִת וָהוֹן נַחֲלַת אָבוֹת וּמֵיְהוָה אִשָּׁה מַשְׂכָּלֶת:

one's personality, so that he can govern his passions in accord with the laws of morality that he has accepted. This self-mastery is achieved by employing one's rational mind, contemplating the moral law — but only if the rational mind is put to proper use, working to good purpose — "to find good."

9. If, however, the intellect is put to corrupt purposes and draws false conclusions from what it observes, then destruction is the result. It is possible to abuse the faculty of *bina*, rational analysis and comprehension, to arrive at heretical conclusions on matters of faith, even at philosophies that seem attractive and plausible at first. These will betray their shoddiness, however, in the crucible of time.

10. The fool (*k*ᵉ*sil*) ignores his real knowledge of morality for the sake of physical pleasure. This pleasure, however, is not becoming to him, since it puts his soul, which should govern his body, at the mercy of his body instead. This inversion of the natural order is conveyed by the metaphor of a bondservant dominating a prince.

11. It is a mere common sense and self-interest to refrain from lashing out immediately to avenge an injury. It is a higher level of humanity when one can entirely suppress feelings of vengeance even in his heart: this is the "glory" of the morally wise man.

gains a [self-disciplining] heart loves his own soul; one who keeps understanding shall find good. ⁹ A false witness shall not go unpunished, and one who breathes out lies shall perish.

¹⁰ Luxury is not seemly for a fool; much less for a bondservant to rule over princes. ¹¹ It is a man's good sense to be slow to anger, and his glory to pass over a transgression. ¹² A king's vexation is as the roaring of a lion, but his good will is as dew upon the grass. ¹³ A foolish son is the calamity of his father, and the contentions of a wife are a constant fall of droplets. ¹⁴ House and wealth are an inheritance from fathers, but an intelligent wife

12. The young lion does not go out of his den, but tears anyone who tries to approach him. So is a king when he fumes with displeasure. But when he is in a good mood, his blessing radiates and refreshes like dew that spreads lushness and life on each individual blade of grass. So does each individual servant of God benefit from His blessing at such a time, as all are drawn to His radiance.

13. Previously we read that "a foolish son is a vexation to his father" (17:25). If, in addition, a man has quarrels with his wife to contend with, the tension in the household becomes unbearable and the home may fall apart—like a house with a leaking roof.

14. Property and wealth should be passed on from father to son. This, however, depends on the wife, whose function it generally is to help her husband succeed in life, and to manage the house so that all can pass on undiminished to children and grandchildren (cf. 14:1: "The wisdom of women builds her

PROVERBS 19:15-22

טו עַצְלָה תַּפִּיל תַּרְדֵּמָה וְנֶפֶשׁ רְמִיָּה תִרְעָב: שֹׁמֵר מִצְוָה שֹׁמֵר
טז נַפְשׁוֹ בּוֹזֵה דְרָכָיו יוּמָת: מַלְוֵה יְהוָה חוֹנֵן דָּל וּגְמֻלוֹ יְשַׁלֶּם־לוֹ:
יז יַסֵּר בִּנְךָ כִּי־יֵשׁ תִּקְוָה וְאֶל־הֲמִיתוֹ אַל־תִּשָּׂא נַפְשֶׁךָ: גְּדָל־חֵמָה
יח נֹשֵׂא עֹנֶשׁ כִּי אִם־תַּצִּיל וְעוֹד תּוֹסִף: שְׁמַע עֵצָה וְקַבֵּל מוּסָר
יט לְמַעַן תֶּחְכַּם בְּאַחֲרִיתֶךָ: רַבּוֹת מַחֲשָׁבוֹת בְּלֶב־אִישׁ וַעֲצַת
כ יְהוָה הִיא תָקוּם: תַּאֲוַת אָדָם חַסְדּוֹ וְטוֹב־רָשׁ מֵאִישׁ כָּזָב:

house, but skepticism—i.e., a foolishly skeptical woman—with her own hands tears it down").

15. Slothfulness (*'atzla*, laziness) merely brings on fast sleep, and no hunger is felt; idleness (*rᵉmiya*) denotes a worse trait, that leaves a person hungry in his waking life.

16. Even a direction of life that seems straight can lead to perdition. The only certain way in life is to keep the Divine commandments. To despise His ways and gratify despicable cravings is to invite death.

17. When a man gives charity to the poor graciously, expecting no return, it is like "lending to HA-SHEM": He then not only "repays the loan" but also the love that the man thus bestows, which means more than money. Alternatively, the text means that the man's charity is merely the (partial) "repayment" of the gifts "lent" him by HA-SHEM for this very purpose.

18. Never despair of a son turned delinquent, and so give up all attempts to chasten and discipline him. There is always hope. Even if he wails and carries on, do not take it to heart.

19. Only punishment leads a person to calm down from wrath.

200

is from HA-SHEM. [15] Slothfulness casts into a deep sleep, and an idle soul shall suffer hunger. [16] He who keeps the commandment keeps his soul, but one who despises His ways shall die. [17] He who is gracious to the poor lends to HA-SHEM, and his good deed will He repay him. [18] Chasten your son, for there is hope, and do not burden your spirit with his noisy wailing. [19] A man of great wrath shall suffer punishment; for if you would bring rescue, you will only add to it. [20] Listen to advice, and accept moral instruction, that you may be wise in your later years. [21] There are many thoughts in a man's heart, but the plan of HA-SHEM, that shall stand. [22] The mark of a man is his kindness, and a poor man is better than a liar.

Referring this verse to the previous one, it would mean: Discipline your wayward son, and do not try to save him from his punishment, or you will destroy the fruit it will bear.

21. A human being believes himself full of possibilities, potential modes of thought and courses of action, to choose as he wills. Yet the single counsel or plan that actually goes into practical effect is often decided by HA-SHEM, overriding a man's apparent freedom.

22. The kindness that a man does stamps his personality and leaves its imprint on his character. A liar, on the other hand, who promises kindness and does not carry through is worse than a poor man who would like to do acts of kindness but has not the means.

כג יִרְאַת יהוה לְחַיִּים וְשָׂבֵעַ יָלִין בַּל־יִפָּקֶד רָע: טָמַן עָצֵל יָדוֹ
כה בַּצַּלָּחַת גַּם־אֶל־פִּיהוּ לֹא יְשִׁיבֶנָּה: לֵץ תַּכֶּה וּפֶתִי יַעְרִם וְהוֹכִיחַ
כו לְנָבוֹן יָבִין דָּעַת: מְשַׁדֶּד־אָב יַבְרִיחַ אֵם בֵּן מֵבִישׁ וּמַחְפִּיר:
כז חֲדַל־בְּנִי לִשְׁמֹעַ מוּסָר לִשְׁגוֹת מֵאִמְרֵי־דָעַת: עֵד בְּלִיַּעַל יָלִיץ
כט מִשְׁפָּט וּפִי רְשָׁעִים יְבַלַּע־אָוֶן: נָכוֹנוּ לַלֵּצִים שְׁפָטִים וּמַהֲלֻמוֹת
לְגֵו כְּסִילִים:

23. Fear of the Almighty is different from all other fears: Other kinds of fear shorten life, prevent eating and sleeping; but fear of HA-SHEM, on the contrary, induces a person to eat and sleep well and live longer. For this reverent fear is a creative emotion that rids one of all other anxieties and apprehensions, giving him confidence that the Creator will protect him from all evil.

24. "The strong desire of the lazy one will kill him, for his hands refuse to labor" (21:25); he will not move them. Even if, under the direct compulsion of hunger, he takes some small action ("buries his hand in the dish"), for the life of him he cannot follow through; cannot "bring it to his mouth."

25–27. A simple person learns sagacity not from the proofs of reason but from punishment; hence the punishment of scoffers acts on him as a deterrent. A "man of understanding" does not need this sort of lesson, for he responds to rational reproof: if he is told (for example) of how much pain he will cause his parents if he befouls and disgraces them by his actions. Hence the behest of verse 27: My understanding son, you have no need of

²³ The fear of HA-SHEM leads to life, and he who has it will rest satisfied; he will not be visited by evil. ²⁴ The lazy man buries his hand in the dish, and will not even bring it back to his mouth. ²⁵ Smite a scorner, and a simple man will become sagacious; and reprove a man of understanding, and he will understand knowledge. ²⁶ A son who brings foulness and disgrace will desolate his father, and drive away his mother. ²⁷ Avoid, my son, [having] to hear [severe] moral instruction, by straying from the words of knowledge. ²⁸ A lawless witness mocks justice, and the mouth of the wicked devours iniquity. ²⁹ Judgments are prepared for scorners, and whiplashes for the back of fools.

the severe moral instruction and punitive discipline due a scoffer. Learn from the example of the "befouling, disgracing son" to keep "the words of knowledge" well in mind, and thus turn away from the actions of scoffers.

28–29. With his falsehoods, a wicked, lawless witness can cause an innocent man's death, in complete mockery of justice; and the mouth of a wicked judge can "devour" and conceal the iniquity. For such witnesses ("scorners"), however, harsh sentences are in store: what they sought to do to their victims; and for such judges, "whiplashes" of Divine punishment.

כ

א לֵץ הַיַּיִן הֹמֶה שֵׁכָר וְכָל־שֹׁגֶה בּוֹ לֹא יֶחְכָּם: נַהַם
ב כַּכְּפִיר אֵימַת מֶלֶךְ מִתְעַבְּרוֹ חוֹטֵא נַפְשׁוֹ: כָּבוֹד לָאִישׁ שֶׁבֶת
ג מֵרִיב וְכָל־אֱוִיל יִתְגַּלָּע: מֵחֹרֶף עָצֵל לֹא־יַחֲרֹשׁ יִשְׁאַל בַּקָּצִיר
ד וָאָיִן: מַיִם עֲמֻקִּים עֵצָה בְלֶב־אִישׁ וְאִישׁ תְּבוּנָה יִדְלֶנָּה: רָב־
ה וְשָׁאַל

1. Wine makes a man mock and scorn the moral laws, which must be accepted on faith, with integrity, since they cannot be proved. For wine can overpower the heart and turn a man to mindless merrymaking. Strong drink, on the other hand, reduces the mind to nothing, leaving a man a mere animal.

2. Previously (19:12) the master of Proverbs dealt with a fuming king; but even when he is in a good mood, one must beware of the terror that a king imposes—a mysterious awe that emanates from the greatness bestowed on him. If a person is unwary and irreverent in his presence, he will have to pay with his life, just like a rash intruder into a lion's den.

3. It is tempting to pick a quarrel, if one has been insulted in some way. This will not, however, bring him prestige because the quarrel will only make him bear more insults, and thus he defeats his purpose; or because such a response to an insult suggests that there was some basis for the insult in the first place. So, it brings prestige and honor to keep far from a quarrel, thus showing that one is not touched by the insult, and also avoiding an escalation of abuse. The fool, who does not accept these laws of wisdom, will reveal his whole unimpressive self in instant anger and revenge when he is provoked.

4. The cold season is the time to plough, but a lazybones dislikes work at the best of times. When the fine weather comes, naturally he would like to have food to eat, but he has harvested nothing. Similarly, youth is the time to prepare the seed-bed of one's character for moral wisdom to take root. This is the time

20 ¹ Wine is a mocker, strong drink causes uproar; and whoever is misled by it is not wise. ² The terror of a king is like the roaring of a lion; he who provokes him to anger forfeits his life. ³ It is prestige for a man to keep aloof from strife, but every fool will be exposed to shame. ⁴ The sluggard will not plough, because of the [cold] winter; therefore he shall seek in harvest-time, and have nothing. ⁵ Counsel in a man's heart is like deep water, but a man of understanding will draw it out. ⁶ Most men will proclaim each his

for hard work in "pruning" unruly desires, but it is also the least congenial time for such labor, when desires are strong and demanding. If a person gives in to his instincts, however, he will find that in old age, when passion has abated, his character was not properly trained and prepared to attain moral wisdom.

5. The term *'étza* (counsel) denotes the capacity to make the best and most effective choice from the range of possibilities. This range is infinite in human consciousness; a flow of thoughts and ideas can rush through the mind. But to be able to arrive at a correct assessment of the best among the many possible courses of action we must draw from the depths of the mind, as by rope linked to rope, through a process of analogies and comparisons, the "counsel" that lies profoundly hidden and accessible only to the "man of understanding."

6. "Goodness" (*chesed*) refers to voluntary acts of kindness, out of generosity, while "reliability" (*emunim*) applies to morally obligatory or promised acts of compassion. One would imagine that if people do kindness voluntarily, they will certainly fulfill their moral obligations. This, however, is not the case:

ז אָדָם יִקְרָא אִישׁ חַסְדּוֹ וְאִישׁ אֱמוּנִים מִי יִמְצָא: מִתְהַלֵּךְ בְּתֻמּוֹ
ח צַדִּיק אַשְׁרֵי בָנָיו אַחֲרָיו: מֶלֶךְ יוֹשֵׁב עַל־כִּסֵּא־דִין מְזָרֶה בְעֵינָיו
ט כָּל־רָע: מִי־יֹאמַר זִכִּיתִי לִבִּי טָהַרְתִּי מֵחַטָּאתִי: אֶבֶן וָאָבֶן

surprisingly, "reliability" in loving-kindness is a rare commodity, while voluntary goodness is not hard to find. This is because voluntary acts of *chesed* are performed, on the whole, not for their own sake, but for the sake of the publicity and prestige that they bring. Mere performance of duty, however, and fulfillment of obligations, brings no particular recognition; it is much more a private affair of conscience, and so it is much less appealing.

7. The *tzaddik* (righteous man) acts with righteousness, but he has not attained the "steadfast integrity" of the *tamim*, who acts solely for the sake of Heaven, with no regard for prestige and honor. The righteousness of the *tzaddik* can still be unstable, affected by ulterior motives (hence in verse 6, "who can find a man of reliability?")—unless he "walks in his steadfast integrity": in pure devotion of God, uncaring of human praise; then his reward, which does not interest him personally, is kept for his descendants after him.

8–9. Injustice and corruption must prevail in a system of government where each judge deputes authority to a junior colleague, in a chain of irresponsibility. This leaves the poor with no access to appeal to the king or senior judge, since they are at the mercy of petty officials who will not allow any appeals to a higher court. Where the king himself, however, directly supervises the administration of justice, the poor and oppressed have a chance of fair treatment.

This is true on four conditions: (1) that the king holds the reigns of justice in his own hands; (2) that he "*sits on the throne*"—connoting constant application to the task; (3) that

own goodness, but who can find a man of reliability? [7] He who walks in his steadfast integrity as a righteous man, happy are his children after him. [8] A king who sits on the throne of judgment scatters away all evil with his eyes. [9] Who can say, "I have made my heart clean, I am become pure from my sin"? [10] Diverse weights and diverse measures, both of them alike are an

he sits in "judgment" (*din*) and not simply in "justice" (*mishpat*): the term *mishpat* denotes the verdict, while *din* refers to the attentive hearing that people must be given in court, to listen to their pleas without the mediation of skilled but possibly distorting advocates; (4) that in addition to the actual sessions in court, the king moves about among his people, eradicating evil and corruption wherever he finds it: he "scatters away all evil with his eyes." Under such conditions, few can feel completely confident that such an inexorable judge will find them wholly innocent.

This is, of course, a parable for the King of kings, who sits constantly on His throne of justice, listening and watching. Hence no individual can feel confident, either of his private thoughts ("Who can say, 'I have made my heart clean' ") or of his actual deeds (" 'I am become pure from my sin' ").

10. Here follows an example of sin in overt action, even where the conscience is clear. In the case of barter, if one has different weights for his commodity, in order to cheat, the other, too, may perhaps use a different measure in repaying him with *his* wares; and thus the cheating may balance out. In such a case, the buyer may say, "I have made my heart clean"—his conscience is clear—but he cannot say, "I am become pure from my sin"—since *in fact* he has committed the crime of using discrepant weights. Even when "both of them [buyer and

יא אֵיפָה וְאֵיפָה תּוֹעֲבַת יהוה גַּם־שְׁנֵיהֶם: גַּם בְּמַעֲלָלָיו יִתְנַכֶּר־
יב נַעַר אִם־זַךְ וְאִם־יָשָׁר פָּעֳלוֹ: אֹזֶן שֹׁמַעַת וְעַיִן רֹאָה יהוה עָשָׂה
יג גַם־שְׁנֵיהֶם: אַל־תֶּאֱהַב שֵׁנָה פֶּן־תִּוָּרֵשׁ פְּקַח עֵינֶיךָ שְׂבַע־לָחֶם:
יד יה רַע רַע יֹאמַר הַקּוֹנֶה וְאֹזֵל לוֹ אָז יִתְהַלָּל: יֵשׁ זָהָב וְרָב־פְּנִינִים

seller] are alike" and balance each other out, this is an "abomination to HA-SHEM."

11. The term *ma'alalav* ("his doings") refers to actions that depend on one's character, stemming for example from pride or humility, cruelty or mercy. On the other hand, *po'alo* ("his work") refers to actions that leave a person's character unknown. When we read in Scripture that Moses killed an Egyptian, or reproached the disputatious Israelites, we cannot know from his actions alone whether he acted from a sense of justice, or from vengefulness and personal pride. Hence Scripture first describes his "doings": e.g. that he went out among his people and saw their suffering. Thus we know that he acted out of humility and compassion.

12. The senses of hearing and sight give a person access to perception. Hearing comes before sight, for if we have first acquired a concept from others, we will then understand what we are seeing. Both senses were created by God, for His glory, and should be used by us for that purpose: we should listen to the transmitted words of Torah wisdom from scholars, and should then perceive and understand the Almighty's work in nature.

13. Only alertness and alacrity can bring wealth; indolence and long, self-indulgent sleep lead to poverty. This is only a metaphor, however: "Open your eyes" of the mind, throw off spiritual torpor, and use "the hearing ear and the seeing eye"

abomination to HA-SHEM. [11] Even a child is known by his doings, whether his work is pure, and whether it is honest. [12] The hearing ear and the seeing eye, HA-SHEM has made even both of them. [13] Do not love sleep, lest you come to poverty; open your eyes, and you will have bread to satisfaction. [14] "It is bad, it is bad," says the buyer; but when he goes on his way, then he boasts. [15] There is gold, and a multitude of rubies; but the lips of knowledge are a precious jewel.

that the Almighty made for you (verse 12), to gain spiritual satisfaction from the "bread" of Torah and Divine wisdom.

14. It is human nature for a man to deprecate the merchandise that he wishes to buy: he thinks the price excessive, and it seems a pity to spend so much for it. After he has paid, however, and taken possession, he feels pleased with himself for having bought so valuable an object; the high price only adds to his pleasure in its value. Similarly, continuing from the previous verse, we are warned not to love sleep and mental torpor, for Torah is acquired through self-denial, lack of sleep, and an ascetic regime. At the time that we have to pay the price, we may feel, "It is bad, bad!" — for the price really hurts. Afterwards, however, we will feel happy about the Torah we have acquired, and take pride in it.

15. The spiritual gain of moral wisdom, acquired and known as palpably as though seen and heard (by "the hearing ear and the seeing eye" of verse 12) — to the point where it can be clearly expressed by one's "lips of knowledge" — is a most unique and precious jewel. Gold and rubies are far more plentiful, hence not as valuable.

נָכְרִיָּה טז וּכְלִי יָקָר שִׂפְתֵי־דָעַת: לְקַח־בִּגְדוֹ כִּי־עָרַב זָר וּבְעַד נָכְרִים
חַבְלֵהוּ: יז עָרֵב לָאִישׁ לֶחֶם שָׁקֶר וְאַחַר יִמָּלֵא־פִיהוּ חָצָץ:
יח מַחֲשָׁבוֹת בְּעֵצָה תִכּוֹן וּבְתַחְבֻּלוֹת עֲשֵׂה מִלְחָמָה: גּוֹלֶה־סּוֹד
יט הוֹלֵךְ רָכִיל וּלְפֹתֶה שְׂפָתָיו לֹא תִתְעָרָב: מְקַלֵּל אָבִיו וְאִמּוֹ
בָּאִשׁוֹן כא יִדְעַךְ נֵרוֹ בֶּאֱשׁוּן חֹשֶׁךְ: נַחֲלָה מְבֻחֶלֶת בָּרִאשֹׁנָה וְאַחֲרִיתָהּ
מְבֹהֶלֶת

16. A "stranger" (*zar*) is a person from another homestead or city; an "alien" (*nochri*) is from another country. Going surety for a "stranger" can make a person "lose his shirt," but his body is left untouched. With an "alien" he may suffer physically too. Metaphorically, it means that adopting false conceptions and philosophies in place of the Torah's teachings is like sinning with a "strange" woman and being saddled with the burden of surety for her. This will cost him the "garment" of spirituality every Jewish soul acquired at Sinai. Sinning with an alien woman is a metaphor for espousing heresy (idolatry). For this a person will be bodily punished—expelled from the people of HA-SHEM to "her alien domain" to bear responsibility ("surety") for his enormous sin.

17. Wealth acquired by deceit at first seems specially enjoyable, since it has come without effort, but eventually retribution falls, and the enjoyment changes to regret. Symbolically, this refers to heresies and alien philosophies (see verse 16) that seem attractive at first but afterwards torment one's spiritual nature.

18. "Thoughts" (*machashavoth*) denotes the full flow of ideas and notions in the mind; "counsel" (*étza*) means the single purposeful plan that is chosen from the many possibilities in the thinking mind. In war, however, many alternative strategies are needed, to meet every contingency, including the leaking of information to the enemy (cf. 15:22: "Without secret consideration, thoughts are frustrated; but in a multitude of counsellors they are established").

[16] Take his garment who has given surety for a stranger; and hold him in pledge who goes surety for an alien woman. [17] Bread of falsehood is sweet to a man, but afterwards his mouth will be filled with gravel. [18] Thoughts are made firm by counsel; and with good strategies wage war. [19] He who goes about as a talebearer reveals secrets; do not meddle then with one who sets his lips prating foolishly. [20] Whoever curses his father or his mother, his lamp shall be put out in the blackest darkness. [21] An inheritance may be

19. We are warned to beware and keep away from people with loose tongues who are of three types: the first reveals secrets and cannot be relied on; the second "goes about as a talebearer," and incidentally lets out secrets in the midst of his gossip; the third "sets his lips prating foolishly," and because he talks so much and so naively, secrets slip out. With all three it is wisest not to meddle, since any strategy you have planned will be endangered.

20. There are two possible reasons for cursing a parent. One is if a person has a melancholy, pessimistic view of life, regarding the evil in it as more significant and dominant than the good; then he may so regret being born that he will curse his parents for giving him life. Such a person will be plunged into the utter blackness of despair, unrelieved by even a glimmer of hope. The other possibility is that a person will curse a parent because he covets his father's or mother's property and cannot bear that the parent should live and keep him deprived of his inheritance. On this track, the text continues.

21. Property acquired by inheritance is no blessing; only what

כב לֹא־תֹאמַר אֲשַׁלְּמָה־רָע קַוֵּה לַיהוָה וְיֹשַׁע לָךְ׃
כג תּוֹעֲבַת יְהוָה אֶבֶן וָאָבֶן וּמֹאזְנֵי מִרְמָה לֹא־טוֹב׃
כד מִיהוָה מִצְעֲדֵי־גָבֶר וְאָדָם מַה־יָּבִין דַּרְכּוֹ׃
כה מוֹקֵשׁ אָדָם יָלַע קֹדֶשׁ וְאַחַר נְדָרִים לְבַקֵּר׃
כו מְזָרֶה רְשָׁעִים מֶלֶךְ חָכָם וַיָּשֶׁב עֲלֵיהֶם אוֹפָן׃
כז נֵר יְהוָה נִשְׁמַת אָדָם חֹפֵשׂ כָּל־חַדְרֵי־בָטֶן׃ חֶסֶד וֶאֱמֶת

we gain by our own efforts is truly blessed. This is even more true of an inheritance that comes prematurely.

22–23. If you have been cheated in business, do not be tempted to cheat in turn and thus even things out. The example given here is of being sold merchandise by false weight: you may be tempted to use false weights yourself next time in order to get your own back; resist the temptation, as any tampering with scales is hateful to the Almighty. Instead, "hope to HA-SHEM, and He will save you."

24. As explained above (16:9), though a man has free will to choose his course, the physical capacity to carry out his decision comes from the Almighty. If in His ultimate wisdom, He wishes a different turn of events, He has only to prevent the man physically from carrying out his decision. Since human perception is limited, often he may feel frustrated at this blocking of his will, not realizing the consequences of his purpose, as the Almighty does. Hence he may not understand why his way must be otherwise.

25. Crimes of the lips (talk) are definitely among the snares that can bring a man to grief, and so we must be wary: for example, not to be hasty to consecrate things to the Almighty, and not to inquire and seek ways to make vows. So we may easily come to grief, by failing to keep our word, or by fulfilling it too late (*achar*, "after," may connote *acher*, "be late").

acquired hastily at the beginning, but its end shall not be blessed. ²² Do not say, "I will repay evil"; hope to HA-SHEM, and He will save you. ²³ Diverse weights are an abomination to HA-SHEM, and a false balance is not good. ²⁴ A man's life-steps are of HA-SHEM; how then can a man understand his way? ²⁵ It is a snare to a man to say rashly "Holy," and after vows to make inquiry. ²⁶ A wise king scatters the wicked, and turns the wheel over them. ²⁷ The spirit of a man is the lamp of HA-SHEM, searching all the innermost parts. ²⁸ Mercy and truth preserve a king; and by loving-kindness he upholds his throne. ²⁹ The glory of young men

26–27. Even if he is the wisest man, a human, mortal king has need of all sorts of tactics in order to find out the truth about a crime. He can "scatter" the suspects—imprison them separately—torture them on the wheel, compare their confessions, and so possibly arrive at the truth. The Almighty has no need of such tactics; His lamp, by which He can read the innermost secrets of man, is the soul of man himself, which illuminates his whole nature, to reveal every last detail. As the Sages put it, a man may think when he sins unseen, "Who will testify against me?"—but his own life-spirit will bear witness.

28. The pure, inexorable justice of strict truth may make an embittered person strike a king down. Pure clemency and kindness toward his people may make someone unafraid to attack him fatally. It is the judicious mixture of strict justice and merciful kindness that wins the people's love and respect. Then in effect he needs no other guard for his safety.

כט יִצְרוּ־מֶלֶךְ וְסָעַד בַּחֶסֶד כִּסְאוֹ: תִּפְאֶרֶת בַּחוּרִים כֹּחָם וַהֲדַר
ל זְקֵנִים שֵׂיבָה: חַבֻּרוֹת פֶּצַע תַּמְרִיק בְּרָע וּמַכּוֹת חַדְרֵי־בָטֶן: תַּמְרוּק

29–30. Dissolute, licentious living in the flush of youth brings on its own disasters in the form of sickness — surface wounds and painful internal diseases (*petza*, "wounds" denotes the first; *chaburoth*, "bruises," the second) — as well as premature old

is their strength, and the radiant beauty of old men is the hoary head. [30] Bruises and wounds come for outpouring in evil, and so whiplashes in the innermost parts.

age, which, quite unlike the normal, timely "radiant beauty of old men," is not attractive at all. Hence the virile strength granted youth must be used wisely, with discretion.

כא א פַּלְגֵי־מַיִם לֶב־מֶלֶךְ בְּיַד־יְהוָה עַל־כָּל־אֲשֶׁר יַחְפֹּץ יַטֶּנּוּ: כָּל־
ב דֶּרֶךְ־אִישׁ יָשָׁר בְּעֵינָיו וְתֹכֵן לִבּוֹת יְהוָה: עֲשֹׂה צְדָקָה וּמִשְׁפָּט
ג נִבְחָר לַיהוָה מִזָּבַח: רוּם־עֵינַיִם וּרְחַב־לֵב נֵר רְשָׁעִים חַטָּאת:
ד מַחְשְׁבוֹת חָרוּץ אַךְ־לְמוֹתָר וְכָל־אָץ אַךְ־לְמַחְסוֹר: פֹּעַל

1. The will of a king is compared to the mighty torrents of water that rush down from the mountain-tops. They cannot be allowed to follow a merely random course, or they may bring destruction instead of blessing. They have to be channeled so that they flow to irrigate and give life to the soil, rather than end up uselessly in desert areas, or destructively in floods over plains or cities. Similarly, unlike an ordinary man, a king's will is not entirely his own, since the welfare of his whole country depends on it. Because he is a public figure, his "heart" is directed by the Almighty to the ends He wills for the nation—good ends if they are deserving, bad if not.

2. Previously we read (16:2), "All the ways of a man are pure in his own eyes, but HA-SHEM examines the spirits." The term *yashar* (right) applies to the straight line to moral perfection that is the shortest distance between two points—for example, via humility, generosity or compassion. Sometimes, though, a person has to move in an extreme direction for particular reasons, as when pride or even cruelty becomes temporarily necessary. Yet someone may then deceive himself into thinking that he is still on the "straight" road, because he is naturally attracted to such an extreme quality of cruelty and pride. God, however, reads accurately the extent to which one is still on the "straight" path. Then too, a person may still be "straight," adhering to the proper path of life, yet no longer "pure" in his motives, having opportunistic reasons for acting morally. Here too the Almighty "weighs the spirit," the true inner motives for an act.

3. Sacrifices are not a Divinely acceptable end in themselves (as

21 ¹ Like coursing streams of water is a king's heart in the hand of HA-SHEM; he turns it wherever He wishes. ² Every way of a man is right in his own eyes, but HA-SHEM weighs the heart. ³ To do righteousness and justice is more choice to HA-SHEM than sacrifice. ⁴ Haughty eyes and a proud heart — the tillage of the wicked is sin. ⁵ The thoughts of a diligent man lead only to advantage, but everyone that is hasty hastes only to want.

the Prophets emphasized), but a way of expressing total self-abnegation to the Almighty, and dedication to a life of the "righteous and justice" that He commanded, in relations with man and God. Since they are only a means, sacrifices are secondary in importance to the spiritual values they are supposed to express. They are an indirect way of achieving these goals, and therefore cannot be regarded as being "right" or "straight," in the sense explained in the previous verse — characterizing the shortest distance to one's goal. The goal is clearly a state of heart, mind and purpose.

4. "Haughty eyes" — of the mind — denote an arrogant intellect that presumes to know all, including what is beyond human understanding and behind the laws of nature; and he accepts no direction or limitations. The "proud heart" denotes boundless cravings and limitless desires. Both of these act as "tillage" to sin: they weed out any obstructions to the growth of sin which may have been implanted beforehand, by theoretical or practical intelligence. The "haughty eyes" remove the inhibitions of one's theoretical intelligence; the "proud heart" removes the barriers of practical good sense.

5. Though they act quickly, the diligent take time to think and

ז פֹּעַל אוֹצָרוֹת בִּלְשׁוֹן שָׁקֶר הֶבֶל נִדָּף מְבַקְשֵׁי־מָוֶת: שֹׁד־רְשָׁעִים
ח יְגוֹרֵם כִּי מֵאֲנוּ לַעֲשׂוֹת מִשְׁפָּט: הֲפַכְפַּךְ דֶּרֶךְ אִישׁ וָזָר וְזַךְ יָשָׁר
ט פָּעֳלוֹ: טוֹב לָשֶׁבֶת עַל־פִּנַּת־גָּג מֵאֵשֶׁת מִדְיָנִים וּבֵית חָבֶר:
י מִדְיָנִים נֶפֶשׁ רָשָׁע אִוְּתָה־רָע לֹא־יֻחַן בְּעֵינָיו רֵעֵהוּ: בַּעֲנָשׁ־לֵץ יֶחְכַּם־
יא

plan their best mode of action out of all the possibilities. This is part of diligence: the thoughtful, efficient approach to action. While it may delay them, it "leads them to advantage." The hasty person, on the other hand, acts without consideration and without waiting for an opportune moment, and he therefore fails. Alacrity is a good policy in action, but not in thinking and planning; a waiting period in which ideas ripen is a good investment in starting any project.

6. "A lying tongue" denotes false testimony from forged documents. Making a fortune through such means brings no lasting wealth or happiness, for finally the truth comes out, and then the treasures "seek death"—for such forgery may lead to a death penalty.

7. "What the wicked dreads, that shall come upon him" (10:24). The wicked are haunted by a dread foreboding of the disaster that awaits them; and it comes—"because they refuse to act with justice" and decency, preferring violence and robbery, or "gathering treasures" by forgery (verse 6). The word *shōd* (calamity) can alternately mean robbery: this can certainly induce a terror of punishment in the criminal.

8. The verse refers to the evildoers of verses 6 and 7. It is basic human nature to go "straight" and love honesty and justice, wanting no part of robbery or violence. Thus society can thrive. The criminals mentioned above, however, have perverted their basic nature as moral social beings. The whole of human society sets itself against them, regarding them as treacherous and alien;

⁶ Gathering treasures by a lying tongue is a wind-swept vapor; they seek death. ⁷ The calamity of the wicked will terrify them, because they refuse to act with justice. ⁸ Treacherously changeable is the way of a man, and strange; but as for a pure man, his activity is right. ⁹ It is better to dwell in a corner of the housetop, than in a house of friendship with a quarrelsome woman. ¹⁰ The soul of the wicked desires evil; his neighbor finds no favor in his eyes. ¹¹ When a scoffer is punished, a

and so they dread anticipated disaster (verse 7). The person who is pure of anything unworthy, however, has also a clear intellect ("his activity is right"), undistorted by personal prejudices.

9. Although in general it is good to live in a home with friends and companionship, a quarrelsome, contentious wife can turn this into a curse by picking arguments with her husband's friends and turning them into his enemies or antagonists; or she will disgrace him before them. In such circumstances, it is better to live apart from others.

10. Even though, generally, "likes attracts" and people of similar interests enjoy each other's company, wicked people find no pleasure in one another's company — for two reasons: (1) each has a different "career" of evil (one is a rake, another a thief, etc.) and so they actually have nothing in common; (2) even if two indulge in the same kind of wrongdoing, and both are overcome by their desires, when one sees the wickedness in the other he can see its ugliness clearly enough, and he is repelled by it.

11. When a scoffer meets his just punishment, the naïve person

יב פֶּתִי וּבַהֲשְׂכִּיל לֶחָכָם יִקַּח־דָּעַת: מַשְׂכִּיל צַדִּיק לְבֵית רָשָׁע
יג מְסַלֵּף רְשָׁעִים לָרָע: אֹטֵם אָזְנוֹ מִזַּעֲקַת־דָּל גַּם־הוּא יִקְרָא
יד וְלֹא יֵעָנֶה: מַתָּן בַּסֵּתֶר יִכְפֶּה־אָף וְשֹׁחַד בַּחֵק חֵמָה עַזָּה:
טו שִׂמְחָה לַצַּדִּיק עֲשׂוֹת מִשְׁפָּט וּמְחִתָּה לְפֹעֲלֵי אָוֶן: אָדָם תּוֹעֶה
טז מִדֶּרֶךְ הַשְׂכֵּל בִּקְהַל רְפָאִים יָנוּחַ: אִישׁ מַחְסוֹר אֹהֵב שִׂמְחָה

is motivated to accept the moral law, since he sees so clearly that virtue is rewarded and crime punished by Heaven. A person who has already accepted the moral law on faith, however, is given empirical evidence of its validity by the scoffer's fate, and acquires a more rational and definite moral perspective.

12. "House" connotes tranquility: even when a *tzaddik* sees an evil man enjoying peace, he understands the reason: It is because the Almighty is giving the man the illusion of impunity, so that he will not be deterred from continuing his evil actions, and thus his final reckoning can come upon him sooner than expected.

13. The term *dal* (impoverished man) denotes a person who has lost his wealth — generally by having been cheated or robbed. If a judge will not listen to his outcry and will not give him any relief and help, he will suffer the same fate (measure for measure), either through human agency or by Heaven's punishment.

14. The gift that asks for nothing in return has a pacifying effect both on God (if it is to the poor, for instance) and on man (if it is to the rich and powerful). If, on the other hand, it is a bribe given and taken stealthily to distort justice, this *arouses* strong wrath instead, both in the Almighty and in a human ruler when he hears of it.

naïve man is made wise; and when a wise man is instructed, he gains knowledge. [12] The righteous man thoughtfully comprehends the house of a wicked man: He is deluding the wicked toward evil. [13] He who stops his ears at the outcry of an impoverished man, he too shall cry out and will not be answered. [14] A gift in secret pacifies anger, but a bribe in the bosom — strong wrath. [15] The execution of justice is joy to the righteous, but ruin to workers of iniquity. [16] The man who wanders errantly from the way of understanding shall rest in the gathering of the shades. [17] He who loves pleasure will be an indigent man; one who loves wine and oil shall not be rich. [18] The wicked

15. The righteous rejoice when Heaven metes out justice: they know they will be rewarded. Not so the "workers of iniquity" who have lived by lawless might. Their fate is the perdition of descent to Gehinnom (purgatory).

16. "Understanding" (*séchel*) denotes the Divinely-inspired capacity to grasp eternal religious truth, like HA-SHEM's omniscience and His providential relations with the world. The man who strays from these fundamental beliefs is doomed to have no place in the ultimate illumination of His presence in the Afterlife.

17. Addiction to pleasure can give no lasting satisfaction: one constantly feels a renewed craving for fresh pleasure. But physical self-indulgence brings not only this painful experience of dissatisfaction; it also leads to financial ruin.

PROVERBS 21:18–23

יח אֹ֣פֶר לַ֭צַּדִּיק רָשָׁ֑ע וְתַ֖חַת יְשָׁרִ֣ים בּוֹגֵֽד׃ יט טוֹב שֶׁ֥בֶת בְּאֶֽרֶץ־מִדְבָּ֑ר מֵאֵ֖שֶׁת מְדוֹנִ֣ים וָכָֽעַס׃ כ אוֹצָ֤ר ׀ נֶחְמָ֣ד וָ֭שֶׁמֶן בִּנְוֵ֣ה חָכָ֑ם וּכְסִ֖יל אָדָ֣ם יְבַלְּעֶֽנּוּ׃ כא רֹ֭דֵף צְדָקָ֣ה וָחָ֑סֶד יִמְצָ֥א חַ֝יִּ֗ים צְדָקָ֥ה וְכָבֽוֹד׃ כב עִ֣יר גִּ֭בֹּרִים עָלָ֣ה חָכָ֑ם וַ֝יֹּ֗רֶד עֹ֣ז מִבְטֶחָֽה׃ כג שֹׁמֵ֣ר פִּ֭יו וּלְשׁוֹנ֑וֹ שֹׁמֵ֖ר מִצָּר֣וֹת נַפְשֽׁוֹ׃ זֵ֣ד יָהִ֣יר לֵץ

18. "Wicked" and "righteous" are relative terms; one who is Divinely judged to be more wicked than another provides atonement for the other by his death. On the other hand, one who is absolutely (not relatively) upright—a man of honesty and integrity—needs no atonement. Moreover, should a faithless man seek to kill him, he himself will fall victim in his stead, and the upright man will emerge safe.

19. In verse 9 a man was advised to shun society and human company if his wife tended to pick quarrels with his friends. Let him better live "in the corner of a housetop." If, however, the wife is not only "quarrelsome" but "angry" in her very nature, such a shrew will plague him with her angry quarreling even if he stays there. In this case, the husband is advised to run from her even to the wilderness.

20. A wise person tries to keep his wealth by the paradoxical means of giving it away to charity. In this way, he stores up for himself eternal spiritual treasure (equivalent reward for the generosity he has shown) in the world to come. Conversely, a fool consumes his wealth and makes it vanish by thinking to keep hold of it, since he is left finally with nothing, when it is the spiritual equivalents that count. Taken metaphorically, the verse refers to the precious insights and conceptual achievements that the wise man will preserve because of his consistently moral way of life, and that the fool will lose because of his moral corruptibility.

man is an atonement for the righteous one, and a faithless man comes instead of the upright. ¹⁹ It is better to live in a wilderness than with a quarrelsome and angry woman. ²⁰ Desirable treasure and oil are in the dwelling of the wise man, but a foolish man swallows it up. ²¹ He who pursues righteousness and kindness will find life, charity and honor. ²² A wise man scales the city of the mighty, and brings down the stronghold in which it trusts. ²³ He who guards his mouth and his tongue, guards his soul from troubles. ²⁴ A

21. Through his pursuit of perfect relations with God (*tzᵉdaka*, righteousness or charity) and with man (kindness), the wise man retains both the material and spiritual blessings noted in the last verse. His reward will be eternal life, Divine charity and honor — denoting eternal spiritual kindness and happiness.

22-23. A wise man's moral strength is depicted metaphorically as a force great enough to enable one to scale a hill and capture singlehandedly a city full of stalwart warriors, seizing even the fortress tower on which they rely for refuge. Strong and manifold though the forces of physical desires and cravings in a human being may be, while his spiritual and rational powers are generally weak and little, the most powerful arms of desire cannot withstand the sword of moral wisdom and the shield of moral understanding and sense, in the reverent fear of HA-SHEM. The morally wise man can make spirituality triumph in his way of life. To retain the internal victory, however, and prevent a resurgence of the moral enemy within, it is necessary to keep watch over wisdom's fortress: the power of speech. Unguarded, it can admit the enemy (which constantly seeks to attack and regain the upper hand), to besiege the human being within, till all is lost and the fierce inner battle must be waged anew.

כה שְׁמוֹ עוֹשֶׂה בְּעֶבְרַת זָדוֹן: תַּאֲוַת עָצֵל תְּמִיתֶנּוּ כִּי־מֵאֲנוּ יָדָיו
כו לַעֲשׂוֹת: כָּל־הַיּוֹם הִתְאַוָּה תַאֲוָה וְצַדִּיק יִתֵּן וְלֹא יַחְשֹׂךְ: זֶבַח
כז רְשָׁעִים תּוֹעֵבָה אַף כִּי־בְזִמָּה יְבִיאֶנּוּ: עֵד־כְּזָבִים יֹאבֵד וְאִישׁ
כח שׁוֹמֵעַ לָנֶצַח יְדַבֵּר: הֵעֵז אִישׁ רָשָׁע בְּפָנָיו וְיָשָׁר הוּא ׀ יָבִין כט

24. The term *zéd* (malevolent man) denotes a person who disputes, with malice aforethought, the doctrines of moral wisdom and Jewish faith, denying Divine providence and Heavenly reward and punishment, and hence brazenly sinning. He can still be won over, however, by convincing arguments and proofs, as he has not yet turned scoffer. He merely adduces arguments and proofs, but will not mock derisively. Should he be vanquished in discussion, he will yield. If he is arrogant, though, he will be impervious to reason and proof, as he mocks the morally wise and faithful person, and sins outrageously, to no purpose, in violation of nature itself. He is simply carried away by his defiance, beyond all bounds.

25–26. A person may well be lazy about matters that he does not consider very important. Here, however, we have the case of the man whose indolence is not for lack of interest in material goods. On the contrary, his desire is much greater than the industrious man's, who labors all day long and has only the nighttime for brooding over his unfulfilled wishes. The lazy man does nothing but brood and yearn, but so slothful is he that his hands will not obey his desire and save him from death by earning a living. This lack of self-control and inner autonomy is the problem, not any lack of desire. Such a person usually meets with no sympathy or help from society, even if he is on the edge of starvation, since people feel that it is in his own power to do some work and earn his bread. The righteous man, however, has the insight to understand that such a person is sick, in a moral sense *incapable* of working. He will give unstintingly, with compassion.

malevolent, haughty man, scoffer is his name; he acts in overbearing malice. ²⁵ The strong desire of the lazy one will kill him, for his hands refuse to labor. ²⁶ He covets greedily all day long; but a righteous man gives and does not hold back. ²⁷ The sacrifice of the wicked is an abomination; how much more when he brings it with evil contemplation. ²⁸ A false witness shall perish; but a man who listens will speak words that endure. ²⁹ A wicked man hardens his face, but as for an upright man, he will comprehend his way.

27. Even if a wicked man brings an offering with all his heart, with the best of intentions, it will not be acceptable till he repents of his past wickedness. It can be compared to a king's hated enemy bringing him a gift. All the more will the offering, and his very act of bringing it, be abhorrent to the Almighty if at that very time his mind is sunk in thoughts and plans for further evil.

28–29. Unlike verses 19:5 and 9, here the reference is to the moral tradition and heritage of Jewish faith and observance — the great body of sacred teaching, from Divine origins, that concerns the commandments and matters of faith and creed — which must be transmitted from generation to generation. When one attests to a true teaching that he received, his words will endure. If a person testifies, however, to a false tradition that he has invented, whether about the observance of a mitzva or a question of faith, his words will perish. This is ordained by Divine providence: truth alone lives on. Should "a wicked man harden his face" to deny the validity of a true tradition, an upright person with good sense will understand which way the truth lies.

אֵין חָכְמָה וְאֵין תְּבוּנָה וְאֵין עֵצָה לְנֶגֶד יהוה: סוּס מוּכָן לְיוֹם מִלְחָמָה וְלַיהוה הַתְּשׁוּעָה:

30–31. In private matters a man generally has free will, and by proper planning and zeal he can succeed. Matters of public significance, however, affecting for example an entire nation, are pre-ordained; there the Divine will pervails. Human beings must act and make their necessary preparations — for example, planning military strategy and arranging forces and equipment

30 There is no wisdom and no understanding and no counsel against HA-SHEM. **31** The horse is prepared for the day of battle, but the victory is by HA-SHEM.

for battle — but only the Almighty will decide the outcome. In such matters affecting an entire people, no received wisdom, innate understanding and perception, or planning by skilled intelligence that can gauge the future, is of any avail against His will.

כב

נִבְחָר שֵׁם מֵעֹשֶׁר רָב מִכֶּסֶף א
וּמִזָּהָב חֵן טוֹב: עָשִׁיר וָרָשׁ נִפְגָּשׁוּ עֹשֵׂה כֻלָּם יהוה: עָרוּם ב ג
רָאָה רָעָה וְיִסָּתֵר וּפְתָיִים עָבְרוּ וְנֶעֱנָשׁוּ: עֵקֶב עֲנָוָה יִרְאַת ד וְנִסְתָּר
יהוה עֹשֶׁר וְכָבוֹד וְחַיִּים: צִנִּים פַּחִים בְּדֶרֶךְ עִקֵּשׁ שׁוֹמֵר נַפְשׁוֹ ה
יִרְחַק מֵהֶם: חֲנֹךְ לַנַּעַר עַל־פִּי דַרְכּוֹ גַּם כִּי־יַזְקִין לֹא־יָסוּר ו

1. Riches are an illusory external wealth, which can be suddenly lost. A good name, once gained through good deeds, is an inherent treasure that cannot be taken away. Again, honor and influence are certainly better attained by a good name than by excessive riches. Silver and gold have no great intrinsic worth but only a high *market* value — how people rate them. Beneficent grace, the quality that makes a person find favor and affection, also depends on the reaction and response of others — but it is innate in the individual, and can have more effect on people in high position than silver and gold.

2. Wealth and poverty are not stable, permanent conditions. People's fortunes are constantly variable, as they move up or down on the ladder of life. Thus the turning wheel of fortune can make "rich man and poor man meet," as the first one's condition goes downward and the second one's improves — all by the regulation of the Almighty. A good name (verse 1) is therefore better in its constancy and security than mercurially uncertain wealth.

3. Without knowing the laws of moral wisdom, *'arum*, a shrewd, sagacious man, is yet guided by his good sense. Hence he looks ahead and is forewarned; cf. 14:8. A naïve, simple person does not look ahead; he blindly "passes on" even into clear and present trouble, and is punished for failing to take care.

4. A sense of the Creator's infinite greatness and power makes a

22

1 A good name is more choice than great riches, and beneficent grace than silver and gold. **2** Rich man and poor man meet together; HA-SHEM is the Maker of them all. **3** A shrewd man sees the evil, and hides himself; but simpletons pass on, and are punished. **4** In the wake of humility comes the fear of HA-SHEM, riches, and honor, and life. **5** Thorns, snares are in the way of a perverse man; one who guards his soul will move far from them. **6** Train a child according to his way; even when

human being aware of his puny insignificance, whatever he may attain in this world; and this puts a reverent fear of the Almighty in his heart, to dissuade him from disobeying or displeasing Him. By acquiring such humility, one acquires Heaven's reward of wealth and honor, as well as eternal life by avoiding evil. Arrogance, on the other hand, removes all fear of the Almighty, and thus leads to death.

5. The proper path in life is the golden mean; any extreme of excess or deficiency is a "perverse way" — just as a temperate climate is best for health, while excessive heat or cold can cause illness and death. (The term *tzinim*, "thorns," connotes *tzina*, "cold," and *pachim*, "snares," means "coals" in Psalms 11:6, where it is followed by "fire and brimstone" — and hence it can denote heat.)

6. Two directives are given here: On the one hand, the parent is urged to begin educating his child early in life to moral and spiritual values; for the impressions of childhood are imprinted deep in the psyche and have a much stronger effect, even into old age, than later impressions. On the other hand, a child should be educated "according to his way": for everyone has his own mental ability, talents and propensities, which can be

ז מִמֶּנָּה: עָשִׁיר בְּרָשִׁים יִמְשׁוֹל וְעֶבֶד לֹוֶה לְאִישׁ מַלְוֶה: זוֹרֵעַ
ט עַוְלָה יִקְצוֹר־אָוֶן וְשֵׁבֶט עֶבְרָתוֹ יִכְלֶה: טוֹב־עַיִן הוּא יְבֹרָךְ
י כִּי־נָתַן מִלַּחְמוֹ לַדָּל: גָּרֵשׁ לֵץ וְיֵצֵא מָדוֹן וְיִשְׁבֹּת דִּין וְקָלוֹן:
יא אֹהֵב טְהָור־לֵב חֵן שְׂפָתָיו רֵעֵהוּ מֶלֶךְ: עֵינֵי יְהוָה נָצְרוּ דָעַת
יג וַיְסַלֵּף דִּבְרֵי בֹגֵד: אָמַר עָצֵל אֲרִי בַחוּץ בְּתוֹךְ רְחֹבוֹת אֵרָצֵחַ:
יד שׁוּחָה עֲמֻקָּה פִּי זָרוֹת זְעוּם יְהוָה יפול־שָׁם: אִוֶּלֶת קְשׁוּרָה
טו יִפָּל־

recognized and should be respected. Then his education will be a lasting one. Any training that goes against a pupil's nature will not be longlasting.

7–9. In times of old, when a loan (at exorbitant interest) could not be paid, the creditor could take the debtor and his wife and children as slaves, to treat them as cruelly as he wished. When a person lost his fortune and borrowed at exorbitant interest rates, he was soon reduced to abject poverty, and thus soon found himself enslaved. As a result, however, there would be an explosion of anger from time to time, as the enslaved, downtrodden poor rebelled, killing the wealthy in revenge. Then everyone "who sowed injustice" by treating his slaves inhumanly would "reap dire trouble" as the "rod of his wrath" that he wielded over his slaves "failed." But the rich who were generous, assisting the poor with their food and money, would find themselves blessed and honored by the people.

10–11. Hating everyone, a scoffer stirs up trouble among people, creating contention and disputes that send them to the law courts, to endure the onerous litigation and disgrace that ensue. Once the scoffer is cast out of human society, the trouble vanishes. His opposite is one who loves human beings, harboring pure benevolent feelings in his heart as on his lips. He is fit company for even the most honored member of society.

he is old, he will not depart from it. ⁷ The rich man rules over the poor, and the borrower is bondservant to the lender. ⁸ He who sows injustice shall reap dire trouble, and the rod of his wrath shall fail. ⁹ He who has a generous eye shall be blessed, for he gave of his bread to the poor. ¹⁰ Cast out a scoffer, and contention will depart; and litigation and disgrace will cease. ¹¹ He who loves, pure of heart, with grace on his lips, the king shall be his friend. ¹² The eyes of HA-SHEM preserve knowledge, but He distorts the words of the faithless. ¹³ The sluggard says, "There is a lion outside; I shall be slain in the streets." ¹⁴ The mouth of strange women is a deep pit; he who is abhorred by HA-SHEM shall fall into it. ¹⁵ Skep-

13. "Outside" refers to the private courtyards adjacent to houses, and "streets" denote the central marketplace. While there might be wild beasts in a forest and bandits on the highways, a town's courtyards and marketplace are certainly safe enough. Yet in his indolence a lazy person imagines impossible terrors there as an excuse for remaining idle at home. This applies as well to one who is lazy to study and learn Torah and wisdom, and imagines untold difficulties and spiritual perils.

14. This is a metaphoric description of the snare of heretical philosophies, which may entrap a person so that he cannot escape.

15. When skepticism about moral law is found in an adult, it is already deeply rooted in his psyche and has become permanent;

טז בְּלֶב־נָעַר שֵׁבֶט מוּסָר יַרְחִיקֶנָּה מִמֶּנּוּ: עֹשֵׁק דָּל לְהַרְבּוֹת לוֹ
יז נֹתֵן לְעָשִׁיר אַךְ־לְמַחְסוֹר: הַט אָזְנְךָ וּשְׁמַע דִּבְרֵי חֲכָמִים וְלִבְּךָ
יח תָּשִׁית לְדַעְתִּי: כִּי־נָעִים כִּי־תִשְׁמְרֵם בְּבִטְנֶךָ יִכֹּנוּ יַחְדָּו עַל־
יט שְׂפָתֶיךָ: לִהְיוֹת בַּיהוָה מִבְטַחֶךָ הוֹדַעְתִּיךָ הַיּוֹם אַף־אָתָּה:
כ שָׁלִישִׁים הֲלֹא כָתַבְתִּי לְךָ שָׁלִשׁוֹם בְּמוֹעֵצוֹת וָדָעַת: לְהוֹדִיעֲךָ קֹשְׁטְ
כב אִמְרֵי אֱמֶת לְהָשִׁיב אֲמָרִים אֱמֶת לְשֹׁלְחֶיךָ: אַל־

cf. 15:5 and 27:22. In a child, however, such scoffing doubt is generally not yet embedded but only "bound up in the heart"—as though by a thread that can be snapped. At this stage he can be made to lose his skepticism by corrective education.

16. A person may exploit and oppress a poor man in order to amass a tidy sum, then give it to a rich man to be used to gain interest, so that he can finally give the poor person a great deal of money at once; or he may withhold the salary payments of a poor worker over a long period, and then pay him everything at once, with interest, thus "giving to a rich man," for the lump sum will make the worker wealthy. Yet such "benevolence" cannot compensate for the months or years of suffering and want. Morality, therefore, is a matter of steady, continued correctness and compassion. Magnanimous ends cannot make up for oppressive means.

17–18. Since the laws of moral wisdom cannot be demonstrated, they must be learned from tradition, by "hearing the words of the wise." Once taken on faith, they can be studied and known well by "applying your heart." If, however, you merely "keep them within you" (literally, "in your belly") without learning to express them with a clear, mature perception of their truth, "they will be wandering" and vague in your

ticism is bound up in the heart of a child; but the rod of discipline will drive it far from him. [16] If one exploits an indigent man to increase his gain, giving to a rich man, it only makes for want. [17] Incline your ear, and hear the words of the wise, and apply your heart to my knowledge. [18] For they will be wandering if you keep them within you; let them be established all together on your lips. [19] That your trust may be in HASHEM, I have made them known to you this day, indeed to you. [20] Have I not written for you thirds, of counsels and knowledge? — [21] to make you know the certainty of the words of truth, in order to bring back words of truth to those who sent you?

mind, with no absolute clarity or stability in your perception of the world.

19. Here again are the two stages of *chochma* (wisdom) and *da'ath* (knowledge). First there is trust in God who gave the laws of wisdom and knows their necessity. Then comes the personal knowledge and understanding that acknowledges the wisdom of His law.

20-21. "Thirds" — because the Book of *Mishley* basically falls into three parts: chapters 1-9, 10-24, 25-31. It is filled with "counsels" for ourselves, guides to personal conduct; and with "knowledge" to comprehend clearly and transmit to others. The proverbs of *Mishley* will "make you know the certainty" of the "counsels" for yourself; once you fully understand the received truth, with a clear grasp of its reasons and details, you

PROVERBS 22:22-29

כג אַל־תִּגְזָל־דָּל כִּי דַל־הוּא וְאַל־תְּדַכֵּא עָנִי בַשָּׁעַר: כִּי־יהוה יָרִיב
כד רִיבָם וְקָבַע אֶת־קֹבְעֵיהֶם נָפֶשׁ: אַל־תִּתְרַע אֶת־בַּעַל אָף
כה וְאֶת־אִישׁ חֵמוֹת לֹא תָבוֹא: פֶּן־תֶּאֱלַף אֹרְחֹתָו וְלָקַחְתָּ מוֹקֵשׁ
כו לְנַפְשֶׁךָ: אַל־תְּהִי בְתֹקְעֵי־כָף בַּעֹרְבִים מַשָּׁאוֹת: אִם־אֵין־לְךָ
כז לְשַׁלֵּם לָמָּה יִקַּח מִשְׁכָּבְךָ מִתַּחְתֶּיךָ: אַל־תַּסֵּג גְּבוּל עוֹלָם
כט אֲשֶׁר עָשׂוּ אֲבוֹתֶיךָ: חָזִיתָ אִישׁ מָהִיר בִּמְלַאכְתּוֹ לִפְנֵי־מְלָכִים
יִתְיַצָּב בַּל־יִתְיַצֵּב לִפְנֵי חֲשֻׁכִּים:

will be able "to bring back" this mature knowledge of yours to others, to make its truth transparently clear.

22-23. In addition to the normal prohibition of any robbery, of rich or poor, it is particularly heinous to rob the indigent, just because of their poverty. It is equally dreadful to "crush" them at law (in ancient times the local judges sat "in the gate") because no one will champion and defend them. If the victim is a rich man, it is only a money matter; but if he is indigent and helpless, it is not so at all—as the text continues.

24-25. "Anger" (*af*) is expressed outwardly, and an angry man, who takes vengeance immediately, is therefore not the kind of friend to seek. "Wrath" (*chéma*) is even worse, however: it denotes harboring resentment in one's heart. Hence the wrathful person is to be avoided altogether.

26-27. When a debtor cannot meet his obligations, the creditor may not enter his home and seize whatever he pledged as security (Deuteronomy 24:10). A guarantor, who with a firm handshake gives surety for a borrower, has no such protection in the Torah's law.

28. This echoes the Torah's prohibition, "Do not remove your

²² Do not rob an impoverished man, because he is impoverished, and do not crush a poor man in the gate. ²³ For HA-SHEM will champion their cause and despoil of life those who despoil them. ²⁴ Do not make friends with a man given to anger, and with a wrathful man you shall not go: ²⁵ lest you learn his ways, and get a snare to your soul. ²⁶ Do not be one of those who clasp hands, who become surety for debts. ²⁷ If you do not have with what to pay, why should he take your bed from under you? ²⁸ Do not remove an ancient landmark which your fathers set. ²⁹ Do you see a man diligent in his work? — he will stand before kings; he shall not stand before obscure men.

neighbor's landmark which men of old set in your inheritance" (Deuteronomy 19:14). There, however, the reference is to physical property rights, while this refers metaphorically to ancient customs which should not be changed. Thus we find in *Yalkut Shim'oni* (ad loc.): "If you see a custom instituted by your ancestors, do not change it; for example, Abraham instituted the morning prayer," etc. (Similarly, see *Sifré* 188.)

29. An artisan who becomes so highly skilled in his craft that kings employ him can no longer work for ordinary people. He is overqualified for their crude tastes and will not even be appreciated by them, since his art is far beyond their understanding. Metaphorically, this principle applies also to the task of a man in this world: He is "employed" (assigned) by the Divine, supreme King to achieve spiritual ends, and hence should no longer set himself to work intensely on material or physical interests. His spiritual caliber is so fine that he has no place or function in a world of vulgarity and materialism.

כג

א כִּי־תֵשֵׁב לִלְחוֹם אֶת־מוֹשֵׁל
ב בִּין תָּבִין אֶת־אֲשֶׁר לְפָנֶיךָ: וְשַׂמְתָּ שַׂכִּין בְּלֹעֶךָ אִם־בַּעַל נֶפֶשׁ
ג אָתָּה: אַל־תִּתְאָו לְמַטְעַמּוֹתָיו וְהוּא לֶחֶם כְּזָבִים: אַל־תִּיגַע
ד לְהַעֲשִׁיר מִבִּינָתְךָ חֲדָל: הֲתָעִיף עֵינֶיךָ בּוֹ וְאֵינֶנּוּ כִּי עָשֹׂה
ה יַעֲשֶׂה־לּוֹ כְנָפַיִם כְּנֶשֶׁר וְעוּף הַשָּׁמָיִם: אַל־תִּלְחַם אֶת־לֶחֶם
ו רַע עָיִן וְאַל־תִּתְאָו לְמַטְעַמֹּתָיו: כִּי | כְּמוֹ־שָׁעַר בְּנַפְשׁוֹ כֶּן־הוּא
ז אֱכוֹל וּשְׁתֵה יֹאמַר לָךְ וְלִבּוֹ בַּל־עִמָּךְ: פִּתְּךָ־אָכַלְתָּ תְקִיאֶנָּה
ח וְשִׁחַתָּ דְּבָרֶיךָ הַנְּעִימִים: בְּאָזְנֵי כְסִיל אַל־תְּדַבֵּר כִּי־יָבוּז לְשֵׂכֶל

1–3. When invited to dine with a sovereign, bear in mind constantly that you are in the presence of high authority, even though in the course of such a meal one is sometimes tempted to forget it (at his peril). Thus, take care not to overeat, either because you have a large appetite, or because the food is so appetizing. The meal is "deceptive"—set out not for your benefit and enjoyment, but as a preliminary to the business he has in his mind—something he wants from you. In Ecclesiastes 4:13 "an old and foolish king" denotes the element of appetites and desires in a human being. This "sovereign" invites the real, rational self to "dine with him" and indulge in pleasures. Then we must resist the internal blandishments and not "overeat" and overstep the boundaries of propriety. What this element offers is "deceptive food," fit not for the human being as a man but only for his animal side.

4–5. Beware not only of appetites and desires, but also of an inordinate drive to wealth. It will distract you from the study of Torah, and may make you "desist from your understanding" and be left without wisdom. For understanding and perception must be consciously, strongly retained by effort and application. If you but "blink your eyes" and avert your attention for a moment, it can disappear from the mind like a bird in your

23 ¹ When you sit down to eat with a ruler, understand well who is in front of you; ² and put a knife to your throat if you are a man of appetite. ³ Do not crave his savory dishes, for it is deceptive food. ⁴ Do not weary yourself to grow rich, [lest you] desist from your own understanding. ⁵ Should you blink your eyes at it, it is gone: for it will surely make itself wings, like an eagle that flies toward heaven. ⁶ Do not eat the bread of an evil-eyed man, and do not crave his delicacies. ⁷ For like the vileness in his soul, so is he. "Eat and drink," he says to you; but his heart is not with you. ⁸ Your morsel that you have eaten you will vomit up, and lose your sweet words. ⁹ Do not speak in the ears of a fool, for he will despise the good

hand that takes wing and soars when you briefly forget about it.

6–8. The very food that a person of "evil eye" — of a jaundiced nature — serves is contaminated by the poison of his nature. He may invite you to share a tempting meal, but the result will be sickness and emptiness. The end-phrase, however — "your sweet words" — is a clue that this too is a parable: for the study of metaphysical questions. In this we should not be guided by teachers whose own personalities are warped and whose understanding of these basic questions is therefore distorted. They may offer plausible theories that seem like sound food for the mind, but their hearts are not governed, so that their teachings will undermine even the modicum of wisdom you had previously. (That *shaʿar* in verse 7 can mean vileness, see Jeremiah 29:17.)

9. Since *kᵉsil* (a fool) is a person who knows the truth of the

יְ מְלִיךָ: אַל־תַּסֵּג גְּבוּל עוֹלָם וּבִשְׂדֵי יְתוֹמִים אַל־תָּבֹא: כִּי־
יא גֹאֲלָם חָזָק הוּא־יָרִיב אֶת־רִיבָם אִתָּךְ: הָבִיאָה לַמּוּסָר לִבֶּךָ
יב וְאָזְנֶךָ לְאִמְרֵי־דָעַת: אַל־תִּמְנַע מִנַּעַר מוּסָר כִּי־תַכֶּנּוּ בַשֵּׁבֶט
יג לֹא יָמוּת: אַתָּה בַּשֵּׁבֶט תַּכֶּנּוּ וְנַפְשׁוֹ מִשְּׁאוֹל תַּצִּיל: בְּנִי אִם־
יד חָכַם לִבֶּךָ יִשְׂמַח לִבִּי גַם־אָנִי: וְתַעְלֹזְנָה כִלְיוֹתָי בְּדַבֵּר שְׂפָתֶיךָ
טו

laws of moral wisdom, yet will not let it interfere with his pleasures, there is no point in attempting to teach him any moral wisdom.

10. Unlike 22:28 (and Deuteronomy 19:14), this concerns the "ancient landmark" or "general boundary" of the right of the poor to gather certain produce in any man's field: *leket* (dropped gleanings; Leviticus 19:9–10), *shich-cha* (forgotten sheaves; Deuteronomy 24:19), and *pé'a* (an unreaped edge or corner of a field; Leviticus 19:9). As *Midrash Sifra* teaches, this verse is a warning not to rob the poor of this produce that is their due. No one should be tempted by the apparent helplessness of the poor and the orphaned: for they have a Divine champion to defend them, as the text continues.

11. A redeemer of a field is ordinarily a relative who has the right to claim the property. The Almighty Himself acts in this capacity for the poor and the orphaned, and He will certainly be punitive.

12. Listening to the moral teachings of the sages does not always provide a person with sufficient defenses against the power of evil, to master his heart. The inner struggle between destructive and constructive desires can be affected for the good by paying attention to "words of knowledge" (as opposed to words of wisdom)—to the evidences of God and His purposeful creation in the world around. This "natural morality" gained from a study of human life and the nature of

sense of your words. [10] Do not remove the ancient landmark, nor enter the fields of the fatherless. [11] For their Redeemer is mighty, and will champion their cause against you. [12] Apply your heart to moral instruction, and your ears to words of knowledge. [13] Do not withhold moral discipline from a child; though you beat him with the rod, he will not die. [14] You shall beat him with the rod, and will save his soul from the netherworld. [15] My son, if your heart is wise, my heart will be glad, indeed mine will, [16] and my conceiving mind will dance for joy when your lips speak right things.

the world will "apply your heart to moral instruction" and subdue a person to a salutary awe of the Almighty deeply and sincerely felt.

13-14. Even if a young lad is not old enough to take seriously any warnings of Divine punishment for sin, strong moral discipline will do him no harm, and may indeed save him spiritually from a serious fate.

15. These are the actual words of moral discipline that the father addresses to his son. If the son attains one of the highest achievements of moral wisdom, to make his heart become wise and control his desires and drives; if he has become so imbued with ethical probity that no more struggle remains—the joy of the father will also be perfect, reaching *his* very heart.

16. This is the father's response to an even higher achievement, in which the son has so integrated the laws of moral probity, through his own understanding, that there is no further need for inner battle to attain moral self-mastery. At such a level, the son

יז מֵישָׁרִים: אַל־יְקַנֵּא לִבְּךָ בַּחַטָּאִים כִּי אִם־בְּיִרְאַת־יְהֹוָה כָּל־
יח הַיּוֹם: כִּי אִם־יֵשׁ אַחֲרִית וְתִקְוָתְךָ לֹא תִכָּרֵת: שְׁמַע־אַתָּה בְנִי
כ וַחֲכָם וְאַשֵּׁר בַּדֶּרֶךְ לִבֶּךָ: אַל־תְּהִי בְסֹבְאֵי־יָיִן בְּזֹלֲלֵי בָשָׂר לָמוֹ:
כא כִּי־סֹבֵא וְזוֹלֵל יִוָּרֵשׁ וּקְרָעִים תַּלְבִּישׁ נוּמָה: שְׁמַע לְאָבִיךָ זֶה
כב כג יְלָדֶךָ וְאַל־תָּבוּז כִּי־זָקְנָה אִמֶּךָ: אֱמֶת קְנֵה וְאַל־תִּמְכֹּר חָכְמָה

can confidently communicate his own moral vision to others: he can "speak right things." This brings the most intense joy to his father, greater than the happiness expressed in the previous verse.

17. Envy can be either a positive or a negative force. It is destructive to envy the apparent success of sinners and to wish one were like them. Envy of the God-fearing and their pure way of life and good deeds, however, is constructive, since it will dispose a person to emulate them.

18. This is the reason for envying the God-fearing rather than the wicked: it is a question of the ultimate fate of the two categories. The "future" of eternal joy belongs only to the righteous, and they are provided too with their needs for this world, about which one is uncertain but has hope.

19. Now the father addresses the son who is far from having attained these goals of perfection. Being far from the necessary wisdom, he must "hear" and accept it, "and be wise." Then will come his inner battles to subdue his passions and cravings— but this only if he "guides his heart along the way" of wisdom and not foolishness.

20. If the son has not yet attained moral wisdom, he should at least avoid the excesses of food and drink. (The text connotes that the "eaters of meat" are in fact eating their *own* flesh— wasting their very being.)

¹⁷ Let your heart not envy sinners, but be in the fear of HA-SHEM all day; ¹⁸ for certainly there is a future, and your hope shall not be cut off. ¹⁹ Hear you, my son, and be wise, and guide your heart along the way. ²⁰ Do not be among wine-guzzlers, among gluttonous eaters of meat: ²¹ for a drunkard and glutton shall come to poverty, and drowsiness will clothe one with rags. ²² Listen to your father who begot you, and do not despise your mother when she has grown old. ²³ Buy truth, and do not sell it — wisdom, and moral

21. From a purely practical point of view, it is clear that indulgence and laziness lead to poverty in this world. Metaphorically, they lead also to spiritual and intellectual impoverishment. Any wisdom he has will disappear.

22. The son is urged not to doubt the truth of the moral law that his father teaches him. The biological relationship of father and son ensures that he would not willingly give him false guidelines for life. Similarly, the son should not scorn his mother's practices on the grounds that she is old and they are therefore old-fashioned.

23. It is worth paying a high price for truth, even the cost of denying youthful desires and pleasures, but it is wrong to "sell" truth — to make use of it for the sake of other gains, such as honor or wealth. Truth should be acquired at all costs, for its own sake.

Then, the father explains the nature of truth. It is the revealed and received moral tradition of the Torah, which in many ways is uncongenial to human nature. This wisdom can be acquired therefore only through "moral instruction" and the

PROVERBS 23:24–29

כד גִּיל יָגִיל / וְיוֹלֵד יִשְׂמַח כה וּמוּסָר וּבִינָה: גּוֹל יָגוּל אֲבִי צַדִּיק יוֹלֵד חָכָם וְיִשְׂמַח־בּוֹ: יִשְׂמַח־
כו אָבִיךָ וְאִמֶּךָ וְתָגֵל יוֹלַדְתֶּךָ: תְּנָה־בְנִי לִבְּךָ לִי וְעֵינֶיךָ דְּרָכַי
כח תִּצְּרְנָה תִּרְצֶנָה: כִּי־שׁוּחָה עֲמֻקָּה זוֹנָה וּבְאֵר צָרָה נָכְרִיָּה: אַף־הִיא
כט כְּחֶתֶף תֶּאֱרֹב וּבוֹגְדִים בְּאָדָם תּוֹסִף: לְמִי אוֹי לְמִי אֲבוֹי לְמִי

consequent discipline of drives and passions which fear of God inspires. This in turn leads to "understanding": the rational capacity to discriminate between true and false in matters of perception.

24. These apparently synonymous lines refer to two different situations. A "righteous" son is one who instinctively follows a moral way of life, while "a wise child" denotes one who has received a tradition of moral wisdom, which he has then learned and accepted for himself. Righteousness is dependent purely on one's free will, and therefore the "father of a righteous son" (which connotes spiritual parenthood—the educator) has *gil* in his achievements: a joy that is ever renewed but can never let one rest in full confidence for the future. On the other hand, fathering a "wise" child depends partly on hereditary factors, and therefore the biological father will have a constant and confident joy (*simcha*) in the nature of his son who has learned and accepted the moral law from infancy and even earlier. (Our Sages teach that at its conception, an unborn child is brought by an angel before the Heavenly Court, where the Almighty decides if it will be wise or foolish: it is not decided if the child will be righteous or wicked.)

25. Here the verbs of rejoicing are reversed. If the son becomes truly wise in heart, so that virtue becomes second nature for him, beyond conflicts or doubts, then his spiritual guardian (metaphorically "father and mother") will experience the constant, confident kind of joy (*simcha*), while the biological parents ("who bore you") will know not only this joy in the

instruction, and understanding. **24** The father of a righteous son will greatly rejoice, and he who begets a wise child will have joy of him. **25** Let your father and your mother be glad, and let her who bore you rejoice. **26** My son, give me your heart, and let your eyes watch my ways. **27** For a harlot is a deep pit, and an alien woman is a narrow well. **28** She also lies in wait like a robber, and increases the faithless among men. **29** Who cries "Woe"? — he who has strong desire. Who

basic soundness of the child's nature, but also an ever-recurring exultation (*gil*) in the strength and consistency of their son's virtue.

26. Here "heart" refers to an inner control by the moral law that obviates all doubts, denials and heresies. Similarly, "eyes" denote cravings and sinful fantasies engendered through the senses; if the eyes focus solely on God's ways, a person is saved from the havoc that lust can create.

27. "Let your eyes watch my ways" (verse 26) to avoid harlots. The temptations of debauchery are snares that are hard to escape from ("a deep pit"). The "alien woman" refers to heresies, which kill a person spiritually as surely as "a narrow well" kills anyone who falls into it. Therefore, "My son, give me your heart" (verse 26).

28. Sensuality ambushes a man and catches him unawares, so that he commits acts that he would never have contemplated in his right mind. Heresy is inventive in fabricating plausible theories to seduce a man from loyalty to the true God.

29. The root of *avoy* (woe) is the verb *ava*, "desired" — thus

PROVERBS 23:30-35

מְדָיָנִים מָדוֹנִים ׀ לְמִי שִׂיחַ לְמִי פְּצָעִים חִנָּם לְמִי חַכְלִלוּת עֵינָיִם:
לֹא לַמְאַחֲרִים עַל־הַיָּיִן לַבָּאִים לַחְקֹר מִמְסָךְ: אַל־תֵּרֶא יַיִן כִּי
בַּכּוֹס לֹב יִתְאַדָּם כִּי־יִתֵּן בַּכִּיס עֵינוֹ יִתְהַלֵּךְ בְּמֵישָׁרִים: אַחֲרִיתוֹ כְּנָחָשׁ
יִשָּׁךְ וּכְצִפְעֹנִי יַפְרִשׁ: עֵינֶיךָ יִרְאוּ זָרוֹת וְלִבְּךָ יְדַבֵּר תַּהְפֻּכוֹת:
לה וְהָיִיתָ כְּשֹׁכֵב בְּלֶב־יָם וּכְשֹׁכֵב בְּרֹאשׁ חִבֵּל: הִכּוּנִי בַל־חָלִיתִי
הֲלָמוּנִי בַּל־יָדָעְתִּי מָתַי אָקִיץ אוֹסִיף אֲבַקְשֶׁנּוּ עוֹד:

denoting powerful cravings and drives. "Raving talk," senseless gossip and babble, indeed leads to quarrels. And should you ask, "Who has redness of eyes?" the text that follows gives the answer.

30. These are habitual drinkers, who after a night of carousal will surface only to inquire for a good mixer of wine, and will then return with renewed vigor to their cups.

31. The son is cautioned not to be attracted to the warm red color of the wine, glowing in the cup, or to the smooth, harmless way it seems to slide down the throat. Metaphorically, the "cup" refers to the drinker himself, who becomes red from the wine although at first he drinks easily and comfortably.

32. Ultimately the wine becomes like poison: the instant poison of the snake or the slower-acting venom of the viper whose secretions bring death.

33. Under the influence of wine the senses are inflamed to lust, and the intellect conceives alien, heretical notions (see verses 26-28).

has quarrels? — he who has raving talk. Who has wounds without cause? — he who has redness of eyes — [30] those who linger over the wine; those who go to try mixed wine. [31] Do not look at wine when it is red, when it gives its color in the cup, when it glides down smoothly. [32] At the end it bites like a serpent, and stings like a viper. [33] Your eyes will see strange things, and your heart will utter confusions; [34] and you shall be like one who lies down in the midst of the sea, or like one who lies on the top of a mast. [35] "They struck me, and I did not sicken; they beat me, and I did not know it. When shall I awake? I shall continue, I will seek it yet again."

34. The turbulence that the drinker experiences progressively worsens: from that of a man tossed among the waves to that of a man on the point of being hurled from the heights of a ship's mast to the depths of the sea.

35. This is the tragic case of the drunkard: increasingly numb to the world (at first he feels the blows but simply does not fall ill from them, while afterwards, even under savage beatings, he has no sensation), he longs to waken from his stupor, for a return of sensation, not in order to change his life but in order to start another bout of drinking. Addiction to drink thus becomes a paradigm for the senseless, suicidal compulsiveness of sin.

כד

א בְּאַנְשֵׁי רָעָה וְאַל־תִּתְאָו לִהְיוֹת אִתָּם: כִּי־שֹׁד יֶהְגֶּה לִבָּם וְעָמָל אַל־תְּקַנֵּא
ב שִׂפְתֵיהֶם תְּדַבֵּרְנָה:
ג בְּחָכְמָה יִבָּנֶה בָּיִת וּבִתְבוּנָה יִתְכּוֹנָן:
ד וּבְדַעַת חֲדָרִים יִמָּלְאוּ כָּל־הוֹן יָקָר וְנָעִים: גֶּבֶר־חָכָם בַּעוֹז
ה וְאִישׁ־דַּעַת מְאַמֶּץ־כֹּחַ: כִּי בְתַחְבֻּלוֹת תַּעֲשֶׂה־לְּךָ מִלְחָמָה
ו וּתְשׁוּעָה בְּרֹב יוֹעֵץ: רָאמוֹת לֶאֱוִיל חָכְמוֹת בַּשַּׁעַר לֹא יִפְתַּח־
ז פִּיהוּ: מְחַשֵּׁב לְהָרֵעַ לוֹ בַּעַל־מְזִמּוֹת יִקְרָאוּ: זִמַּת אִוֶּלֶת חַטָּאת
ח

1–2. This is a double warning: not to envy the wicked and wish to act like them, and not even to seek their company for the sake of practical profit, without intending to emulate them. The first warning is given because, despite their apparent prosperity, the wicked are deeply anxious about the ruin that they sense must befall them; to envy or copy them is therefore sheer folly. The second warning, not to seek their company, is explained next: As all their talk is of evil, you will be influenced to imitate their lifestyle, even if that was not your original intention.

3–4. This depicts the construction of a proper moral life: The laws of moral wisdom are gathered like bricks, and its rules and lessons are taken to heart, and like bricks are set into a solid structure. Then they are studied by the understanding mind, to comprehend all their consequences—analogous to adding a roof and ceiling to a constructed house. When *da'ath*, clear knowledge, is attained, and all is lucidly grasped, it is like filling the house "with all precious and pleasant riches" from the radiance of the Torah.

5. A person who has accepted the moral tradition and behaves accordingly has the force to control his urges. But a really reliable and consistent moral energy is found only in one who has gone further, and internalized the received traditions so well

24

¹ Do not be envious of evil men, nor desire to be with them: ² for their heart ponders destruction, and their lips talk of wrongdoing. ³ Through wisdom is a house built, and by understanding is it established; ⁴ and by knowledge are the chambers filled with all precious and pleasant riches. ⁵ A wise man is with might, and a man of knowledge maintains strength. ⁶ For with [wise] strategies you shall make your war, and with a multitude of counsellors there is victory. ⁷ Wisdom for a skeptic is as gems from on high; in the gate he does not open his mouth. ⁸ If one schemes to do evil, others shall call him a man of evil devices. ⁹ The licentious thought of skepticism is

that their truth is as clear to him as any matter of experience or sense-perception.

6. As explained previously (11:14), one strategy is insufficient in war, because one has to be prepared with several alternate possibilities to meet whatever strategy the enemy uses. Therefore many counsellors and advisors are needed. Similarly, in the struggle against evil, one needs all the resources of wisdom, understanding and knowledge in order to outwit the wily enemy.

7. Doubting everything, a skeptic knows nothing clearly and certainly. Hence moral wisdom, derived from "on high," is over his head. In times of old, the fiercest battle against a city took place "in the gate": the city had to stay the enemy there, or it was lost. Wisdom can win the fierce inner battle against desires and urges; but lacking it, the skeptic cannot "open his mouth" to know and express any part of it clearly.

PROVERBS 24:10-18

יא וְתוֹעֵבַת לְאָדָם לֵץ: הִתְרַפִּיתָ בְּיוֹם צָרָה צַר כֹּחֶכָה: הַצֵּל
יב לְקֻחִים לַמָּוֶת וּמָטִים לַהֶרֶג אִם־תַּחְשׂוֹךְ: כִּי־תֹאמַר הֵן לֹא־
יָדַעְנוּ זֶה הֲלֹא־תֹכֵן לִבּוֹת ׀ הוּא־יָבִין וְנֹצֵר נַפְשְׁךָ הוּא יֵדָע
יג וְהֵשִׁיב לְאָדָם כְּפָעֳלוֹ: אֱכָל־בְּנִי דְבַשׁ כִּי־טוֹב וְנֹפֶת מָתוֹק עַל־
יד חִכֶּךָ: כֵּן ׀ דְּעֶה חָכְמָה לְנַפְשֶׁךָ אִם־מָצָאתָ וְיֵשׁ אַחֲרִית וְתִקְוָתְךָ
טו לֹא תִכָּרֵת: אַל־תֶּאֱרֹב רָשָׁע לִנְוֵה צַדִּיק אַל־תְּשַׁדֵּד רִבְצוֹ:
טז כִּי שֶׁבַע ׀ יִפּוֹל צַדִּיק וָקָם וּרְשָׁעִים יִכָּשְׁלוּ בְרָעָה: בִּנְפֹל אוֹיִבְךָ
יח אַל־תִּשְׂמָח וּבִכָּשְׁלוֹ אַל־יָגֵל לִבֶּךָ: פֶּן־יִרְאֶה יְהוָה וְרַע בְּעֵינָיו
וְהֵשִׁיב מֵעָלָיו אַפּוֹ:

9. Doubting and flouting the moral law is akin to licentiousness. And if a skeptic turns scoffer, he will do abominable things openly, scorning all standards of decency.

10–11. This is measure for measure: If one can save others from death and does nothing, he will find himself without strength, feeble and helpless, when he faces his own dire troubles.

12. If the person (verses 10-11) tries to excuse himself for not going to the help of the distressed by saying that he was not aware of their plight or of his ability to help them, he may convince other people, but God knows the truth of the heart, and will deal with him as he has dealt with others.

14. Wisdom has all the immediate sweetness of honey, but also the additional characteristic of a pleasure that lasts for eternity.

15. A wicked man may intend to rob the righteous of his money, or out of envy or vengeance he may intend to rob him of his tranquility.

sin; and a scoffer is an abomination to men. [10] You shall have been feeble in a day of adversity, your strength small, [11] if you hold back from rescuing those taken to their death, and those on the verge of being slain. [12] If you say, "Behold, we did not know this," does not He who weighs hearts comprehend? and does He who guards your soul not know? And will He not repay every man according to his action? [13] My son, eat honey, for it is good, and the honeycomb is sweet to your taste. [14] Know that so is wisdom for your soul; if you have found it, then there will be a future, and your hope will not be cut off. [15] Do not lie in wait, O wicked man, at the dwelling of a righteous man; do not despoil his resting-place: [16] For a righteous man falls seven times, and rises up again, but the wicked stumble under adversity. [17] When your enemy falls do not rejoice, and when he stumbles, let your heart not be glad, [18] lest HA-SHEM see it, and it displease Him, and He turn away His wrath from him.

16. The righteous recover again and again from misfortune, while the wicked fall into the very pit they have prepared for others, and cannot extricate themselves.

17–18. The noun of "rejoice," *simcha*, denotes a steady happiness over something constant; on the other hand, *gil*, the noun of "be glad," denotes a temporary spurt of happiness over something new and momentary, such as good news. We are strongly advised here not to feel a constant gladness when an

PROVERBS 24:19-26

יט אַל־תִּתְחַר בַּמְּרֵעִים אַל־תְּקַנֵּא בָּרְשָׁעִים: כִּי ׀ לֹא־תִהְיֶה
כא אַחֲרִית לָרָע נֵר רְשָׁעִים יִדְעָךְ: יְרָא־אֶת־יְהוָה בְּנִי וָמֶלֶךְ
כב עִם־שׁוֹנִים אַל־תִּתְעָרָב: כִּי־פִתְאֹם יָקוּם אֵידָם וּפִיד שְׁנֵיהֶם
מִי יוֹדֵעַ:
כג גַּם־אֵלֶּה לַחֲכָמִים הַכֵּר־פָּנִים בְּמִשְׁפָּט בַּל־טוֹב: אֹמֵר ׀
כה לְרָשָׁע צַדִּיק אָתָּה יִקְּבֻהוּ עַמִּים יִזְעָמוּהוּ לְאֻמִּים: וְלַמּוֹכִיחִים
כו יִנְעָם וַעֲלֵיהֶם תָּבוֹא בִרְכַּת־טוֹב: שְׂפָתַיִם יִשָּׁק מֵשִׁיב

enemy's fortunes change drastically, nor to gloat in a burst of joy if he stumbles and falls: because pleasure in an enemy's distress repels the Creator, and when He sees such cruelty and vengefulness, He may begin to see your enemy in a relatively good light. The result may be that He shifts some of His anger from the enemy to you, the vengeful person.

19-20. We are warned against two possible reactions to the wicked: One is plain envy and a desire to emulate them. The other happens when the wicked man's actions are so patently ugly that we have no wish to copy them but are still irritated by the unpunished prosperity of evil in the world. Both reactions are unwarranted because the success of the wicked is short lived and anxiety-ridden even at its height.

21-22. God is to be feared in religious matters and the king in matters of law and social order. Dissenters and revolutionaries who seek to change the social order should be avoided, for they break the Divine law—which commands obedience to human authority—as well as the law of man. Moreover, when the revolutionary conspiracy is discovered, then the rebels are doomed. And even if the revolution succeeds, it is not certain if the new regime will be better. It may be worse than the old, with anarchy and violence the order of the day.

¹⁹ Do not vex yourself because of evildoers, and do not be envious of the wicked: ²⁰ for there will be no future for an evil man; the lamp of the wicked will ebb out. ²¹ My son, fear HA-SHEM and the king; do not meddle with dissenters: ²² for their calamity shall arise suddenly; and who knows the ruin from their dissension?

²³ These [sayings] also are from the wise: To show respect for persons in judgment is not good. ²⁴ If one says to a wicked man "You are righteous," peoples shall curse him, nations shall storm at him; ²⁵ but those who give rebuke will have delight, and a good blessing shall come upon them. ²⁶ His lips should be kissed who answers

23-24. Up to this point, we have read the Proverbs of Solomon. From here till the end of the chapter, we have a collection of aphorisms by other sages.

It is wrong for a judge to favor even a righteous man in court though he knows him to be virtuous. In court he must impartially hold both parties potentially guilty till the case is clarified. And it is certainly outrageous to justify the guilty party in court: that is to undermine the whole structure of justice and law. This is the thrust of "peoples shall curse him, nations shall storm at him." "Peoples" (*'amim*) are held together by a common culture and civilization, which is ruined by such perversion of justice; while "nations (*lᵉ'umim*) also have a religious faith in common, which is equally undermined by injustice.

25. The consequence of proper judicial treatment of the wicked is the intrinsic satisfaction and delight that comes from right action, and the blessing and approval of society.

כז דְּבָרִים נְכֹחִים: הָכֵן בַּחוּץ׀ מְלַאכְתֶּךָ וְעַתְּדָהּ בַּשָּׂדֶה לָךְ אַחַר וּבָנִיתָ בֵיתֶךָ:

כח אַל־תְּהִי עֵד־חִנָּם בְּרֵעֶךָ וַהֲפִתִּיתָ בִּשְׂפָתֶיךָ: אַל־תֹּאמַר כַּאֲשֶׁר עָשָׂה־לִי כֵּן אֶעֱשֶׂה־לּוֹ אָשִׁיב לָאִישׁ כְּפָעֳלוֹ:

ל עַל־שְׂדֵה אִישׁ־עָצֵל עָבַרְתִּי וְעַל־כֶּרֶם אָדָם חֲסַר־לֵב: וְהִנֵּה עָלָה כֻלּוֹ׀ קִמְּשֹׂנִים כָּסּוּ פָנָיו חֲרֻלִּים וְגֶדֶר אֲבָנָיו נֶהֱרָסָה:

לב וָאֶחֱזֶה אָנֹכִי אָשִׁית לִבִּי רָאִיתִי לָקַחְתִּי מוּסָר: מְעַט שֵׁנוֹת

26. When a person is wise in giving rebuke and can give a telling rebuttal when someone tries to dispute him, he will be loved and admired.

27. Before taking a wife and establishing a family, we should prepare our means of earning an income and providing support: prepare fields well-sown and ready to harvest for the household's food. Otherwise, we will have to turn to charity or theft, or be forced to neglect Torah-study. This can be taken also on a general metaphorical level: Before any act, proper, thoughtful preparations should be made.

28–29. We are warned against giving false testimony, whether for the sake of money or for the sake of revenge.

30–31. A field needs hard work — sowing, plowing, etc. — which a lazybones will not invest in his land. Even he, however, is capable of looking after a vineyard, which simply needs to be guarded against deterioration. But a man "lacking a heart" to discipline himself at all does not even realize the importance of this passive care, so that even the vineyard is neglected.

with right words. ²⁷ Prepare your work outside, and make it fit for yourself in the field; afterwards build your house.

²⁸ Do not be a witness against your neighbor without cause, so that you will earn food with your lips. ²⁹ Do not say, "I will do so to him as he has done to me; I will pay the man back for what he has done."

³⁰ I passed by the field of a lazy man, and by the vineyard of a man lacking a [self-disciplining] heart: ³¹ and behold, it was all grown over with thistles, its surface was covered with nettles, and its stone fence was broken down. ³² Then I saw and applied my heart; I looked, and learned a

---

32. Literally, the master of Proverbs sees the field and the vineyard, and draws moral conclusions from their neglect. Metaphorically, he contemplates inwardly the potential fertility of the soul, and the painful consequences of its neglect. The image of the field conveys that the soul requires constant tending through positive precepts (*mitzvoth 'aséh*) and active intellectual inquiry. The lazy man is reluctant to labor in this way. The vineyard depicts one who has already planted the vines of wisdom, and he only needs to safeguard it from degeneration, through observance of the negative commandments (*mitzvoth lo-ta'aseh*). A person "lacking in heart" does not have sufficient self-control in the face of his desires to keep even this minimal negative program to protect his spiritual integrity. Overgrown with weeds, the vineyard of the soul cannot bring forth its fruit.

לד מְעַט תְּנוּמוֹת מְעַט חֲבֻק יָדַיִם לִשְׁכָּב: וּבָא־מִתְהַלֵּךְ רֵישֶׁךָ
וּמַחְסֹרֶיךָ כְּאִישׁ מָגֵן:

33. It is delightful, but quite unnecessary, to doze and stay in bed after sufficient full sleep. In his languor, an indolent person is loth to rise resolutely and get dressed—and he suffers the consequences:

moral lesson. [33] Yet a little slumber, yet a little dozing, a little folding of the hands to lie abed: [34] so shall your poverty come like a stroller, and your want like an armed man.

34. The state of poverty comes imperceptibly, without violent impact; it is hardly felt at all. But the condition of want which follows is a drastic calamity, like the attack of an armed warrior, against which one may struggle and fight in vain.

א גַּם־אֵלֶּה מִשְׁלֵי שְׁלֹמֹה אֲשֶׁר הֶעְתִּיקוּ אַנְשֵׁי ׀ חִזְקִיָּה מֶלֶךְ־
ב יְהוּדָה: כְּבֹד אֱלֹהִים הַסְתֵּר דָּבָר וּכְבֹד מְלָכִים חֲקֹר דָּבָר:
ג שָׁמַיִם לָרוּם וָאָרֶץ לָעֹמֶק וְלֵב מְלָכִים אֵין חֵקֶר: הָגוֹ סִיגִים
ד מִכָּסֶף וַיֵּצֵא לַצֹּרֵף כֶּלִי: הָגוֹ רָשָׁע לִפְנֵי־מֶלֶךְ וְיִכּוֹן בַּצֶּדֶק כִּסְאוֹ:
ו אַל־תִּתְהַדַּר לִפְנֵי־מֶלֶךְ וּבִמְקוֹם גְּדֹלִים אַל־תַּעֲמֹד: כִּי טוֹב
אֲמָר־לְךָ עֲלֵה הֵנָּה מֵהַשְׁפִּילְךָ לִפְנֵי נָדִיב אֲשֶׁר רָאוּ עֵינֶיךָ:
ח אַל־תֵּצֵא לָרִב מַהֵר פֶּן מַה־תַּעֲשֶׂה בְּאַחֲרִיתָהּ בְּהַכְלִים אֹתְךָ

2. In matters of metaphysics and gnosticism, honor lies in discretion and silence, especially in those mystical areas where human intellect is lost. In these areas, human thought can only be indirect, figurative and suggestive; and the Sages spoke only in symbol and metaphor. In matters of governmental rule, on the other hand, openness and clarity are virtues, as they demonstrate the justice and goodness of the sovereign authority. Concealment would generally indicate something amiss or corrupt.

3. Just as neither the infinite reaches of the heavens nor the far depths of the earth can be plumbed, so can we never know all the intricate details and nuances of a government's sovereign rule, extending as it does over innumerable people and their individual destinies.

4–5. The purpose of a sovereign's rule is the execution of justice. Since the king needs many counsellors and ministers to help in achieving a just administration, it is important that these aides be themselves uncorrupted: then the king's throne is of pure, unadulterated silver, as it were. If some of these counsellors are corrupt, however, then justice will be perverted. This alloy in the pure silver of the throne must be purged before the throne can again serve its pure purpose.

25 ¹ These also are proverbs of Solomon, which the men of Hezekiah king of Judah copied out. ² It is the glory of God to conceal a thing, but the glory of kings is to search out a matter. ³ The heaven for height and the earth for depth, and the heart of kings is unsearchable. ⁴ Remove the dross from the silver, and a vessel emerges for the refiner; ⁵ take away the wicked from the presence of a king, and his throne shall be established in righteousness. ⁶ Do not glorify yourself in the presence of the king, and do not stand in the place of great men; ⁷ for it is better that you should be told, "Come up here," than that you should be put down in the presence of a nobleman whom your eyes have seen. ⁸ Do not go out hastily to be discordant, lest you do not know what to do in the end, when your neighbor has put you to

6–7. It is most disrespectful to preen ourselves in a king's presence, when our own honor should be completely overshadowed by his (Divinely bestowed) majesty. Similarly, we should withdraw to a discreet position, beneath our true level of esteem, when great men are present, rather than thrust our way to a prominent place. In a humble position, we will be invited to move higher — which brings honor. Having pushed into an important place, however, even before someone "whom your eyes have seen" as your equal, only invites demotion and disgrace. Again, the last phrase may denote, "*because* your eyes have seen": taking a lower position will bring elevation because your action indicates insight, tact and decorum.

8. We should always make sure that our actions will not end in

ט רֵעֶךָ: רִיבְךָ רִיב אֶת־רֵעֶךָ וְסוֹד אַחֵר אַל־תְּגָל: פֶּן־יְחַסֶּדְךָ
יא שֹׁמֵעַ וְדִבָּתְךָ לֹא תָשׁוּב: תַּפּוּחֵי זָהָב בְּמַשְׂכִּיּוֹת כָּסֶף
יב דָּבָר דָּבֻר עַל־אָפְנָיו: נֶזֶם זָהָב וַחֲלִי־כָתֶם מוֹכִיחַ חָכָם
עַל־אֹזֶן שֹׁמָעַת:
יג כְּצִנַּת־שֶׁלֶג ׀ בְּיוֹם קָצִיר צִיר נֶאֱמָן לְשֹׁלְחָיו וְנֶפֶשׁ אֲדֹנָיו
יָשִׁיב:
יד נְשִׂיאִים וְרוּחַ וְגֶשֶׁם אָיִן אִישׁ מִתְהַלֵּל בְּמַתַּת־שָׁקֶר: בְּאֹרֶךְ

a result precisely contrary to what we want to achieve. Hence let us not rush to start a quarrel in order to avenge an insult; the end-result may be further insult and more humiliation, instead of the satisfaction of revenge and restored honor.

9-10. Even if you must quarrel with a neighbor over a grievance, be careful to air out only the grievance, and not another person's secrets, in the heat of passion. For then you will be humiliated not only by your opponent but by all bystanders for being a defamatory gossip; and afterward it will be impossible to retract your slander even if you want to, and so your disgrace will remain a permanent stain.

11. If the setting of an ornament is valuable, the ornament itself must be yet more precious; no one would set iron or copper in silver. Similarly, human speech is a setting (as it were) for the invisible spirit, indicating its concealed thoughts and emotions. If a person's basic self is estimable, his mind worthy of honor for its integrity, his speech will be worthy of esteem, free of anything gross or vile. His words will always be chosen with care for their purpose. Evil gossip and slander, however, indicate a base, coarse spirit.

12. His words of wisdom will equally "adorn" the inner ear of an obedient listener, earning him grace.

shame. ⁹ Have your discordant quarrel out with your neighbor, but do not reveal the secret of another, ¹⁰ lest he who hears it will cast shame upon you, while your slander cannot be taken back. ¹¹ Like apples of gold in settings of silver is a word apt for its purpose. ¹² As an earring of gold, and an ear-ornament of fine gold, so is a wise reprover on an obedient ear.

¹³ As the cold of snow in the time of harvest, so is a faithful messenger to those who send him: for he revives the soul of his master.

¹⁴ Like clouds and wind without rain is one who boasts of a false gift. ¹⁵ By long patience is a ruler

13. Should a man feel a king's wrath like the heat of a blazing summer sun, putting his life in danger, he would have to send a mediator to plead for him with the king and abate his rage. If the mediator is a "faithful messenger" who carries out his mission well, the man is of course tremendously relieved. Symbolically, this concerns the human being as an emissary in this world, sent to fulfill his set task. If he does it faithfully, he will "return the spirit of his Master" (literal translation): at his expiration he will relinquish the Divine spirit with which he was endowed for his lifetime, and will fear no Divine burning wrath at his judgment in the Afterlife.

14. When a gift is promised and never given, it is comparable to clouds that promise rain and are then swept away by the winds. Such empty promises, say the Sages, are actually punished by the curse of drought.

15. If we have angered a person in authority, we should not try to win a full pardon immediately, but rather persuade him to

PROVERBS 25:16–22

טז אַפַּיִם יְפֻתֶּה קָצִין וְלָשׁוֹן רַכָּה תִּשְׁבָּר־גָּרֶם: דְּבַשׁ מָצָאתָ אֱכֹל
יז דַּיֶּךָּ פֶּן־תִּשְׂבָּעֶנּוּ וַהֲקֵאתוֹ: הֹקַר רַגְלְךָ מִבֵּית רֵעֶךָ פֶּן־יִשְׂבָּעֲךָ
יח וּשְׂנֵאֶךָ: מֵפִיץ וְחֶרֶב וְחֵץ שָׁנוּן אִישׁ־עֹנֶה בְרֵעֵהוּ עֵד שָׁקֶר:
יט שֵׁן רֹעָה וְרֶגֶל מוּעָדֶת מִבְטָח בּוֹגֵד בְּיוֹם צָרָה: מַעֲדֶה־בֶּגֶד ו
כא בְּיוֹם קָרָה חֹמֶץ עַל־נָתֶר וְשָׁר בַּשִּׁרִים עַל לֶב־רָע: אִם־רָעֵב
כב שֹׂנַאֲךָ הַאֲכִלֵהוּ לָחֶם וְאִם־צָמֵא הַשְׁקֵהוּ מָיִם: כִּי גֶחָלִים

defer punishment and show patience. Gradually his fury will subside, and he will forgive us. Likewise, if a carnivorous beast can break bones with its tongue when it eats its prey, surely a human can "break" Heaven's stern judgment, to win Divine forbearance by prayer, and eventual remission through entreaty.

16–17. Even though honey is good to eat and you have the additional pleasure of having "found" it without effort, eat it only in moderation, and do not make yourself sick over it. Likewise, even if you are as beloved to your neighbor as honey, do not overstay your welcome in his house.

18. The three instruments of destruction represent three different effects of false testimony. Like a hammer, it splits people apart; like a sword, it can instantly fell its victim; and like an arrow, it can have a remote, long-distance effect—for instance, when it takes the form of slander secretly spoken.

19. It is as unnerving to depend on something and be let down when it is needed, as to crunch down on a shaky tooth or to set out on a journey and find out that one's foot has become dislocated.

20. Light ornamental clothing may be attractive on a warm day, but in cold weather not only is it not attractive but it does nothing to warm the body, chilled as it is by the winter cold. In

won over, and a soft tongue breaks a bone. **16** Have you found honey? Eat only enough for you, lest you be filled with it and vomit it. **17** Let your foot be seldom in your neighbor's house, lest he become fed up with you and hate you. **18** A hammer, and a sword, and a sharp arrow — this is a man who bears false witness against his neighbor. **19** Confidence in a traitorous man in time of trouble is like a broken tooth, and a foot out of joint. **20** Like one who adorns himself with a garment on a cold day, and like vinegar on *nether* earthenware, so is one who sings songs to a heavy heart. **21** If your enemy is hungry, give him bread to eat, and if he is thirsty, give him water to drink: **22** For you will be heaping coals of fire

the same way, songs have no cheering effect on a melancholy mood, but on the contrary, may only deepen the sadness. Similarly, vinegar would destroy a soft, thin, fragile earthenware vessel (*nether*: see Rambam, commentary to Mishna, *Kélim* ii 1) that is not strong enough to withstand it. Symbolically this refers to the introduction of any substance into a receptable unfit for it — for instance, teaching Torah to a student who has not conditioned himself to receive it by engaging in good deeds.

21–22. If we want to take great revenge on an enemy, we should not refuse him food and drink, but on the contrary should treat him well — thus gaining two objects: Firstly, the enemy will remember his own bad behavior and feel shame that he has now to accept food and drink from one whom he has wronged; and secondly, we will be rewarded by Heaven for acting charitably.

PROVERBS 25:23–28

כג אֲתָה חֹתֶה עַל־רֹאשׁוֹ וַיהוָה יְשַׁלֶּם־לָךְ: רוּחַ צָפוֹן תְּחוֹלֵל
כד גֶּשֶׁם וּפָנִים נִזְעָמִים לְשׁוֹן סָתֶר: טוֹב שֶׁבֶת עַל־פִּנַּת־גָּג מֵאֵשֶׁת
מִדְיָנִים   מדונים וּבֵית חָבֶר:
כה מַיִם קָרִים עַל־נֶפֶשׁ עֲיֵפָה וּשְׁמוּעָה טוֹבָה מֵאֶרֶץ מֶרְחָק: מַעְיָן
כו נִרְפָּשׂ וּמָקוֹר מָשְׁחָת צַדִּיק מָט לִפְנֵי־רָשָׁע: אָכֹל דְּבַשׁ הַרְבּוֹת
כח לֹא־טוֹב וְחֵקֶר כְּבֹדָם כָּבוֹד: עִיר פְּרוּצָה אֵין חוֹמָה אִישׁ אֲשֶׁר
אֵין מַעְצָר לְרוּחוֹ:

23. Just as rain is brought by the winds which are not visible, so when we see an angry countenance, we know it is caused by the poison of evil gossip from a tongue wagging in secret, even though it is kept well concealed.

24. Just as the north wind engenders rain (verse 23), the spirit of a quarrelsome woman engenders altercations and rancor; "better (then) to live in a corner" of the roof, unprotected from the rain, than to live within the shared house unprotected from her.

25. When a person grows faint from thirst in a place without water, and water is brought from elsewhere, it is highly refreshing. Just so is good news brought from afar of the well-being and prosperity of family relations.

26. The "source" is the deep, hidden origin from which the fountain springs. In general, if a righteous man fails in his fortunes, his economic stability will be damaged, but not the "source" of his life, his profound belief in the Almighty. If, however, his misfortunes are due to a wicked man, then not only does he suffer in financial, worldly terms, but even his deep faith is affected, as he begins to question God's justice.

27. Just as eating too much honey is sickening, so too much probing about the "honor" (estimable well-being) of the righ-

upon his head, and HA-SHEM will reward you. ²³ The north wind engenders rain and a backbiting tongue a fuming face. ²⁴ It is better to live in a corner of the housetop than in a house of companionship with a quarrelsome woman.

²⁵ As cold water to a thirsting soul, so is good news from a far country. ²⁶ As a troubled fountain and a polluted source, so is a righteous man who falters before a wicked person. ²⁷ It is not good to eat much honey, and [not any] honor for men to [unduly] search out their honor. ²⁸ Like a city broken down and without a wall, so is a man with no restraint on his spirit.

teous brings no "honor" or worthwhile results. It is one of the mysteries of Divine providence why "a righteous man falters before a wicked person" (verse 26), and excessive querying can only be as harmful as too much honey. True, quintessential honor awaits the righteous in the world-to-come—a reward beyond human comprehension, which can only be taken on faith. The honor of the righteous which the wicked can damage or destroy is only the illusory esteem of this world.

28. The human being has been likened to "a small city" attacked and besieged by "a great king" (Ecclesiastes 9:14): i.e. his evil inclination, imagination and fantasies of passion and pride seek to overpower him. With his good inclination he must subdue his imaginative, fantasying spirit, setting a curb, like a wall, to the multifarious destructive forces of pride, envy, vengefulness, etc. Our text depicts the result if he fails to use his power to achieve inner moral victory and control. He will remain at the mercy of his evil impulses, with no "restraining wall."

PROVERBS 26:1-7

א כַּשֶּׁ֤לֶג ׀ בַּקַּ֗יִץ וְכַמָּטָ֥ר בַּקָּצִ֑יר כֵּ֤ן לֹא־נָאוֶ֬ה לִכְסִ֥יל כָּבֽוֹד׃
ב כַּצִּפּ֣וֹר לָ֭נוּד כַּדְּר֣וֹר לָע֑וּף כֵּ֥ן קִֽלְלַ֥ת חִ֝נָּ֗ם לֹ֣א תָבֹֽא׃
ג שׁ֣וֹט לַ֭סּוּס מֶ֣תֶג לַחֲמ֑וֹר וְ֝שֵׁ֗בֶט לְגֵ֣ו כְּסִילִֽים׃
ד אַל־תַּ֣עַן כְּ֭סִיל כְּאִוַּלְתּ֑וֹ פֶּֽן־תִּשְׁוֶה־לּ֥וֹ גַם־אָֽתָּה׃
ה עֲנֵ֣ה כְ֭סִיל כְּאִוַּלְתּ֑וֹ פֶּן־יִהְיֶ֖ה חָכָ֣ם בְּעֵינָֽיו׃
ו מְקַצֶּ֣ה רַ֭גְלַיִם חָמָ֣ס שֹׁתֶ֑ה שֹׁלֵ֖חַ דְּבָרִ֣ים בְּיַד־כְּסִֽיל׃
ז דַּלְי֣וּ שֹׁ֭קַיִם מִפִּסֵּ֑חַ וּ֝מָשָׁ֗ל בְּפִ֣י כְסִילִֽים׃

1. Rain and snow help to make the earth fertile, if they fall at the right time in the yearly cycle. If they fall in summer or at harvest-time, then they only make the harvest rot. Similarly, honor may benefit the wise man, who has "plowed and sown" the field of his soul; it can act as a further incentive to his spiritual growth, encouraging him to fulfill his potential. The fool, however, who has "sown" nothing in himself, can only be damaged by honor, as it reinforces his conceit.

2. In its written form the text means, "so shall a curse for no cause not come home": Just as a sparrow may fly about from place to place, and a swallow may fly far from its nest, so will a curse without reason not affect its intended victim. As read, however, the verse literally states that the curse will "come home to him": As these birds ultimately do return to their nests, so the malediction will come home to roost, striking the one who uttered it.

3. Senseless brutes need restraint and discipline to keep them on the right road. A man, endowed with intellect, should be able to steer a good course without such discipline; but the fool, who evades the self-discipline of wisdom for the sake of his appetites, needs castigating to keep him on the proper path.

4–5. This is the fool (*kᵉsil*) whose theoretical knowledge of the

26 ¹ Like snow in summer, and like rain in harvest, so honor is not seemly for a fool. ² Like the wandering sparrow, like the flying swallow, so shall a curse for no cause come home. ³ A whip for the horse, a bridle for the donkey, and a rod for the back of fools. ⁴ Do not answer a fool according to his skepticism, lest you also become like him. ⁵ Answer a fool according to his skepticism, lest he be wise in his own eyes. ⁶ He who sends a message by the hand of a fool cuts off his own feet, drinking damage. ⁷ The thighs hang limp from a lame man: so is a parable in the mouth of fools.

moral law is undercut by the power of his desires, for they dictate his practices and beliefs. Arguing theology with such a person is useless, for his skepticism is merely a front for his anarchic desires; and getting too involved in such discussions may make us appear his equal, affected by the doubts and uncertainties that he prates. Verse 5, however, directs us to answer him. This apparent contradiction suggests that there is a legitimate mode of reply. So that the fool should not remain with a sense of his own cleverness, we may answer briefly, without getting involved in complex arguments, just to show up his folly. An example of such a reply follows.

6–7. The sensual fool, living undisciplined in the gratification of his cravings, is "drinking damage" as a drunkard guzzles wine. When the drunkard is so inebriated that he can no longer walk on his feet, it is as if his feet were cut off. Then this might "send" him "a message by the hand of a fool" to cut off his thighs too, because they seem to serve no purpose now. This is "a parable" to put "in the mouth of fools": Having yielded to his passions like a drunkard to alcohol, he may think he can

ט אֶבֶן בְּמַרְגֵּמָה כֵּן־נוֹתֵן לִכְסִיל כָּבוֹד: חוֹחַ עָלָה בְיַד־שִׁכּוֹר
י וּמָשָׁל בְּפִי כְסִילִים: רַב מְחוֹלֵל־כֹּל
יא וְשֹׂכֵר כְּסִיל וְשֹׂכֵר עֹבְרִים: כְּכֶלֶב שָׁב עַל־קֵאוֹ כְּסִיל שׁוֹנֶה
יב בְאִוַּלְתּוֹ: רָאִיתָ אִישׁ חָכָם בְּעֵינָיו תִּקְוָה לִכְסִיל מִמֶּנּוּ: אָמַר
יד עָצֵל שַׁחַל בַּדָּרֶךְ אֲרִי בֵּין הָרְחֹבוֹת: הַדֶּלֶת תִּסּוֹב עַל־צִירָהּ
טו וְעָצֵל עַל־מִטָּתוֹ: טָמַן עָצֵל יָדוֹ בַּצַּלָּחַת נִלְאָה לַהֲשִׁיבָהּ אֶל־

dismiss moral wisdom entirely, as superfluous; but this is like the drunkard's cutting off his thighs...

8. Wrapping a stone in a sling may seem to be paying honor to the stone, but it is only a preparation for hurling it and injuring someone. So the honor of a lengthy reply would only give a fool ammunition to vanquish more innocent people with his perverse, heretical views.

9-10. Left without the use of legs and thighs (verses 6-7), the drunkard would then go walking on his hands, and would likely get a thorn in his hand. Yet his counterpart, the fool, will persist with his parable, undermining the religious beliefs that make for a moral life. Thus he will argue that since God is the Creator of all men, both the moral and dissolute, all natures and actions are of His making, and not the result of man's free will. Therefore (supposedly) He rewards the criminal as well as the moral man, since each must act in accordance with the nature that the Almighty has given him.

11. This is the reason why any serious argument with this kind of fool (*k^esil*) is useless. Like the dog returning to swallow a second time the food that has made it sick, the fool keeps coming back to his skeptical notions, even though he knows that they are foully destructive and wrong. No amount of argument, therefore, will influence him.

⁸ As if wrapping a stone in a sling, so is one who gives honor to a fool. ⁹ Like a thorn that goes into the hand of a drunkard, so is a parable in the mouth of fools.

¹⁰ A Master engenders all; He rewards a fool and rewards transgressors. ¹¹ Like a dog that returns to his vomit, so is a fool that repeats his skepticism. ¹² Do you see a man wise in his own eyes? There is more hope for a fool than for him. ¹³ A lazy man says, "There is a great lion on the road; a small lion is on the highways!" ¹⁴ The door turns on its hinges, and a lazy man is on his bed. ¹⁵ A lazy man buries his hand in the dish; it wearies him to bring

12. It is therefore important to answer such a "wise man," to remove his illusion that his opinions are sagacious. For this is the worst condition, when a person thinks himself enlightened in his skepticism and denies that his doubts are in fact generated by his desires. From this there is no rescue. The fool at least acknowledges in his heart that he is giving a spurious justification for indulging his desires; and thus he has some hope of a return to moral wisdom, when the violence of his passions subsides.

13-14. He will not venture to seek any metaphysical knowledge of Jewish cosmogony or theosophy: for he may succumb (he claims) to the "great lion" of sectarian heresy. Nor will he make the effort to learn ordinary moral wisdom: he would (supposedly) face the danger of a "small lion" — denial of the principles of the Jewish faith. He finds it easy and satisfying to merely become "wise in his own eyes" (verse 12). Hence like the door turning on its hinges, he turns from side to side, but will not budge from his bed.

PROVERBS 26:15–23

טו ‏פִּיו: חָכָם עָצֵל בְּעֵינָיו מִשִּׁבְעָה מְשִׁיבֵי טָעַם: מַחֲזִיק בְּאָזְנֵי־
יח ‏כֶלֶב עֹבֵר מִתְעַבֵּר עַל־רִיב לֹּא־לֹו: כְּמִתְלַהְלֵהַּ הַיֹּרֶה זִקִּים
יט ‏חִצִּים וָמָוֶת: כֵּן־אִישׁ רִמָּה אֶת־רֵעֵהוּ וְאָמַר הֲלֹא־מְשַׂחֵק אָנִי:
כא ‏בְּאֶפֶס עֵצִים תִּכְבֶּה־אֵשׁ וּבְאֵין נִרְגָּן יִשְׁתֹּק מָדֹון: פֶּחָם לְגֶחָלִים
   ‏וְעֵצִים לְאֵשׁ וְאִישׁ מדונים לְחַרְחַר־רִיב: מִדְיָנִים
כב ‏דִּבְרֵי נִרְגָּן כְּמִתְלַהֲמִים וְהֵם יָרְדוּ חַדְרֵי־בָטֶן: כֶּסֶף סִיגִים

15. Even if he is offered food and puts his hand in the dish, he has not the energy to bring the food to his mouth. Metaphorically this denotes a man who is offered spiritual nourishment, for example the narratives of the Written Torah, whereupon he only "puts his hand into the dish," without actually taking the food; in other words, he responds only to the literal level of the narrative, without taking its essence, the real nourishment it has to offer.

16. Even if seven men of great wisdom try to set him straight, it is of no use: cf. verse 12.

17. If a dog is walking along quietly and someone seizes it by the ears, he will have it barking furiously and biting him. Similarly, if he grows furious about some rancorous argument that does not concern him and decides to interfere, he will find himself calumniated and even "bitten" verbally.

18–19. Firebrands burn clothing; ordinary arrows inflict wounds; poisoned arrows kill. Similarly, deceit and swindle can bring monetary damage, then physical illness and injury, and ultimately psychological injury. Yet the wrongdoer may think it all a joke.

20. The word *madon* (from the root *din*, law) denotes disputing and quarreling that lead to litigation at court. This is

it back to his mouth. ¹⁶ A lazy man is wiser in his own eyes than seven men who respond with sense. ¹⁷ Like one who grasps a passing dog by the ears, so is one who becomes impassioned [and meddlesome] over discord that is not his own. ¹⁸ Like a taunting prankster who casts firebrands, arrows, and death, ¹⁹ so is a man who deceives his neighbor, and says, "But I am only joking!" ²⁰ Where there is no wood, the fire goes out; and where there is no grumbler, disputatious quarreling ceases. ²¹ As sparks are to burning coals and wood to fire, so is a quarrelsome man for kindling discord.

²² The words of a grumbler are like stunning blows, and they go down into the innermost parts of the body. ²³ Silver dross overlaid on an earthen

what develops when a person constantly grumbles and complains that he has been wronged. Without such audible bitterness, fed by resentment and hate, quarrels between neighbors will subside before they ever reach the courts—like a fire dying out when it gets no wood to sustain it.

21–22. Just as sparks are not enough to raise a great fire—fuel is necessary—so a merely quarrelsome person may kindle an argument that reaches the courts, but it takes a grumbler, filled with inner resentments, to start a conflagration of violent hatred (=stunning blows that penetrate deep into the body). This is a parable for a resentful man who complains that God has created man for a tragic destiny, and that the world is full of evil (see 18:5–8).

23. Worse still than the resentful grumbler of verse 22 is a

כד מִצָּפֶה עַל־חֶרֶשׂ שְׂפָתַיִם דֹּלְקִים וְלֶב־רָע: בִּשְׂפָתָו יִנָּכֵר שׂוֹנֵא
כה וּבְקִרְבּוֹ יָשִׁית מִרְמָה: כִּי־יְחַנֵּן קוֹלוֹ אַל־תַּאֲמֶן־בּוֹ כִּי שֶׁבַע
כו תּוֹעֵבוֹת בְּלִבּוֹ: תִּכַּסֶּה שִׂנְאָה בְּמַשָּׁאוֹן תִּגָּלֶה רָעָתוֹ בְקָהָל:
כז כֹּרֶה־שַּׁחַת בָּהּ יִפֹּל וְגֹלֵל אֶבֶן אֵלָיו תָּשׁוּב: לְשׁוֹן־שֶׁקֶר יִשְׂנָא
דַכָּיו וּפֶה חָלָק יַעֲשֶׂה מִדְחֶה:

hypocrite who speaks passionately (with "burning lips") of affection and love, while his heart is filled with malice. He is comparable to a vessel that seems to be of silver, but beneath the impressive surface is just crude earthenware.

24-25. In his talk he hides his hatred with a show of love, while within he devises schemes to swindle and cheat. Analogously, a hypocrite will make a pretense of piety and faith; but do not be taken in by his sweet and moving prayer...

26-27. However a dissembling swindler and a hypocrite may hide the hatred in their hearts, they are ultimately revealed for

vessel — such are burning lips and a wicked heart. ²⁴ He who hates dissembles with his lips, but he harbors deceit within himself. ²⁵ When he makes his voice gracious with entreaty, do not believe him, for there are seven abominations in his heart. ²⁶ Though his hatred be covered with darkness, his wickedness will be exposed in the public assembly. ²⁷ He who digs a pit shall fall into it; and if one starts a stone rolling, it will come back upon him. ²⁸ A lying tongue hates its cringing ones, and a flattering mouth produces ruin.

what they are, and they themselves suffer the evil they sought to perpetrate.

28. The hypcritical liar of the previous verses prefers strong, forthright men, and hates those who come furtively, servilely, to whisper evil gossip and slander, afraid to speak aloud — since they make it obvious that all the scurrilous words are empty talk, without substance. Likewise, one "flattering mouth" hates another sycophant, and seeks to harm and ruin him.

כז

א אַל־תִּתְהַלֵּל בְּיוֹם מָחָר כִּי לֹא־
ב תֵדַע מַה־יֵּלֶד יוֹם: יְהַלֶּלְךָ זָר וְלֹא־פִיךָ נָכְרִי וְאַל־שְׂפָתֶיךָ:
ג כֹּבֶד־אֶבֶן וְנֵטֶל הַחוֹל וְכַעַס אֱוִיל כָּבֵד מִשְּׁנֵיהֶם: אַכְזְרִיּוּת
ד חֵמָה וְשֶׁטֶף אָף וּמִי יַעֲמֹד לִפְנֵי קִנְאָה: טוֹבָה תּוֹכַחַת מְגֻלָּה
ה מֵאַהֲבָה מְסֻתָּרֶת: נֶאֱמָנִים פִּצְעֵי אוֹהֵב וְנַעְתָּרוֹת נְשִׁיקוֹת
ו שׂוֹנֵא: נֶפֶשׁ שְׂבֵעָה תָּבוּס נֹפֶת וְנֶפֶשׁ רְעֵבָה כָּל־מַר מָתוֹק:

1. The vicissitudes of time are notorious, and since even the events of a day are still unknown in the morning, it is foolhardy to talk with brazen confidence about tomorrow.

2. Self-praise is obviously worthless; far better to act in life so as to earn praise from others ("strangers") who notice and observe you, and then even from "foreigners," people in other regions who hear of you, as your reputation spreads. Even the fact that you refrain from self-praise ("not your own lips") will "praise you": it will add to your esteem as a mark of modesty.

3. Stone is intrinsically heavy, and a single boulder has tremendous weight, while sand is a burden if borne in large mass. Likewise, each individual outburst of a skeptic's rage is hard to bear; but it is far more difficult to tolerate him if his rages are repeated with a vexing frequency. The Midrash applies this verse to Pharaoh, the paragon of skeptics, who said, "Who is HA-SHEM (the Lord)?... I do not know HA-SHEM" (Exodus 5:2). Every time he "hardened his heart" and refused to release the Israelites, his sin was as heavy as stone; in its cumulative effect his repeated intransigence became a burden like a load of sand.

4. Anger (*af*) is external and instantly expressed; it is often overwhelming in its immediate momentary impact, but not really cruel. Wrath (*chéma*) denotes a hidden inner fury that

27 ¹ Do not boast about tomorrow, for you do not know what a day may bring forth. ² Let a stranger praise you, and not your own mouth; a foreigner, and not your own lips. ³ The heaviness of stone and the weight of sand—yet a skeptic's anger is heavier than both. ⁴ Wrath is cruel, and anger overwhelming; but who can stand firm before jealousy? ⁵ Indeed good is open rebuke out of hidden love. ⁶ Faithful are the wounds of a friend, while the kisses of an enemy are profuse. ⁷ A satiated person loathes a honeycomb, but to a

may not express itself in instant revenge, but enflames a person with cruel intentions. Fuming jealousy, however, combines the worst of both emotions: the person both lashes out in revenge and smolders with suppressed hatred.

5. Open rebuke for wrong behavior is salutary if it arises from hidden love. The classic example is the father who disciplines his son out of love; and so the Almighty Himself acts (cf. 3:12).

6. Even if a true friend chastises a person and strikes him, it is out of loyal love and concern. He wants to return him to the proper path. But even if an enemy showers a person with signs of affection, it is only to encourage him to continue in a misguided way of life; there is no wish for his ultimate welfare.

7. Physical pleasures are a subjective matter. A person accustomed to them no longer feels their delight, while someone unaccustomed will respond keenly. The resulting paradox is that a poor man can be happier than a man of wealth, since his appetites are sharper. To acquire wealth and indulge in material enjoyments may therefore be self-defeating.

ח כְּצִפּוֹר נוֹדֶדֶת מִן־קִנָּהּ כֵּן־אִישׁ נוֹדֵד מִמְּקוֹמוֹ: שֶׁמֶן וּקְטֹרֶת
ט יְשַׂמַּח־לֵב וּמֶתֶק רֵעֵהוּ מֵעֲצַת־נָפֶשׁ: רֵעֲךָ וְרֵעַ אָבִיךָ אַל־
י תַּעֲזֹב וּבֵית אָחִיךָ אַל־תָּבוֹא בְּיוֹם אֵידֶךָ טוֹב שָׁכֵן קָרוֹב
יא מֵאָח רָחוֹק: חֲכַם בְּנִי וְשַׂמַּח לִבִּי וְאָשִׁיבָה חֹרְפִי דָבָר: עָרוּם
יג רָאָה רָעָה נִסְתָּר פְּתָאיִם עָבְרוּ נֶעֱנָשׁוּ: קַח־בִּגְדוֹ כִּי־עָרַב זָר
יד וּבְעַד נָכְרִיָּה חַבְלֵהוּ: מְבָרֵךְ רֵעֵהוּ בְּקוֹל גָּדוֹל בַּבֹּקֶר הַשְׁכֵּים

8. Human nature is in one aspect identical with animal nature. Just as birds may fly far but always seek to return to their nests, so do humans have a deep homing instinct. Thus the spirit yearns to return to its origins, to be again with the Creator, who sent it to live itinerantly in this world like a wandering bird, so that it can be enclosed again in the great Divine matrix of life.

9. Although fresh air to breathe is basically adequate to sustain life and strength, the Almighty has also provided the bounties of perfume and ointment to give extra pleasure to the senses. Similarly, a person can find in his own heart the plans he needs to progress in life, but good advice from a friend in sweet confidential conversation will give him added inner strength.

10. A well-tried friendship that goes back to the previous generation is better even than the love of brothers. Natural as it is, a brother's love flourishes only in good times, when it is not really needed. If calamity strikes, it fades away (cf. 19:7). For this reason, a neighbor who is truly and constantly near in all circumstances is better than a brother who holds himself remote.

11. Even if his son has not accepted the laws of moral wisdom until now, the father appeals to him to heed them now, so that he can put an end to the complaint and defamation heaped upon him for having and raising such a son.

hungry person every bitter thing is sweet. [8] Like a bird that wanders from her nest, so is a man who wanders from his place. [9] Ointment and perfume rejoice the heart; so does the sweet converse of a man's friend by [his] sincere counsel. [10] Your own friend, and your father's friend, do not forsake; and do not go into your brother's house on the day of your calamity. Better a neighbor who is near than a brother far off. [11] Be wise, my son, and make my heart glad, that I may answer him who taunts me. [12] A shrewd man, seeing the evil, hides himself; [while] simpletons, passing on, are punished. [13] Take his garment, who has given surety for a stranger; and if for an alien woman, hold him in pledge. [14] If one blesses his friend with a loud voice, rising early in the morning, it

12. The previous verse that is almost identical (22:3) refers to unfortunate events; this verse, to misfortune arising from a lack of moral wisdom. It thus continues the father's advice and appeal to his son in verse 11.

13. Verse 20:16 was given as a literal truth; this is meant metaphorically, as explained there.

14. A blessing should be given quietly, discreetly, and at an auspicious moment. Before morning prayers is no time for elaborate greetings and blessings (when all one's thoughts should be set on his entreaty before the Creator). Hence a blessing given then, ostentatiously, may be transformed into a curse.

מִדְיָנִים טּ קֶלָלָה תֵחָשֶׁב לוֹ: דֶּלֶף טוֹרֵד בְּיוֹם סַגְרִיר וְאֵשֶׁת מִדְיָנִים
טּז נִשְׁתָּוָה: צֹפְנֶיהָ צָפַן־רוּחַ וְשֶׁמֶן יְמִינוֹ יִקְרָא: בַּרְזֶל בְּבַרְזֶל יָחַד
יח וְאִישׁ יַחַד פְּנֵי־רֵעֵהוּ: נֹצֵר תְּאֵנָה יֹאכַל פִּרְיָהּ וְשֹׁמֵר אֲדֹנָיו
יט יְכֻבָּד: כַּמַּיִם הַפָּנִים לַפָּנִים כֵּן לֵב־הָאָדָם לָאָדָם: שְׁאוֹל וַאֲבַדּוֹ
לֹא תִשְׂבַּעְנָה וְעֵינֵי הָאָדָם לֹא תִשְׂבַּעְנָה:
כא מַצְרֵף לַכֶּסֶף וְכוּר לַזָּהָב וְאִישׁ לְפִי מַהֲלָלוֹ: אִם־תִּכְתּוֹשׁ

15–16. Any attempt to hold back the rain is like trying to imprison the wind. Similarly, such a woman is too stormy to contain. It is useless to try to hide evidence of her anger, since the ointment on his hand betrays the wounds she has inflicted on him.

17. The important characteristic of a sword or knife is its sharpness, and this is maintained by whetting it against another metal. Similarly, the essence of a man is his intellect, and this is sharpened by dialogue with his friend.

18. If one wants to eat the fruit of a fig-tree, he has to go early each morning and pluck the figs as they ripen, a few at a time, before the worms get to them. Similarly, one who attends his master faithfully and learns eagerly his every word of wisdom will finally be honored by being declared his master's worthy successor (e.g. Joshua: cf. Exodus 33:11).

19. As the heart pumps back into the system the blood it receives, thus maintaining life, water reflects back to a person the countenance that he presents; and the heart reflects a person's thoughts and impulses, presaging good or evil results. Analogously, a king (the "heart" of a country) will channel back, beneficially, the taxes he receives; and a Torah scholar (the spiritual "heart" of a community) will bring his community Heaven's blessing of abundance for the merit of sustaining

shall be counted a curse to him. ¹⁵ A continual dripping on a rainstormy day and a quarrelsome woman are alike: ¹⁶ He who would hide her will have hidden the wind, and the ointment of his right hand betrays itself. ¹⁷ Iron sharpens iron, and one man sharpens the mind of another. ¹⁸ He who watches a fig-tree faithfully shall eat its fruit, and one who attends upon his master shall be honored. ¹⁹ As in water face answers to face, so the heart of a man to a man. ²⁰ The netherworld of hell and perdition are never satisfied, and the eyes of a man are never satisfied.

²¹ The refining pot is for silver, and the furnace for gold; and a man is tried according to his praise. ²² Though you pound a skeptic among grain in a

him. The maintenance of the holy Temple in Jerusalem likewise brought blessing to all Israel.

20. A mortal man's appetite for physical pleasure can never be satisfied, since by its nature it constantly seeks novelty and loses interest in anything familiar. The volatile nature of man, whose physical self is destined for the netherworld and perdition, is thus always in search of new riches and delights.

21. The more precious the metal, the hotter the fire needed to remove all the dross and impurities from it. In the same way, the more admirable and praiseworthy a man is, the more exacting are the standards of behavior expected of him; and hence, for his purification and refinement, a Torah scholar faces far greater afflictions from Heaven than others, even for minor and inadvertent transgressions.

PROVERBS 27:22-27

אֶת־הָאֱוִיל ׀ בַּמַּכְתֵּשׁ בְּתוֹךְ הָרִיפוֹת בַּעֲלִי לֹא־תָסוּר
מֵעָלָיו אִוַּלְתּוֹ:

כג יָדֹעַ תֵּדַע פְּנֵי צֹאנֶךָ שִׁית לִבְּךָ לַעֲדָרִים: כִּי לֹא לְעוֹלָם חֹסֶן
וְאִם־נֵזֶר לְדוֹר דוֹר: גָּלָה חָצִיר וְנִרְאָה־דֶשֶׁא וְנֶאֶסְפוּ עִשְּׂבוֹת
הָרִים: כְּבָשִׂים לִלְבוּשֶׁךָ וּמְחִיר שָׂדֶה עַתּוּדִים: וְדֵי ׀ חֲלֵב עִזִּים
לְלַחְמְךָ לְלֶחֶם בֵּיתֶךָ וְחַיִּים לְנַעֲרוֹתֶיךָ:

22. Forever insisting on his doubts of the disciplining laws of moral wisdom, the skeptic remains incorrigible: No amount of affliction can "refine" him and remove the "dross" from him. He is irredeemable. On the other hand, a *kᵉsil*, a fool who knows the validity of moral wisdom but will not let it interfere with his amoral pleasures, can be re-educated by Heaven's punishment; and so too a *pethi*, a simpleton who lets himself be swayed by others, unthinkingly. Now wheat and barley must be pounded in a mortar to remove the chaff, because it is strongly attached. Even if a skeptic realizes that Heaven is "pounding" him for the same purpose, as it were, and he sees others thus repenting, he remains intransigent with his doubts and denials.

23. Do not leave your business affairs to others. Give them close personal attention and invest effort to make them yield profits, like sheep producing whole flocks.

24. With the greatest fortune, a person can yet be reduced to poverty; and even if he has been crowned for life, to spend his

mortar with a pestle, his skepticism will not depart from him.

²³ Know well the condition of your sheep; give your attention to your flocks. ²⁴ For a treasure is not forever; and does the crown endure for all generations? ²⁵ When the hay is mown, and tender grass shows itself, and the herbs of the mountain are gathered in: ²⁶ there will be lambs for your clothing, and goats the price for a field; ²⁷ and goat's milk enough for your food, for the food of your household; and maintenance for your maidens.

years in royal pomp and wealth, there is no certainty that his children will inherit the throne.

25-27. If you gather the hay from your field for fodder when your livestock must be kept in the barn (in the winter), and there is grass in the field for pasture in fair weather, and in addition you gather fodder from the mountains, where your livestock cannot go—you will have prosperity: lamb's wool provides clothing; by the sale of goats a field can be bought; and goat's milk can provide healthy, nourishing food for everyone in the home, even the servant-girls who eat there only occasionally. (Hence, following verse 23, industriousness is both necessary and rewarding.)

כח

א נָ֣סוּ וְאֵין־רֹדֵ֣ף רָשָׁ֑ע
וְצַדִּיקִ֗ים כִּכְפִ֥יר יִבְטָֽח׃
ב בְּפֶ֣שַֽׁע אֶ֭רֶץ רַבִּ֣ים שָׂרֶ֑יהָ וּבְאָדָ֥ם מֵבִ֥ין
יֹ֝דֵ֗עַ כֵּ֣ן יַאֲרִֽיךְ׃
ג גֶּ֣בֶר רָ֭שׁ וְעֹשֵׁ֣ק דַּלִּ֑ים מָטָ֥ר סֹ֝חֵ֗ף וְאֵ֣ין לָֽחֶם׃
ד עֹזְבֵ֣י תֽ֭וֹרָה יְהַלְל֣וּ רָשָׁ֑ע וְשֹׁמְרֵ֥י ת֝וֹרָ֗ה יִתְגָּ֥רוּ בָֽם׃
ה אַנְשֵׁי־רָ֭ע לֹא־יָבִ֣ינוּ מִשְׁפָּ֑ט וּמְבַקְשֵׁ֥י יְ֝הוָ֗ה יָבִ֥ינוּ כֹֽל׃
ו טֽוֹב־רָ֭שׁ הוֹלֵ֣ךְ בְּתֻמּ֑וֹ מֵעִקֵּ֥שׁ דְּ֝רָכַ֗יִם וְה֣וּא עָשִֽׁיר׃
ז נוֹצֵ֣ר תּ֭וֹרָה

1. The anxiety of the wicked is so infectious that it will spread in a crowd, even where there is only one wicked man in a large number of decent people. The righteous, on the other hand, have a deep confidence even when really in danger from pursuers.

2. When a nation rebels against its rightful ruler, it may find itself suffering under the multiple tyrannies of many petty princes. Then, only if a wise man can be found who understands how to restore stability, will political and social health return to the land.

3. At times the wretchedly poor revolt and gain the upper hand, and in the ensuing state of anarchy they despoil "the impoverished," the people who lose their property in the maelstrom. This is simply a torrent that benefits no one but sweeps everyone and everything before it to destruction.

4. In times of turbulence (see verses 2–3), the wicked rise to positions of power, and then those who have abandoned the Torah with its moral values and Divine truth will envy the men of violence who have come to the top. Those who remain true to His Torah, however, will resist this new system in which the corrupt has become admirable.

5. Evil men praise wickedness, because they are blind to the

28 ¹ They flee when no one pursues, [with] a wicked person; but the righteous are as confident as a young lion. ² For the insurrection of a land, many are its ruling princes; but by an understanding man who knows to make sound order, it will recover. ³ An upsurge of the indigent oppressing the impoverished is like a sweeping rain that leaves no food. ⁴ Those who forsake Torah praise the wicked, but those who keep Torah contend with them. ⁵ Men of evil do not understand justice, but those who seek HA-SHEM understand everything.

⁶ Better is a poor man who walks in his steadfast integrity than someone perverse in his ways, though he be rich. ⁷ A wise son keeps Torah

---

Almighty's system of justice, which dooms the wicked to punishment. By the Torah, however, the righteous know His system of justice, and they give the wicked short shrift. Alternatively, the wicked cannot appreciate the value of true justice and decency, preferring their own murderous system of jungle law.

6. Two ways in life are possible: One begins in thorny difficulty and struggle, but pursued in integrity it ends in gratifying equanimity and rightness. Taken steadfastly by the poor, this road leads straight to its rewarding goal. The other way, taken by the unbred rich, is mellifluously smooth in the beginning, but it ends in vexing frustration and failure.

7. A wise son refrains from indulging his passions but is faithful to the Torah, which curbs the enjoyment of his desires. The

PROVERBS 28:8-13

ח בֵּן מֵבִין וְרֹעֶה זוֹלְלִים יַכְלִים אָבִיו: מַרְבֶּה הוֹנוֹ בְּנֶשֶׁךְ
ט וְתַרְבִּית לְחוֹנֵן דַּלִּים יִקְבְּצֶנּוּ: מֵסִיר אָזְנוֹ מִשְּׁמֹעַ תּוֹרָה גַּם־
י תְּפִלָּתוֹ תּוֹעֵבָה: מַשְׁגֶּה יְשָׁרִים ׀ בְּדֶרֶךְ רָע בִּשְׁחוּתוֹ הוּא־יִפּוֹל
יא וּתְמִימִים יִנְחֲלוּ־טוֹב: חָכָם בְּעֵינָיו אִישׁ עָשִׁיר וְדַל מֵבִין
יב יַחְקְרֶנּוּ: בַּעֲלֹץ צַדִּיקִים רַבָּה תִפְאָרֶת וּבְקוּם רְשָׁעִים יְחֻפַּשׂ
יג אָדָם: מְכַסֶּה פְשָׁעָיו לֹא יַצְלִיחַ וּמוֹדֶה וְעֹזֵב יְרֻחָם: אַשְׁרֵי

dissolute, rebellious son shames his father, for with his actions, it would have been better had he never been born, as his life leads to the waste and destruction of an outlaw.

8. This is an illustration of the principle in verse 6, of the two ways in life. One man spends his youth accumulating wealth by unscrupulous means, but in the end he loses it and becomes poor. Another is consistently kind and generous to the poor whatever the cost, even if his way in life is thorny and uphill; but in the end he acquires the wealth of the first man, and ends his days in ease.

9. If a person makes himself deaf to the Divine words of the Torah, e.g. he leaves a Torah lesson even if it is because the time for prayer has come, he is ignoring the source of eternal life, and nothing can compensate for that loss. Torah bestows eternal life, but prayer only temporary help.

10. Decent and good by nature, the upright rely on their insight and understanding in their way of life, without particularly studying the laws of moral wisdom. Hence they can be led astray — but woe betide anyone who tries to mislead them (cf. 26:27). On the other hand, *t^emimim*, the steadfastly sincere, serve HA-SHEM loyally without regard to their own understanding, and thus are not vulnerable to plausible lies; and in the end they are well rewarded.

faithfully, but the companion of gluttons shames his father. ⁸ He who increases his wealth by interest and usury gathers it for one who is beneficent to the poor. ⁹ If one turns away his ear from hearing Torah, even his prayer is an abomination. ¹⁰ He who leads the upright astray on an evil road will himself fall into his pit; but the steadfastly sincere shall inherit good. ¹¹ A rich man is wise in his own eyes, but an understanding impoverished man will probe him through. ¹² When the righteous exult, there is great glory; but when the wicked ascend, a man becomes disguised. ¹³ He who covers up his willful transgressions will not prosper, but one who confesses and forsakes them shall obtain mercy.

11–12. Earlier (26:12) we were well taught that anyone "wise in his own eyes" is worse than a fool: he cuts off all hope of change and rectification. The fool (*kᵉsil*) knows the laws of wisdom, but won't let them interfere with his pleasures. The self-styled "wise man," however, thinks that his ways *are* the ways of wisdom, and he scorns Divine moral law. One form of this disease occurs in a wealthy man who sees his wealth as a validation of his amoral way of life. But a poor man who can observe and analyze will know that his success is no real good fortune, but mere animal gratification. Truly good fortune and human glory are to be found only in the spiritual joy of the righteous. When the wicked rise to power, the human spiritual element in them is disguised and hidden under the animal surface that is the personality they cultivate.

13. A person who invests all his energy in concealing and

יד אַשְׁרֵי אָדָם מְפַחֵד תָּמִיד וּמַקְשֶׁה לִבּוֹ יִפּוֹל בְּרָעָה: אֲרִי־נֹהֵם וְדֹב
שׁוֹקֵק מוֹשֵׁל רָשָׁע עַל עַם־דָּל:
טו נָגִיד חֲסַר תְּבוּנוֹת וְרַב מַעֲשַׁקּוֹת שֹׂנֵא בֶצַע יַאֲרִיךְ
יָמִים:
יז אָדָם עָשֻׁק בְּדַם־נָפֶשׁ עַד־בּוֹר יָנוּס אַל־יִתְמְכוּ־בוֹ: הוֹלֵךְ
יח תָּמִים יִוָּשֵׁעַ וְנֶעְקַשׁ דְּרָכַיִם יִפּוֹל בְּאֶחָת: עֹבֵד אַדְמָתוֹ יִשְׂבַּע־

disguising his wrongs and faults will ultimately be exposed and shamed for his incorrigible hypocrisy. A man who confesses his sins openly, on the other hand, shows his sincere contrition and will easily find forgiveness and compassion.

14. This verse speaks not of a haunting fear from guilt but of the prudent fear of a man of clear conscience, who is aware of the dangers of evil and acts with due caution. A person who "hardens his heart" (like Pharaoh) experiences punishment for his wrongdoings, yet resists the pressure to fear the Almighty (even for his own practical benefit).

15. The term *nohém* (roaring) denotes a lion's roar when it lacks for prey and is therefore at its most dangerous. Both it and a bear thirsting for blood metaphorically describe a wicked ruler whose people are too poor to provide him with the wealth and pleasures he lusts for.

16. A tyrant who is also a fool will not allow a class of successful merchants to develop in his country, to pay taxes and enrich both him and the country: he kills them right away and confiscates their wealth. In such a state, only those who earn no great fortunes will live long; the others are instant prey of the ruler's avarice.

17. The wealthy merchants to which verse 16 refers are indeed

¹⁴ Fortunate is a person who fears always, but one who hardens his heart shall fall into misfortune.
¹⁵ A roaring lion and a bloodthirsty bear; such is a wicked ruler over an impoverished people.
¹⁶ A nobleman who lacks understanding is also a great oppressor; then one who hates profit shall prolong his days.
¹⁷ When a man is persecuted to his very life-blood, he shall flee fugitive up to the pit; none will support him. ¹⁸ He who walks in steadfast integrity will be saved; but one who is perverse in his ways shall fall in every one [of them]. ¹⁹ He who tills his land will have bread to satisfaction,

doomed: The tyrannical ruler wants not only such a person's property but also his life. If he wants to flee, others will not help him: they will pay with their lives if they do (cf. the plight of Navoth in I Kings 21).

18. At every turn in life we can act humbly or proudly, kindly or cruelly: two ways are open (*d^erachayim*, "ways," denotes a pair of opposite roads that can be taken). The choice must be made with wisdom and discrimination: for instance, we should be humble toward the righteous, and proud before the wicked. Taken with steadfast integrity, such a way keeps a person safe from life's disasters. If, however, one always chooses perversely between life's alternatives—for example, if he is humble to the wicked and haughty to the righteous; generously accommodating toward transgression but disdainful toward the Torah's commandments—every such choice of path will bring him to grief. The text goes on to give an example.

19–20. Industriousness and laziness are opposite life-ways. An

כ לֶחֶם וּמְרַדֵּף רֵיקִים יִשְׂבַּע־רִישׁ: אִישׁ אֱמוּנוֹת רַב־בְּרָכוֹת וְאָץ
כא לְהַעֲשִׁיר לֹא יִנָּקֶה: הַכֵּר־פָּנִים לֹא־טוֹב וְעַל־פַּת־לֶחֶם יִפְשַׁע־
כב גָּבֶר: נִבֳהָל לַהוֹן אִישׁ רַע עָיִן וְלֹא־יֵדַע כִּי־חֶסֶר יְבֹאֶנּוּ: מוֹכִיחַ
כג אָדָם אַחֲרַי חֵן יִמְצָא מִמַּחֲלִיק לָשׁוֹן: גּוֹזֵל ׀ אָבִיו וְאִמּוֹ וְאֹמֵר
כה אֵין־פָּשַׁע חָבֵר הוּא לְאִישׁ מַשְׁחִית: רְחַב־נֶפֶשׁ יְגָרֶה מָדוֹן

industrious farmer works hard on his land and is rewarded with rich harvests. He is "a faithful man," dependably loyal to his duties. His opposite, a lazy man, rejects hard work, preferring to "chase phantoms": he will have to suffer poverty as a result. There is, however, also a good form of "idleness": the calm passive trust that the hard-working man has in the Almighty that He will send blessing on what he plants. And there is, as well, a bad form of industriousness: the eager readiness of a lazy man to get rich quick, by whatever methods come to hand, even theft or murder. This is an example of the ways in which qualities can become either constructive or destructive depending on the context and the purpose.

21. Even if you know someone to be a moral and reliable person, do not depend on his reputation and treat him too generously, for poverty can make a man do unexpected things.

22. A miserly man "of evil eye" who is unwilling to share his wealth with others but only "hastens after riches" will finally lose everything to the wicked who will arise and strip him of all he owns (cf. 22:7–9). The want and hunger that the poor suffer because he is so miserly "will come upon him" and leave him poverty-stricken.

23. Ordinarily it would seem that a person who rebukes no one for his sins thus gains popularity, and all the more so if he

but one who pursues phantoms shall have his fill of poverty. [20] A faithful man will have blessings aplenty, but one who hastens to get rich will not go unpunished. [21] To recognize favorably is not good, for a man will transgress for a piece of bread. [22] A man of evil eye hastens after riches, and does not know that want will come upon him. [23] He who rebukes a man will afterward find more favor than one who flatters with his tongue. [24] If one robs his father or his mother, and he says, "It is no transgression," he is the companion of a man of destruction. [25] A person of greedy spirit stirs up quarrel, but one who puts his trust in HA-

indulges in flattery. Ultimately, however, when Heaven's punishment strikes and retribution comes for the crimes of society, people will realize that those who could have rebuked them and refrained, preferring to give flattery, did them no good; it was the so-called prophet of doom who sincerely had their good at heart.

24. This is a most extreme example of flattery. Stealing from one's own parents is the worst possible crime; a loyal son should guard their property for them. Yet the flatterer assures this scoundrel that it is no crime! He is in effect the equal of a vandal, as he aids and abets the sinful son; and he will be "a companion," a full partner, to the destruction that will inevitably befall this criminal.

25. A person dominated by boundless desires and cravings is doomed to frustration and bitterness, and then he accuses the Almighty of having created the world for misfortune and misery. On the other hand, a man of faith who believes

כו וּבֹטֵחַ עַל־יהוה יְדֻשָּׁן: בּוֹטֵחַ בְּלִבּוֹ הוּא כְסִיל וְהוֹלֵךְ בְּחָכְמָה
כז הוּא יִמָּלֵט: נוֹתֵן לָרָשׁ אֵין מַחְסוֹר וּמַעְלִים עֵינָיו רַב־מְאֵרוֹת:
כח בְּקוּם רְשָׁעִים יִסָּתֵר אָדָם וּבְאָבְדָם יִרְבּוּ צַדִּיקִים:

implicitly that the Creator will provide all his needs, makes do with what he has, and he derives true comfort and pleasure at finding himself provided for.

26. Moral wisdom educates a man, so that he can escape the fantasies and impulses of desire that fill his imagining heart. To *trust* in this heart, this breeding-ground of evil, as a guide in life is the height of folly. Rather than evade the laws of moral wisdom like this fool (cf. 18:2), a sensible person will utilize them to battle and overcome his amoral impulses.

27. Giving charity never brings a person any real loss: "for on account of this matter HA-SHEM your God will bless you" (Deuteronomy 15:10). The reverse is true: for turning a blind

SHEM shall be abundantly gratified. ²⁶ He who trusts in his own heart is a fool, but one who walks in wisdom—he shall escape. ²⁷ He who gives to the poor shall have no lack, but one who hides his eyes will suffer many a curse. ²⁸ When the wicked rise, a human being hides himself; but when they perish, the righteous increase.

eye to the poor, not only is there an abysmal lack of Divine blessing, but "many a curse" strikes home.

28. When lawless men come to power, those who remain truly human (in the Divine image) are obliged to hide themselves, for that is a time when God's ways are abandoned and men behave like animals. Afterwards, however, retribution falls on the wicked, and everyone recognizes His providence and power, whereupon the numbers of "righteous" God-fearing men increase.

אִישׁ תּוֹכָחוֹת ‎ כט

ב מַקְשֶׁה־עֹרֶף פֶּתַע יִשָּׁבֵר וְאֵין מַרְפֵּא: בִּרְבוֹת צַדִּיקִים יִשְׂמַח
ג הָעָם וּבִמְשֹׁל רָשָׁע יֵאָנַח עָם: אִישׁ־אֹהֵב חָכְמָה יְשַׂמַּח אָבִיו
ד וְרֹעֶה זוֹנוֹת יְאַבֶּד־הוֹן: מֶלֶךְ בְּמִשְׁפָּט יַעֲמִיד אָרֶץ וְאִישׁ
ה תְּרוּמוֹת יֶהֶרְסֶנָּה: גֶּבֶר מַחֲלִיק עַל־רֵעֵהוּ רֶשֶׁת פּוֹרֵשׂ עַל־
ו פְּעָמָיו: בְּפֶשַׁע אִישׁ רָע מוֹקֵשׁ וְצַדִּיק יָרוּן וְשָׂמֵחַ: יֹדֵעַ צַדִּיק

1. A person can generally be brought to his senses by rational argument and proof that he has taken a wrong way in life — unless he is argumentative and disputes every point of moral force. Then afflictions come, till the fear of punishment deters him. If, however, he "hardens his neck" and stubbornly disregards this too, he becomes spiritually incurable and will simply "be broken."

2. When a state is governed with justice, the people live in peace and ease. A righteous governor, unlike the wicked, does not "rule" in the usual sense, in autocratic tyranny, but by wise consultation; and under his humane regime "the righteous are augmented" either in number or in status. A wicked ruler, harshly autocratic, favors no one, and the people feel accursed.

3. It is well to use one's natural capacity for love to develop a liking for such good qualities as wisdom, goodness and justice. When moral wisdom comes to rule his heart, a person then brings his father happiness. If, however, the inclination to love is devoted to harlots, one will simply squander his father's wealth. In the metaphorical sense, if someone loves alien, amoral wisdom indiscriminately, he will lose the "wealth" of his soul, the virtue and probity gathered from the laws of true moral wisdom.

4. A king's function has always been to establish social justice

29 ¹ A disputatious man who hardens his neck shall suddenly be broken, and beyond healing. ² When the righteous are augmented, the people rejoice; but when the wicked rule, the people sigh. ³ He who loves wisdom makes his father rejoice, but one who keeps company with harlots wastes his wealth. ⁴ A king by justice establishes the land, yet a man of Heaven's gifts can demolish it. ⁵ A man who smoothly brushes away his neighbor's wrongdoing spreads a net for his feet. ⁶ In the transgression of an evil man, there is a snare; but a righteous man will sing and rejoice. ⁷ A righteous

in the land, while of yore the *kohén gadol* (high priest) was always in charge of the religious life of the nation and the people. Even if a king functions properly, but a *kohén gadol* and his underlings are interested only in *t^erumoth*, the gifts due them by the Torah's law, not caring a bit for the people's religious life, they can tear down everything the king builds up. Without a sound structure of worship, study and faith, the best Jewish social system is unstable.

5. The apparently superfluous *al* in the Hebrew (disregarded in the usual English rendering, "A man who flatters his neighbor") is connected with *a-vel*, wrongdoing. If with a smooth tongue of flattery a person airily dismisses someone's evil deeds as nothing, he prepares the way for that man to become deeply ensnared in the trap of utter evil, to his destruction.

6. Criminal acts are themselves the snare that entraps a man of evil; and then the righteous are glad, because Divine justice is demonstrated most clearly by the evident connection between crime and punishment; and this is the most effective deterrent to sin.

ח דִּין־דַּלִּים רָשָׁע לֹא־יָבִין דָּעַת׃ אַנְשֵׁי לָצוֹן יָפִיחוּ קִרְיָה וַחֲכָמִים
ט יָשִׁיבוּ אָף׃ אִישׁ־חָכָם נִשְׁפָּט אֶת־אִישׁ אֱוִיל וְרָגַז וְשָׂחַק וְאֵין
י נָחַת׃ אַנְשֵׁי דָמִים יִשְׂנְאוּ־תָם וִישָׁרִים יְבַקְשׁוּ נַפְשׁוֹ׃ כָּל־רוּחוֹ
יב יוֹצִיא כְסִיל וְחָכָם בְּאָחוֹר יְשַׁבְּחֶנָּה׃ מֹשֵׁל מַקְשִׁיב עַל־דְּבַר־

7. Whereas *mishpat* ("judgment") denotes a person's clear rights or due under the law, *din* conveys a claim on which the law is as yet unclear. Involved with justice and charity, a righteous person will know even the *din* of the poor—what they are entitled to, although the law about it is unclear. In contrast, a wicked man will not even have any awareness and comprehension of "knowledge": clear facts of definite law.

8. The verb *yafichu* (enflame) literally means "blow, infuse," but it also connotes *mapach nefesh*, dismaying anguish, and *pach*, a snare. Scoffing cynicism spreads a destructive, inflammatory atmosphere of slander and lies that breeds anguish and despair. Men who act according to the laws of moral wisdom, however, know how to bring a healing calm and avert the Divine wrath that the cynical scoffers incur for the city, by inspiring repentance and prayer.

9. Any attempt to argue and discuss religion or morality with a "doubting Thomas" who does not accept the moral law is a frustrating experience. Talk with a *k^esil*, a "fool" who won't let the moral law interfere with his pleasures, warrants a show of anger at his conscious defiance and evasion. With a *pethi*, a credulous simpleton with no understanding of moral law, a wise man can use laughter to explain things in good humor. With the skeptic he may grow angry when he finds the man understanding the laws of moral wisdom, yet rejecting them out of doubt; and he may turn to humor and cajolery, realizing that the man is not willful. Yet neither approach will bring the wise man *nachath*, contentment or satisfaction; and *nachath* also

man knows the lawful claim of the poor; a wicked man will not apprehend knowledge. ⁸ Men of scorn enflame a city, but wise men turn away wrath. ⁹ If a wise man disputes with a skeptical man, he will be vexed and laugh, but will have no contentment. ¹⁰ Men of blood hate one who is steadfastly sincere, and upright men; they seek his life. ¹¹ A fool expresses all his spirit, but a wise man quells it back within. ¹² If a ruler listens to

connotes *no-ach*, "easy, convenient," and *hanchoth*, "lead, guide": There is simply no easy way to guide the skeptic aright. Again, whether the Almighty punishes him (in "anger") or deals lovingly with him (in "good-humored laughter") his doubts about Divine providence will remain.

10. Alternatively this can mean that upright, decent people hate "men of blood" who seek to kill an innocent person of steadfast integrity. They will intervene on his behalf, to defend him.

11. The "spirit" denotes the imagination that fills the mind with fantasies of egotistic gratification. Ignoring moral wisdom in favor of his sensual pleasures, the fool (*kᵉsil*) gives active vent to every whim of his unrestrained imagination. The wise man, who lives in accordance with moral law, however, puts a rein on these fantasies, so that they play no significant role in his conscious life.

12. If the sovereign head of a realm pays heed to lies, all his officers and servitors will be infected by the "fashion" of lying and slander, till the whole court is corrupted. Metaphorically, this refers to the inner world of a man: If a person's heart "rules" in wise morality and he refuses to listen to lies from the

יג שָׁקֶר כָּל־מְשָׁרְתָיו רְשָׁעִים׃ רָשׁ וְאִישׁ תְּכָכִים נִפְגָּשׁוּ מֵאִיר־
יד עֵינֵי שְׁנֵיהֶם יְהוָה׃ מֶלֶךְ שׁוֹפֵט בֶּאֱמֶת דַּלִּים כִּסְאוֹ לָעַד יִכּוֹן׃
טו שֵׁבֶט וְתוֹכַחַת יִתֵּן חָכְמָה וְנַעַר מְשֻׁלָּח מֵבִישׁ אִמּוֹ׃ בִּרְבוֹת
טז רְשָׁעִים יִרְבֶּה־פָּשַׁע וְצַדִּיקִים בְּמַפַּלְתָּם יִרְאוּ׃ יַסֵּר בִּנְךָ וִינִיחֶךָ וְיִתֵּן מַעֲדַנִּים לְנַפְשֶׁךָ׃
יח בְּאֵין חָזוֹן יִפָּרַע עָם וְשֹׁמֵר תּוֹרָה אַשְׁרֵהוּ׃ בִּדְבָרִים לֹא־יִוָּסֶר

passions, then the imaginative thoughts that rise into the conscious mind will be healthy ones, in accord with wisdom. If, however, the heart "listens to" amoral "falsehood," it will be served by "ministers" of libertinism and moral aberration. Thus the text continues the theme of verse 11.

13. A midrashic fable relates that since Noah would admit only couples to the ark, he refused poverty admittance; whereupon poverty met deceit coming, and they made a "marriage of convenience," with the understanding that anything gained by deceit would be consumed by poverty. The first part of this verse could well serve as a proof-text. The point, of course, is that neither survives alone in the world: it is a lesson of Divine enlightenment that deceit and mendacity bring no fortune or happiness, and some other way out of poverty must be sought.

14. Justice gives a king's reign stability (29:4, 16:12, Isaiah 32:1). At times people attempt deceit, but if the king goes to great efforts to attain true justice, his reign will endure, just as truth is one of the enduring elements in human life.

15. Both physical punishment and words of discipline, appealing to reason, can make a child grow properly with the laws of moral wisdom. Words alone are generally not enough to counter his powerful fantasies. A permissive upbringing,

falsehood, all his ministers turn wicked. ¹³ A poor and a deceitful man met together; HA-SHEM gives light to the eyes of both. ¹⁴ If a king truthfully judges the poor, his throne shall be established forever. ¹⁵ The rod and reproof give wisdom, but a child left free brings shame to his mother. ¹⁶ When the wicked increase, transgression increases; but the righteous shall witness their fall. ¹⁷ Discipline your son, and he will bring you rest, and will give delight to your soul.
¹⁸ Where there is no vision, a people becomes unrestrained, but one who keeps Torah, fortunate

however, leaving him to himself, is certain to lead to agonizing disaster.

16. The wicked may grow, whether in number or in importance, but finally their time comes, and they fall. The righteous, however, have the foresight to be aware, even at the height of their prosperity, of their impending downfall.

17. A father's excessive indulgence leads to a child's eventual contempt of him, and disturbed family relations. Proper disciplining guidance of the child results in peaceful, loving relations later on; and under the influence of moral wisdom, the child will bring his parents increased affection and honor.

18. When prophecy came to an end in Israel, moral chaos threatened. Without the guiding adjurations and reminders of the prophets, the people seemed ready to run amok. From this time, therefore, faithful observance of the Torah became all-important. Hence the last words of the last prophet, Malachi: "Behold, I am sending you Elijah the prophet... Remember the Torah of Moses My servant..." (Malachi 3:23, 22).

כ ‏עֶבֶד כִּי־יָבִין וְאֵין מַעֲנֶה: חָזִיתָ אִישׁ אָץ בִּדְבָרָיו תִּקְוָה לִכְסִיל
כא ‏מִמֶּנּוּ: מְפַנֵּק מִנֹּעַר עַבְדּוֹ וְאַחֲרִיתוֹ יִהְיֶה מָנוֹן: אִישׁ־אַף יְגָרֶה
כב ‏מָדוֹן וּבַעַל חֵמָה רַב־פָּשַׁע: גַּאֲוַת אָדָם תַּשְׁפִּילֶנּוּ וּשְׁפַל־רוּחַ
כד ‏יִתְמֹךְ כָּבוֹד: חוֹלֵק עִם־גַּנָּב שׂוֹנֵא נַפְשׁוֹ אָלָה יִשְׁמַע וְלֹא יַגִּיד:
כה ‏חֶרְדַּת אָדָם יִתֵּן מוֹקֵשׁ וּבוֹטֵחַ בַּיהוָה יְשֻׂגָּב: רַבִּים מְבַקְשִׁים

19. A slave generally does not respond to moral arguments: even if he understands them, his nature is too physical to achieve self-control without physical discipline. A free man, however, should have enough ability to be influenced by words alone. Metaphorically, this refers to a morally recalcitrant human being who can be persuaded to obey his Creator only by fear of punishment.

20. The *k^esil* (fool) knows the Divine laws of moral wisdom; only the strength of his physical desires prevents him from acquiescing to them. For him there is hope then: let his cravings leave him, and the moral knowledge he has repeatedly thrust away will surface and move him to a rectifying self-control. However, when a man is "hasty with his words" and makes snap conclusions about Divine providence and moral wisdom — for him there is no hope.

21. If a person spoils his young servant because "he is still only a child," not yet grown to his full strength, the owner may find that afterwards all he has for his money is a drain on it (*manon*, rendered as "knave," is related to *ona'a*, "wronging, cheating"): grown to maturity, the servant is now inured to idleness. Metaphorically, this refers to the folly of indulging one's body in youth: The body should be the servant of the soul, and if it is not trained early to labor in Torah and spiritual activity, in maturity it will certainly not submit to the demands of the Divine word.

is he. [19] A bondservant will not be disciplined by words: for though he understands, there will be no submission. [20] Have you seen a man hasty with his words? There is more hope for a fool than for him. [21] Let one pamper his bondservant from childhood, and in the end he will be a knave. [22] An angry man stirs up a litigious quarrel, and a wrathful man abounds in transgression. [23] A person's pride shall bring him low, but one of lowly spirit will sustain honor. [24] He who co-operates with a thief hates his own soul; he hears the adjuration for testimony and discloses nothing. [25] Terror of a human being sets a snare;

22. A man of *af* (anger) has only a surface rage, and while fuming at his opponent seeks to hurt him at the law courts. If, however, a person is possessed by *chéma* (wrath) — if he seethes within with deep resentment, he will seek no legal pretense but will strike out against his enemy without benefit of law or justice.

23. If he preens with pride, a person is blind to any modest evaluation of his true worth: and this itself will bring him to grief; an opposite self-appraisal brings a gratifyingly opposite result (cf. 16:18).

24. Even if a person has stolen nothing himself but is the confidant of a thief, privy to his crimes, he will come to loathe himself. He will hear the court's imprecation on anyone who can testify about a crime of the thief and holds back (see Leviticus 5:1), and he will maintain silence.

25. We have learned previously that "fortunate is a person who

כו פְּנֵי־מוֹשֵׁל וּמֵיהוה מִשְׁפַּט־אִישׁ: תּוֹעֲבַת צַדִּיקִים אִישׁ עָוֶל וְתוֹעֲבַת רָשָׁע יְשַׁר־דָּרֶךְ:

fears always" (28:14). That does not apply, however, to an onset of terror: sudden panic betrays a lack of trust in the Almighty. True faith in Him will lift a person above the fear of any personal calamity.

26. When a person faces a death penalty, he will almost naturally implore the persons in power for mercy; but it is far

but one who puts his trust in HA-SHEM shall be raised on high. ²⁶ Many seek the favor of a ruler, but a man's judgment comes from HA-SHEM. ²⁷ An unjust man is an abomination to the righteous, and someone upright in his way is an abomination to the wicked.

more important to entreat the Almighty: It is He who determines the verdict, by influencing judges and rulers.

27. The conflict of right and wrong, good and evil, is fundamental, uncompromising, and passionate: nothing can mitigate their mutual antagonism and loathing.

PROVERBS 30:1-5

ל

א דִּבְרֵי ׀ אָגוּר בִּן־יָקֶה הַמַּשָּׂא נְאֻם הַגֶּבֶר לְאִיתִיאֵל לְאִיתִיאֵל
ב וְאֻכָל: כִּי בַעַר אָנֹכִי מֵאִישׁ וְלֹא־בִינַת אָדָם לִי: וְלֹא־לָמַדְתִּי
ג חָכְמָה וְדַעַת קְדֹשִׁים אֵדָע: מִי עָלָה־שָׁמַיִם ׀ וַיֵּרַד מִי אָסַף־
ד רוּחַ ׀ בְּחָפְנָיו מִי צָרַר־מַיִם ׀ בַּשִּׂמְלָה מִי הֵקִים כָּל־אַפְסֵי־אָרֶץ
ה מַה־שְּׁמוֹ וּמַה־שֶּׁם־בְּנוֹ כִּי תֵדָע: כָּל־אִמְרַת אֱלוֹהַּ צְרוּפָה

1. In this chapter, King Hezekiah's scribes [see 25:1] copied out the words of a sage called Agur the son of Yakeh, who was in charge of ceremonial music (cf. *massa* in I Chronicles 15:22), in response to questions put to him once by Ithiel, and on another occasion by Ithiel and Ucal, two men of wisdom.

2-3. The two evidently posed questions about the origins of the world, and abstruse details of Creation, in a philosophical quest of metaphysical knowledge; and they propounded theories of their own. Agur replies that the knowledge they seek cannot be attained by human intellect but only by a supernal revelation to men of great sanctity ("the knowledge of holy people"). Modestly he disclaims any such rank or knowledge: he lacks the ascending levels of *chochma*, Divinely revealed (undemonstrable) moral wisdom; *bina*, understanding to absorb and apply this wisdom; and *da'ath*, a clear, palpable grasp of the moral wisdom, which paves the way for Divine bestowal of "the knowledge of holy people." Moreover, he insists he is "boorish" and lacks even the plain good sense of ordinary people, or the simplest conceptions of logic; he has not the common understanding of ordinary persons, and certainly no learned wisdom.

4. The five parts of the verse denote a series of questions on the creation of the universe: (1) How did the two kinds of primary

30

¹ The words of Agur son of Yakeh, the music master; the declaration of the man to Ithiel, to Ithiel and Ucal: ² I am surely too boorish for a man, and have not a human's understanding; ³ and I have not learned wisdom, that I should possess the knowledge of holy people. ⁴ Who has ascended to heaven and descended? Who has gathered the wind in his fists? Who has wrapped up the waters in the garment? Who has established all the ends of the earth? What is his name, and what is his son's name?—You would but know? ⁵ Every word of God is refined; He is a

matter or energy arise which became (respectively) heaven and earth? Who assigned them their places and set their dimensions? (2) Who set the strata of atmosphere around the earth, to make breathing possible? (3) Who ordered the universe by the laws of gravitation and gravity, to give the earth its stability, "hanging" in space? (4) Who gathered the cosmic waters into oceans bounded by land that prevent the earth from being utterly inundated? These questions involve all four basic elements of Creation: fire (heaven), air, water and earth. (5) Finally, the questioner asks about the First Cause and its emanation, the primary Intellect, which two of the classical philosophers called Father and Son. To demand or claim knowledge of all these mysteries, answers Agur, is presumption: they are not accessible to human investigation.

5. In all these questions we must rely on the Torah's testimony, that the cosmos was created *ex nihilo* (from nothing) by the sheer creative Word of God. The Torah's account of Creation is

מָגֵן הוּא לַחֹסִים בּוֹ: אַל־תּוֹסְףְּ עַל־דְּבָרָיו פֶּן־יוֹכִיחַ בְּךָ וְנִכְזָבְתָּ: שְׁתַּיִם שָׁאַלְתִּי מֵאִתָּךְ אַל־תִּמְנַע מִמֶּנִּי בְּטֶרֶם אָמוּת: שָׁוְא ׀ וּדְבַר־כָּזָב הַרְחֵק מִמֶּנִּי רֵאשׁ וָעֹשֶׁר אַל־תִּתֶּן־לִי הַטְרִיפֵנִי לֶחֶם חֻקִּי: פֶּן אֶשְׂבַּע ׀ וְכִחַשְׁתִּי וְאָמַרְתִּי מִי יְהֹוָה וּפֶן־אִוָּרֵשׁ וְגָנַבְתִּי וְתָפַשְׂתִּי שֵׁם אֱלֹהָי:

like precious metal "refined"—pure of every falsehood—while the ancient philosophers achieved at best an alloyed truth. The Creator "is a shield to those who take refuge in Him" and are not led astray by specious philosophizing.

6. We should not try to conjecture about these abstruse matters: Our inadequate knowledge, even about human life—its origins, anatomical details, the relations between the physical and the psychological—can betray us. And if we know so little about these most immediate and humanly relevant matters, how can we presume to speak of the creation of worlds?

7. Agur prays to be granted two requests, so that he may not meet a spiritual death by entanglement, through error, in the spider's webs of the philosophers.

shield to those who take refuge in Him. **⁶** Do not add to His words, lest He rebuke you, and you are found to be a liar.

⁷ Two things I have asked of You; do not deny me them before I die: **⁸** Remove far from me falsehood and a lying word: give me neither poverty nor riches; provide me my allotted bread; **⁹** lest I be full, and deny, and say, "Who is HA-SHEM?" or lest I be poor, and steal, and clasp the name of my God.

8. He pleads that he be granted neither intellectual poverty, which might make him gullible to any baseless and superstitious beliefs, nor intellectual riches, which might make him arrogant, until he overreaches himself in heresies and falsehoods. He asks simply to be given the right measure of intellectual nutriment from the Torah's wisdom — the perfect, most wholesome food for the soul.

9. An excessive wealth of knowledge of what lies behind nature's laws can lead to a denial of the Creator's very existence. Too little intellectual understanding of reality invites superstition and idolatry: we may naïvely adopt ("steal") aberrant foreign notions and attach ("clasp") the Creator's name to them, as valid religious beliefs.

אַל־

יא ‏ תַּלְשֵׁן עֶבֶד אֶל־אֲדֹנָו פֶּן־יְקַלֶּלְךָ וְאָשָׁמְתָּ׃ דּוֹר אָבִיו יְקַלֵּל

10. This too is part of Agur's reply. From here to the end of the chapter, however, the text lends itself to two distinct levels of interpretation: the literal and the symbolic — which are best given separately:

THE LITERAL LEVEL

The background to this chapter concerns a tyrannical idolatrous king of the times who had two wives, daughters of one woman, Aluka (verse 15). These wives corrupted the people, and at their instigation the king imposed ruinous decrees and countless death sentences. It was moreover a time of disastrous drought and wildfires. Now this king, prompted by his wives, had gained power by banishing his own parents from the throne; and he was deposed in turn through a plot initiated by a slave-woman S'mamith (verse 28), who seduced him: Aided by her intrigues, her husband, Alkum (verse 31), led a successful rebellion, murdered the king, and fed his body to the vultures; and the two assumed the throne. Knowing of the brewing

THE SYMBOLIC LEVEL

Taken allegorically, the balance of this chapter is a dialogue between Agur and those heretic philosophers who deny the existence of a Creator and Divine providence and regulation. For them the world arose and exists "naturally," and hence man faces no moral demands and no reward or punishment for his actions. Consequently they would mock all devout faith and worship. [In this commentary to the end of the chapter, words in italic give alternative translations of the Hebrew text, in keeping with the interpretation.]

10. Says Agur, *Do not slander a servant to his Master* — i.e. a loyal servant of the Almighty: for in His watchful supervision

10 Do not inform against a bondservant to his master, lest he curse you, and you are found guilty. **11** This is a generation that curses its father,

THE LITERAL LEVEL

rebellion beforehand, Ithiel and Ucal had asked Agur's advice whether they should reveal everything to the king in time.

10. Agur advises them to keep still: Alkum has always been a loyal bondservant to the king, and he may show himself innocent, whereupon their accusation will boomerang. Unable to prove their charges, they will be sentenced to death. Moreover, explains Agur in the next sentences, the king and his followers deserve their impending fate:

11-14. The whole generation has been corrupted by the king's example in banishing his parents to usurp their throne (verse 11). Blandly convinced of their innocence, the people are immersed in every abomination, haughty and arrogant as they viciously sin against both God and man. They therefore face Divine retribution.

THE SYMBOLIC LEVEL

He will know, and may curse you; and if you lead such a man astray into heresy, you will bear his guilt.

11. Moreover, your heresies may produce *a generation that curses its Father* in heaven, denying as you do any Creator who watches and regulates the world according to human deeds. Nor will this generation have any blessing for "mother earth," the setting for its existence: for it will see the world as a source of corruption and violence, where evil predominates. Such atheists call for no honor to parents, since they consider human existence a curse and hate their own parents for bringing them into life.

יב וְאֶת־אִמּוֹ לֹא יְבָרֵךְ: דּוֹר טָהוֹר בְּעֵינָיו וּמִצֹּאָתוֹ לֹא רֻחָץ: דּוֹר
יג מָה־רָמוּ עֵינָיו וְעַפְעַפָּיו יִנָּשֵׂאוּ: דּוֹר ׀ חֲרָבוֹת שִׁנָּיו וּמַאֲכָלוֹת
מְתַלְּעֹתָיו לֶאֱכֹל עֲנִיִּים מֵאֶרֶץ וְאֶבְיוֹנִים מֵאָדָם:
יד לַעֲלוּקָה ׀ שְׁתֵּי בָנוֹת הַב ׀ הַב שָׁלוֹשׁ הֵנָּה לֹא תִשְׂבַּעְנָה אַרְבַּע
טו לֹא־אָמְרוּ הוֹן: שְׁאוֹל וְעֹצֶר רָחַם אֶרֶץ לֹא־שָׂבְעָה מַּיִם וְאֵשׁ

THE LITERAL LEVEL

15. The avarice of the king's wives (thus symbolized) has brought widespread violence and corruption; but the lust for blood they have unleashed will not be satisfied with the three groups or types described: those who curse their parents, those who are pure in their own eyes, and those whose eyes are lofty. The fourth too, described in verse 14, will be "devoured" in Divine retaliation.

THE SYMBOLIC LEVEL

12. Abandoned to their lusts and perversions, such people see no need to purge themselves of their moral filth. As they acknowledge no Divine authority, they are "pure in their own eyes," insisting that their debased behavior is in accord with nature.

13. With "lofty eyes" they brazenly probe and stare at the mysteries of Creation and phenomena of nature; their "eyelids are lifted up," as they refuse even to blink in awe before the unknowable, infinite domain that is God's alone.

14. Social violence is another result of their perverse, perverted "philosophy": no moral law restrains their murderous rapacious behavior against the poor and the weak.

15. Now Agur explains the conceptions of Aluka, one exponent of the views of the heretical philosophers, which lead to a denial

and does not bless its mother; [12] a generation that is pure in its own eyes, yet has not been washed of its filth; [13] a generation, O how lofty are its eyes, and its eyelids lifted up; [14] a generation whose teeth are swords, and its fangs are knives, to devour the poor from the earth, and the impoverished from humankind.

[15] Aluka (the leech) has two daughters [crying] *Give, give!* With three they will not be satisfied; with four they will not have said *Enough!* [16] *Sh^{e}ol* (the netherworld of the grave), and the realm of

THE LITERAL LEVEL

16. Thus the people were punished by the hell (*sh^{e}ol*) of the reign of these two sisters (that *'otzer* can denote a realm or reign, cf. Judges 18:7; *racham* = strumpet has a similar meaning in Job 24:20); in addition there will be the ravages of drought in the fields and conflagrations in all the cities.

THE SYMBOLIC LEVEL

of the Creator. They believe the world to have evolved of itself from a primary matter (for which *aluka*, "leech," may rather be their symbolic name) which is insatiably destructive to everything it engenders. This is now clarified.

16. "Aluka (the leech) has two daughters" (verse 15): *Sh^{e}ol and the realm of the womb*. The two inherent characteristics of the primary matter of Creation (says this philosopher) is that it brings everything into existence (as a symbolic womb) and makes everything end in perdition (*Sh^{e}ol*). And so (they claim) the four basic elements in the world's creation — earth, water, air and fire — constantly intermingle and interact destructively. ("Water" in the text connotes air as well, since chemically the two are fairly similar.)

יז לֹא־אָמְרָה הוֹן: עַיִן ׀ תִּלְעַג לְאָב וְתָבֻז לִיקֲּהַת אֵם יִקְּרוּהָ
עֹרְבֵי־נַחַל וְיֹאכְלוּהָ בְנֵי־נָשֶׁר:
יח שְׁלֹשָׁה הֵמָּה
יט נִפְלְאוּ מִמֶּנִּי וְאַרְבָּעָ לֹא יְדַעְתִּים: דֶּרֶךְ הַנֶּשֶׁר ׀ בַּשָּׁמַיִם
דֶּרֶךְ נָחָשׁ עֲלֵי צוּר דֶּרֶךְ־אֳנִיָּה בְלֶב־יָם וְדֶרֶךְ גֶּבֶר בְּעַלְמָה:
כ כֵּן ׀ דֶּרֶךְ אִשָּׁה מְנָאָפֶת אָכְלָה וּמָחֲתָה פִיהָ וְאָמְרָה לֹא־
פָעַלְתִּי אָוֶן:

THE LITERAL LEVEL

17. This is the final fate awaiting this king who despised his royal parents. Ravens are totally indifferent to their mother-birds, while eagles are notably faithful to both their mother-birds and their young. Hence the first will bring his death, and the second will benefit from it.

18–20. Now, in four successive parables, Agur deals with the new king and his regime. First he considers the new queen, S‘mamith, the former slave-woman who was adulterously intimate with her master, the previous king, then wiped away all traces of affection and turned traitor against her lover. Three phenomena, says the parable, vanish strikingly without trace:

THE SYMBOLIC LEVEL

17. Agur replies vividly: "The eye" of this philosopher "mocks" the Creator, the Father of all creation who brought the cosmos into being from nothing (*ex nihilo*); and he has only antipathy and acrimony for the primary matter, the "mother" that engendered the universe. With no Creator, no Divine providence, this is a world of pure random chance for him. Hence a dreadful fate will befall him, as if by random chance.

18–20. Agur proves this philosophy fallacious by pointing to

the strumpet; earth did not have its fill of water, and fire did not say *Enough!* [17] The eye that mocks a father, and despises to obey a mother, the ravens of the valley shall pick it out, and the young eagles shall eat it.

[18] Three things are too wondrous for me; four I do not know: [19] the way of the eagle in the sky, the way of a serpent on a rock, the way of a ship in the midst of the sea; and the way of a man with a young woman. [20] So is the way of an adulterous woman; she eats, and wipes her mouth, and says, "I have done no wickedness."

THE LITERAL LEVEL

the paths made by an eagle, a serpent, and a ship—moving respectively in air, on earth, and in water. But in the fourth of the basic elements of Creation, fire, there is also something that disappears as though it had never been: "the way of a man with a young woman"—when an adulteress denies and expunges her immoral behavior, no trace of the fire of blazing passion remains.

THE SYMBOLIC LEVEL

the mystery of procreation, that keeps every created species in existence. But like other phenomena that leave no trace ("the way of the eagle," etc.) the act of mating is apparently obliterated from consciousness after the fires of passion ("the way of a man," etc.) have died away; it is as though nothing happened; the entire experience can be denied. (An adulterous woman can "eat, wipe her mouth, and say," etc.) Yet this is indisputably a Divine element in the plan of Creation, for the continuity of life.

כא תַּחַת שָׁלוֹשׁ רָגְזָה אֶרֶץ וְתַחַת אַרְבַּע לֹא־תוּכַל שְׂאֵת: תַּחַת
כב עֶבֶד כִּי יִמְלוֹךְ וְנָבָל כִּי יִשְׂבַּע־לָחֶם: תַּחַת שְׂנוּאָה כִּי תִבָּעֵל
וְשִׁפְחָה כִּי־תִירַשׁ גְּבִרְתָּהּ:
כה אַרְבָּעָה הֵם קְטַנֵּי־אָרֶץ וְהֵמָּה חֲכָמִים מְחֻכָּמִים: הַנְּמָלִים עַם

THE LITERAL LEVEL

21–23. In the second of his four parables, Agur turns his attention to the new "royal" couple on the throne. Three outrages, says he, make the very earth tremble: (1) a slave has seized sovereignty from his master; (2) a miserable wretch has become opulent; he is now "filled with food"; yet he remains a wretch, using none of his new-found wealth to help the poor; (3) and as for the new queen, she became odious and hateful by

---

THE SYMBOLIC LEVEL

21–23. Three psychological states, continues Agur, are outrages against a person's proper way of being; and there is a fourth, worst of all: (1) instinctual, uninhibited imagination should be "bondservant" (subservient) to the rational intellect. If the "bondservant reigns" and has the upper hand, lies and illusions will abound in the mind, and the person will become either a skeptic, doubting and scorning every moral truth, or a *pethi* (simpleton), to believe every nonsense. (2) The "wretch" (*naval*) accumulates no laws of moral wisdom but only wretched foolish notions, and imagines himself "filled with the food" of true wisdom. This is the type that is "wise in his own eyes" (26:12, 28:11). (3) When amoral fantasies and perverse tendencies dominate the heart, producing destructive emotions, such as anger, covetousness, arrogance and envy, these become like *an odious woman when she is taken to wife*—controlling "partners" in life—instead of the laws of moral wisdom, which should really be cherished, since they impose harmony among the elements of the psyche. (4) Worst of all is the type that

²¹ Under three things the earth trembles, and under four it cannot endure: ²² under a bondservant when he reigns; and a wretch when he is filled with food; ²³ under an odious woman when she is taken by a man, and a slave-woman that becomes heir to her mistress.

²⁴ Four are small upon the earth, but they are schooled in wisdom: ²⁵ the ants are a people not

THE LITERAL LEVEL

her immoral behavior and vile deeds. A married woman, she became the former king's paramour; and now, worst of all, in blatant usurpation she has "inherited" the throne of her mistress.

THE SYMBOLIC LEVEL

abandons Divine wisdom and the Torah (the proper, ideal "mistress" of one's spiritual "house") and prefers the "slave-woman" of false philosophies that have arisen in human history. This is the "malevolent haughty man" of 21:24, who becomes a willful miscreant.

24. In contrast to the four types just described, Agur notes four small animals with impressive faculties that are not absolutely necessary for their survival, but can ideally teach a human being wisdom.

25. The ant requires very little food for its sustenance, yet it gathers provisions all summer for the coming winter, far in excess of its needs. Thus humans can learn to gather wisdom throughout their lifetime, never complacently deciding, like the "wretch" of verse 22, that they are "filled with food" and have enough.

כו לֹא־עַז וַיָּכִינוּ בַקַּיִץ לַחְמָם: שְׁפַנִּים עַם לֹא־עָצוּם וַיָּשִׂימוּ
כז בַסֶּלַע בֵּיתָם: מֶלֶךְ אֵין לָאַרְבֶּה וַיֵּצֵא חֹצֵץ כֻּלּוֹ: שְׂמָמִית
בְּיָדַיִם תְּתַפֵּשׂ וְהִיא בְּהֵיכְלֵי מֶלֶךְ:
כט שְׁלֹשָׁה הֵמָּה מֵיטִיבֵי צָעַד וְאַרְבָּעָה מֵיטִבֵי לָכֶת: לַיִשׁ גִּבּוֹר

THE LITERAL LEVEL

24–28. Agur's third parable focuses on S‛mamith, the queen. Though one of earth's small, insignificant human beings, she gained great power by the plots she brewed, till she reached the throne "in the king's palaces." Her Hebrew namesake, the spider, exudes a material which it "seizes with her hands" and spins into a web; and thus it can dwell even in a royal palace. So she "exuded" vile schemes from her mind, which she spun into webs of intrigue, and thus she caught the king in her net of endearments, and now ensnared the queen's very throne. Agur finds three analogous small creatures in nature, whose wise and

---

THE SYMBOLIC LEVEL

26. The strengthless rock-badger could well find safety from its natural enemies by burrowing into the earth and settling there. Yet the Creator gave it the instinct to make its haven in mighty crags and rocks. Thus should a human being build his inner world on the mighty foundations of intellect and reason, and not on phantoms of the imagination, that can only bring a distorting skepticism and foolishness. This is the reverse of having "the bondservant reign" (verse 22).

27. Though it exposes them to the danger of mass destruction, the leaderless locusts fly only in one indissoluble group — to teach us that all the faculties of the psyche should be united and welded harmoniously, under the "rule" of moral law. This is the psychological state opposite to "an odious woman taken to wife" (verse 23), in which inner forces inimical to moral wisdom dominate, in psychological anarchy and conflict.

strong, yet they prepare their food in the summer; ²⁶ *the rock-badgers are a folk not mighty, yet they make their houses in the crags;* ²⁷ *the locusts have no king, yet they all go out in solid cluster;* ²⁸ *Sᵉmamith (the spider) seizes with her hands, and she is in a king's palaces.*

²⁹ *Three are outstanding in their gait, four are*

THE LITERAL LEVEL

wily instincts bring them great advantage: the diligent ants with their provision of food for the winter; the rock-badgers with their remote, inaccessible abodes; and the locusts with their organized mass formations. They may symbolize three peoples, all subjected to Sᵉmamith's nefarious rule: (1) those who were diligent in amassing wealth; (2) those who built themselves strong fortress towns; (3) those who lived independently, free of the king's rule, strongly united under one religion.

THE SYMBOLIC LEVEL

28. The spider spins its flimsy, ugly web from its own emitted material; hence, even if "she is in king's palaces," it is removed and killed. Similarly, a man may presume to construct out of his own mind a system of philosophy and conjecture, which he imagines to be a mighty edifice. Yet we exist in the Divine "King's palaces," the mental realm of Torah, if we will but see it. If one insists on his own philosophical quests and conclusions, he does so to his own spiritually fatal detriment — by making "a slave-woman" of fallacious, heretical ideas "heir to her mistress" (verse 23) of proper religious faith.

29. *Three*, says Agur now, *do well in their tread, and four do well in their stride.* With three faculties a person can capably progress and succeed in observing the Torah's commandments, and a

לא בַּבְּהֵמָה וְלֹא־יָשׁוּב מִפְּנֵי־כֹל: זַרְזִיר מָתְנַיִם אוֹ־תָיִשׁ וּמֶלֶךְ
לב אַלְקוּם עִמּוֹ: אִם־נָבַלְתָּ בְהִתְנַשֵּׂא וְאִם־זַמּוֹתָ יָד לְפֶה: כִּי
לג מִיץ חָלָב יוֹצִיא חֶמְאָה וּמִיץ־אַף יוֹצִיא דָם וּמִיץ אַפַּיִם יוֹצִיא
רִיב:

THE LITERAL LEVEL

29–31. The last parable is a scornful appraisal of Alkum, the slave turned king. The lion's strength makes it king of the animals; the greyhound has a regal status by virtue of its speed and agility in the hunt. The he-goat, however, marches proudly at the head of a flock only because it is the sole male; the rest are female. Similarly, Alkum had neither strength and courage, nor agility and cleverness in political action; he came to the head of his country solely on the coat-tails of his wife.

32–33. Says Agur to this slave-turned-king: If you have become a vile scoundrel in ascending to the throne (see verse

---

THE SYMBOLIC LEVEL

fourth can bring achievements in the mind's search for life's verities.

30. The lion represents inner strength to battle and overcome physical desires and animal cravings. Mustering such inner power, a person will not transgress a single one of the Torah's prohibitions.

31. The swift, eager greyhound denotes an enthusiasm and alacrity to observe the Torah's positive commandments, never giving way to laziness. The he-goat symbolizes the male principle, the active force and initiative, which should be imposed on the passive physical elements of one's being. Thus the "male" should "stride ahead" and take the lead with vigor and energy. *And with him a king proof against uprising*: With this, the intellect and its rational faculties should rule and impose control over all the inner forces, allowing no "uprising"

outstanding in their stride: [30] the lion, which is mightiest among beasts, and does not turn away for anyone; [31] the greyhound; otherwise the he-goat, and King Alkum with him. [32] If you became a wretch in your ascendency, and if you devised evil, hand upon mouth, [33] well now, the pressing of milk produces butter, and the pressing of the nose produces blood; and the pressing of anger produces rancorous discord.

THE LITERAL LEVEL

22), you were the same before. Though you plotted rebellion in secret ("hand upon mouth") and succeeded, know that churning milk brings butter to the top, an element of fine quality; but pressing the nose with its repellent discharge can produce only nauseating blood. And now, as the new king presses and seethes with anger, he will produce only rancorous, mutinous discord and unrest in the land, fomenting revolt and anarchy.

THE SYMBOLIC LEVEL

by any physical urges or impulses. Then life's truths can be grasped by the mind's pursuit.

32. Finally Agur warns Ithiel and Ukal that if they find themselves deteriorating spiritually ("if you have become a wretch") it will be because of "your ascendency": their high-flown heretical speculations about the mysteries of Creation and existence. *If you have speculated* and cogitated deeply on these questions, it is best to keep your thoughts to yourself, "hand upon mouth," and give them no voice.

33. The concentrated essence of true wisdom is a truly fine product of the mind, like butter from milk. But if we press false speculations for their essence, derived from ignominious,

לא

א דִּבְרֵי לְמוּאֵל מֶלֶךְ מַשָּׂא אֲשֶׁר־יִסְּרַתּוּ
ב אִמּוֹ: מַה־בְּרִי וּמַה־בַּר־בִּטְנִי וּמֶה בַּר־נְדָרָי: אַל־תִּתֵּן לַנָּשִׁים
ד חֵילֶךָ וּדְרָכֶיךָ לַמְחוֹת מְלָכִין: אַל לַמְלָכִים ׀ לְמוֹאֵל אַל
ה לַמְלָכִים שְׁתוֹ־יָיִן וּלְרוֹזְנִים אֵי שֵׁכָר: פֶּן־יִשְׁתֶּה וְיִשְׁכַּח
ו מְחֻקָּק וִישַׁנֶּה דִּין כָּל־בְּנֵי־עֹנִי: תְּנוּ־שֵׁכָר לְאוֹבֵד וְיַיִן לְמָרֵי
ח נָפֶשׁ: יִשְׁתֶּה וְיִשְׁכַּח רִישׁוֹ וַעֲמָלוֹ לֹא יִזְכָּר־עוֹד: פְּתַח־
ט פִּיךָ לְאִלֵּם אֶל־דִּין כָּל־בְּנֵי חֲלוֹף: פְּתַח־פִּיךָ שְׁפָט־צֶדֶק
וְדִין עָנִי וְאֶבְיוֹן:

---

delusive sources, we end up with repulsive results, as in the case of those philosophers who fulminate against the providential allotment of good and evil in the world, quarreling angrily with the Almighty, as it were, like the fool in Job 5:2.

---

2. His mother calls Lemuel the "choice," most favored of her sons—on three counts: (1) she devoted most of her instruction and education to him; (2) he was born ("of my womb") with unusual natural advantages, the most gifted of her sons; (3) she made great vows and offered up devout prayers to the Almighty before he was ever conceived, in her hopes for him.

3. Invested with such gifts and hopes, the king should use energies for the service of the Almighty, and not squander his strength in debauchery or in behavior that can make nought of his royal descent and disqualify him from sovereignty.

4–5. Drinking and carousing is "not" for kings: it makes nought (says his mother) of your royal status and prestige. Even if royal counsellors and ministers take wine, they should not indulge in strong drink that leaves them inebriated: for thus they may forget the very laws that should ensure the justice which the poor and the wretched seek at their hands.

31

¹ The words of Lemuel king of Massa, with which his mother disciplined him: ² What, my choice one? and what, O choice one of my womb? and what, O choice one of my vows? ³ Do not give your strength to women, nor your ways to what expunges kings. ⁴ It is not for kings, Lemuel, it is not for kings to drink wine; and for counsellors there should be no strong drink — ⁵ lest one drink and forget what was made law, and pervert the justice due to all the children of misery. ⁶ Give strong drink to him who is perishing, and wine to the bitter in soul: ⁷ Let him drink, and forget his poverty, and remember his misery no more. ⁸ Open your mouth for the mute, in the cause of all the children of vicissitude. ⁹ Open your mouth, judge righteously, and plead the cause of the poor and the helpless.

6–7. Strong drink is good only for a person facing doom, to give him relief in oblivion; and wine should properly be used in quantity only to let the wretched and the poor forget their misery in an induced glow of happiness.

8. A king, however, has a sober, solemn duty to champion and plead the cause of those who cannot speak up for themselves in their helplessness; and he must stand by anyone whose fortunes have suddenly gone down, leaving him the impoverished target of persecution and chicanery, in dire need of a strong advocate in the courts of justice.

9. You must see to it that not only the rich receive justice at law.

PROVERBS 31:10-13

אֵשֶׁת־חַיִל מִי יִמְצָא וְרָחֹק מִפְּנִינִים מִכְרָהּ: בָּטַח בָּהּ לֵב בַּעְלָהּ יא
וְשָׁלָל לֹא יֶחְסָר: גְּמָלַתְהוּ טוֹב וְלֹא־רָע כֹּל יְמֵי חַיֶּיהָ: דָּרְשָׁה יב

Having completed the reproving instruction given Lemuel by his mother, evidently a woman of valor, Scripture takes up the theme of a praise-worthy woman of mettle in general. This section too lends itself to two levels of interpretation:

THE LITERAL LEVEL

10. A woman of valor is not likely to be "found" and gained as a wife without effort, but she can be "bought" and acquired in marriage by great striving and exertion: for she is more inaccessible and elusive than precious pearls.

11. Most women tend to squander money, but her husband can feel secure that his earnings and profits are safe with her.

THE SYMBOLIC LEVEL

10. As most commentaries note, this section of *Mishley* is an allegory. The human intellect is depicted as the king that is to rule within a person, and his primary undeveloped soul is conceived as a woman wed to the king, because she listens to him. Of a materialistic nature, the primary undeveloped soul (or element of the psyche) is essentially inimical to spirituality. It can be prepared, however, to yield to instructive ideas of moral wisdom and goodness, either by nature or by effort. Such a pliant soul is denoted as "a woman of valor," which the intellect "finds," for this is indeed a find, an instance of good fortune without effort. Generally, however, "her price is beyond pearls": A primary undeveloped soul can be evolved into a good, harmonious element of the psyche only through inner battle with the intellect. Metaphorically, one must cross distant oceans and plumb the water's depths to find its pearls—the good hidden faculties and powers that are latent in

¹⁰ A woman of valor who can find? — for her price is beyond pearls. ¹¹ The heart of her husband trusted in her, and he would have no lack of gain. ¹² She did him good and not evil, all the days of her life. ¹³ She sought out wool and flax, and

THE LITERAL LEVEL

12. Other women may cause their husbands both happiness and pain; or, if they are a source of good when young and healthy, when all is well, they may bring trouble in old age or adversity. *Her* relations with her husband are of constant, unalloyed goodness in all circumstances.

13. Whatever she chooses to do, she does industriously, cheerfully, and capably — the very opposite of the lazybones whose "hands refuse to labor" (21:25).

THE SYMBOLIC LEVEL

the psyche — and bring them to the surface of conscious behavior.

11. The heart is the governing force in the psyche, to regulate the primary undeveloped soul under the guidance of the intellect (the "royal husband"). If the primary soul is recalcitrant, it will yield only sporadically to discipline and then regress to amorality, making the individual lose what his intellect has gained from the Torah's moral laws. With a "woman of valor," an obedient primary soul, a person can feel secure that there will be no such loss of moral progress in unresolved inner conflicts.

12. Though it has elements of good, yet having experienced primal sin, a primary soul will sometimes fall prey to its evil elements, especially in the years of unruly youth. A good, heedful primary soul, however, can make for a consistent life of decent, moral behavior.

יד צֶמֶר וּפִשְׁתִּים וַתַּעַשׂ בְּחֵפֶץ כַּפֶּיהָ: הָיְתָה כָּאֳנִיּוֹת סוֹחֵר
טו מִמֶּרְחָק תָּבִיא לַחְמָהּ: וַתָּקָם ׀ בְּעוֹד לַיְלָה וַתִּתֵּן טֶרֶף לְבֵיתָהּ
טז וְחֹק לְנַעֲרֹתֶיהָ: זָמְמָה שָׂדֶה וַתִּקָּחֵהוּ מִפְּרִי כַפֶּיהָ נָטְעָה כָּרֶם:
יז חָגְרָה בְעוֹז מָתְנֶיהָ וַתְּאַמֵּץ זְרוֹעֹתֶיהָ: טָעֲמָה כִּי־טוֹב סַחְרָהּ

THE LITERAL LEVEL

14. Should she decide on some business venture or activity outside the home, she will not be loth to go to great lengths, literally and figuratively, for greater profits.

15. For the internal needs of the home, she is ready to rise well before dawn and prepare the food for the family and the rations for the servants.

THE SYMBOLIC LEVEL

13. Good character traits and virtues are depicted as clothing for the soul, to be realized and acquired through proper action and behavior. Virtuous actions and good deeds are consequently described as wool and flaxen cloths. A good, compliant primary soul seeks and welcomes good deeds, to acquire its "garments" of praiseworthy character traits; it does not have to be coerced and compelled to become inured to virtuous actions.

14. Factual, worldly education can be acquired by "trading" in human experience, gaining knowledge by knowledge, as it were, to profit in one's development. One must embark on the high seas of this profound, wide-ranging knowledge, to bring such "food from afar" for the soul; for the faculties of wisdom, intellect and spiritual awareness are innately distant from the physical world. Though normally the primary soul is prone to cravings and evil desires, a good soul, purified of such tendencies, will "sail forth" unimpeded, flag unfurled, into the "sea" of valid knowledge.

worked with the willingness of her hands. [14] She was like a merchant's ships: she would bring her food from afar. [15] Then she rose while it was still night, and gave food to her household, and a portion to her maids. [16] She planned for a field, and acquired it; with the fruit of her hands she planted a vineyard. [17] She girded her loins with vigor, and made strong her arms. [18] She perceived

THE LITERAL LEVEL

16–17. If she decides on agricultural work outside the home, or makes calculations and plans to acquire farmland—for this as well as for any far-ranging business venture (verse 14) she "girds her loins" for her outside activity, while she "makes her arms strong" for her domestic duties (verse 17).

THE SYMBOLIC LEVEL

15. In this world the light of intellect and spirituality is greatly darkened by the physical human condition. A good soul, however, will arise from its torpor in the dark night of earthly existence and "give" the "food" of Torah study to "her household," the faculties of intellect and understanding; and "rations" of observance of religious commandments and moral precepts for the training of the "maids," the physical self and its natural tendencies.

16. By nature, the primary soul is able and willing to "plant Divine seeds" of good action in the psyche, if the human being does his "farming" properly by moral study and conduct; and then there is a "harvest" of reward in the world-to-come for all his good deeds. The field of study and mental growth is symbolized as a vineyard, in which proper conceptions are "planted" to develop into an essential part of the psyche, which remains through eternity.

PROVERBS 31:18-21

יט לֹא־יִכְבֶּ֣ה בַלַּ֣יְלָה נֵרָֽהּ: יָ֭דֶיהָ שִׁלְּחָ֣ה בַכִּישׁ֑וֹר וְ֝כַפֶּ֗יהָ תָּ֣מְכוּ פָֽלֶךְ:
כא כַּ֭פָּהּ פָּרְשָׂ֣ה לֶעָנִ֑י וְ֝יָדֶ֗יהָ שִׁלְּחָ֥ה לָֽאֶבְיֽוֹן: לֹא־תִירָ֣א לְבֵיתָ֣הּ

THE LITERAL LEVEL

18. Realizing that with her work and activities beyond the home she can benefit and gratify others too, by charity and good deeds, she increases her efforts and stays up late at night.

19-20. With her "hands" — i.e. with the whole hand, openly — she gives to an *evyon*, an indigent man who can do nothing for himself and has lost all sensitivity about begging alms. With her "palm," discreetly, she aids a poor man who can

---

THE SYMBOLIC LEVEL

17. Intellectual pursuits in religious development are akin to walking, to proceed steadily from concept to concept. The good soul "girds her loins" so that the individual can make steady gains in his understanding. As regards action, the performance of the Torah's commandments and good deeds, "she makes her arms strong" and enables the individual to act forthrightly, unhampered by laziness or reluctance.

18. As it progresses well toward its own perfection, a good soul wishes to improve others too, both in their moral understanding and in their actions, to "gain profit" by "selling the merchandise" that it has found so good. Thus a great, abiding merit is earned, as the individual shares in the reward that others gain by their moral progress; and so "her lamp will not go out in the night" of terminated life: After his death, such an individual's good and religious deeds, and the Torah he taught, will continue to cast their influence like a shining light.

19-20. The distaff connotes a wooden beam to which prisoners were pinioned or tied, suggesting the coarse physicality of this world that "ties" and hampers the human psyche,

that her merchandise was good; her lamp would not go out at night. ¹⁹ She set her hands to the distaff, and her palms held the spindle. ²⁰ She opened her palm to a poor man, and stretched out her hands to a hopelessly needy man. ²¹ She would not be afraid for her household in snow-

THE LITERAL LEVEL

still help himself and is therefore ashamed to seek or accept charity openly.

21. Though she has generously given the poor and the hopelessly indigent clothing derived from her spindle, she has no anxiety that her family may be cold in the winter, the season of snow, for all have clothes enough made from her spinning

THE SYMBOLIC LEVEL

reducing it to hopeless poverty. Here the good soul "sets her hands" to the performance of commandments and good deeds, to refine the physical self and release it from its bonds. It furthermore helps a "hopelessly needy man," overcome by physical desires and drives, by setting an example for him to emulate, thus to gain mastery of his gross physical nature. Again, for growth in religious awareness, "her palms hold the spindle" to weave the insights for progressive understanding; and the good soul can "open her palms to a" spiritually "poor man," to teach him the Divine word and holy knowledge of the Torah, that will stand him in good stead in the world-to-come.

21. A good primary soul that has developed well will feel no fear of death, the "time of snow" that freezes off the natural warmth of life; for it has no anxiety about its "household" of spiritual forces and faculties in the psyche, that they will remain without "clothes" (see verse 13): *for all her household are clothed in* the *manifold garments* of Torah and good deeds. (The word

כב מִשְׁלֵי כִּי כָל־בֵּיתָהּ לָבֻשׁ שָׁנִים: מַרְבַדִּים עָשְׂתָה־לָּהּ שֵׁשׁ
כג וְאַרְגָּמָן לְבוּשָׁהּ: נוֹדָע בַּשְּׁעָרִים בַּעְלָהּ בְּשִׁבְתּוֹ עִם־זִקְנֵי־אָרֶץ:
כד סָדִין עָשְׂתָה וַתִּמְכֹּר וַחֲגוֹר נָתְנָה לַכְּנַעֲנִי: עוֹז־וְהָדָר לְבוּשָׁהּ
כה

THE LITERAL LEVEL

(*shanim* = the plural of *shani*, denoting *tola'ath shani*, scarlet cloth).

22. Heaven rewards her with affluence, as it bestows its blessing on the good work she does.

23. She supports and encourages her husband in his Torah studies, to become a learned scholar, till he can rank and sit among the distinguished elders called upon to settle disputes and render decisions. (In ancient times the elders who served as a court of law would literally "sit in the gates" of the city, to be accessible to all who came and went.)

THE SYMBOLIC LEVEL

shanim, "scarlet," is now understood as *shonim*, various or manifold.)

22. This soul has moreover made for itself "precious ornaments" of the perceptions and ideas gained in a lifetime of religious study; and it has most splendid "garments" out of such study and observance, a spiritual status to adorn it in the Hereafter.

23. The "husband" of the good primary soul, the guiding intellect of the psyche, will be "known" and have a telling effect when "they shall speak with the enemies in the gate" (Psalms 127:5), i.e. in confronting and battling the inner forces of evil impulse, to impose discipline with moral law. Again, it will make its mark in "sitting with the elders of the land," i.e. in studying moral perceptions and religious ideas, to gain an elder's mastery of understanding.

324

time, for all her household would be clothed in scarlet. ²² She made precious ornaments for herself; her clothing was fine linen and cloth of royal purple. ²³ Her husband was known in the gates, when he would sit among the elders of the land. ²⁴ She made linen clothing and would sell it, and gave many a belt to the trader. ²⁵ Strength and dignity were her clothing, and she smiled at

THE LITERAL LEVEL

24–25. The linen clothing and the belts that she sells provides the money for her charity to the poor and the indigent. This endows her with a "spiritual garment" of strength and dignity that she will "put on" when her final day on earth comes and she must leave behind the physical body that has "clothed" her spirit during her lifetime, to go "smiling" in confidence to the world-to-come.

THE SYMBOLIC LEVEL

24. The gaining of understanding that integrates a person's acquired perceptions and insights is symbolized as the weaving of linen clothing. This the good soul "sells" by applying it in the individual's inner life, and by sharing it with others, which in turn increases and enriches one's own religious maturation. The belt denotes the strength of wisdom to overcome temptation and impulse and choose only the good in behavior. This too "she gives to a trader" to pass on to others as an example to learn from.

25. Out of a life of Divine education and good deeds, the good soul will be "clothed in garments" of spiritual splendor when the final day of earthly existence is to be faced. There will be happiness and joy as well for this good soul, that has brought merit and virtue to others by precept and example, thus earning a radiant reward in the Hereafter.

PROVERBS 31:26-31

כו וַתִּשְׂחַק לְיוֹם אַחֲרוֹן: פִּיהָ פָּתְחָה בְחָכְמָה וְתוֹרַת־חֶסֶד עַל־
לְשׁוֹנָהּ: כז צוֹפִיָּה הֲלִיכוֹת בֵּיתָהּ וְלֶחֶם עַצְלוּת לֹא תֹאכֵל: קָמוּ
כח בָנֶיהָ וַיְאַשְּׁרוּהָ בַּעְלָהּ וַיְהַלְלָהּ: רַבּוֹת בָּנוֹת עָשׂוּ חָיִל וְאַתְּ
ל עָלִית עַל־כֻּלָּנָה: שֶׁקֶר הַחֵן וְהֶבֶל הַיֹּפִי אִשָּׁה יִרְאַת־יְהֹוָה הִיא
לא תִתְהַלָּל: תְּנוּ־לָהּ מִפְּרִי יָדֶיהָ וִיהַלְלוּהָ בַשְּׁעָרִים מַעֲשֶׂיהָ:

THE LITERAL LEVEL

26. On that "final day" when she faces her judgment in the Hereafter, she will be able to speak up for herself, having lived by the laws of moral wisdom; and "on her tongue" will be all the acts of kindness she performed in her lifetime, over and above any call of duty. This will be her splendid vindication before the Almighty.

27-28. The fact that she was an industrious homemaker, who looked well after the progress of her family and worked hard for their wellbeing—for this she will receive praise from her husband and children, but not beyond the home, since it is happily quite common for women ("many daughters") to excel in these ways.

THE SYMBOLIC LEVEL

26. The good soul will then point to a lifetime choice of good over evil by the laws of moral wisdom. The tongue, within the mouth, denotes inner understanding—which the good soul gained, while on earth, of the esoteric meaning of much in the Torah (designated as *torath chesed*, "the Torah of kindness," since it goes amply beyond the plain meaning as kindness goes beyond the call of law and duty).

27-28. If a good soul has "kept watch" only over its own "household" to achieve self-perfection by alertness and zeal, there will be no public, general praise. Only "her children," the good deeds performed and the good faculties developed in the

the final day. ²⁶ She opened her mouth with wisdom; and the system of kindness was on her tongue. ²⁷ She kept watch over the ways of her household, and would not eat the bread of idleness. ²⁸ Her children rose up and called her blessed; her husband too, and he praised her: ²⁹ "Many daughters have done valiantly, but you have excelled them all." ³⁰ Charm is deceitful, and beauty is vapid; but a woman who fears HA-SHEM, she shall be praised. ³¹ Give her of the fruit of her hands, and let her deeds praise her in the gates.

THE LITERAL LEVEL

29–30. However, "you have excelled them all" by taking no pride in beauty or attractiveness but only in being pious and devout. For this virtue of spiritual wisdom she will receive her reward ("the fruit of her hands") in the world-to-come and will be praised in the world beyond her home as well.

THE SYMBOLIC LEVEL

psyche, will bring reward; and for all the effort and energy invested in holy study to attain Divine truth, "her husband," the intellect, will be grateful for having been able to take this clear, blessed path in life.

29–31. Many good souls have pursued their own perfection, gaining spiritual "charm and beauty" by intellectual attainments and good deeds. Such gains, however, are "false and vapid" as it were, in comparison with the achievements of good souls whose life has been marked by a devout awareness and reverence of the Almighty, which has inspired them to exert a profound influence on others. Such a soul's reward is extremely great, and its name remains a source of blessing wherever the Torah's wisdom and righteousness are valued.